Praise, Praise, Praise For Beer For Dummies!

"Even smart beer drinkers, including those who consider themselves experts, will learn from *Beer For Dummies*. Authors Marty Nachel and Steve Ettlinger are obviously no 'lite' weights when it comes to beer knowledge. Presented in a user-friendly style, this book is witty and weiss, with comprehensive information about every aspect of the fascinating world of beer."

— Charles Finkel, Founder and Creative Director, Merchant du Vin and the Pike Brewing Co.

"*Beer For Dummies* is mistitled. Rather, *Beer — Become an Expert!* would be more appropriate! Marty Nachel and Steve Ettlinger provide a comprehensive, fun, and enlightening read for all beer lovers!"

— Jake Leinenkugel, President, Jacob Leinenkugel Brewing Co.

"I believe that great beer has all the complexity and nobility of fine wines. Learning about beer is a wonderful and tasty educational process. *Beer For Dummies* will teach you how to choose, appreciate, buy, and even brew great beer. Cheers!"

— Jim Koch, Brewer, Samuel Adams Boston Lager Beer

"A wonderful book about one of life's great pleasures. *Beer For Dummies* is as satisfying to the soul as a rich pale ale."

— Gordon Johnson, CPA and beer enthusiast

"*Beer For Dummies* will make you smart about beer history and culture and the beer revolution in America. It will enrich your appreciation of this wonderful, inexpensive beverage. You'll never say, 'Gimme a beer' again."

— Steve Hindy, Cofounder and President, Brooklyn Brewery

"Written by an acknowledged authority in the field, *Beer For Dummies* provides a fun and entertaining way to learn about a complex and sophisticated subject, beer."

— Steve Johnson, author of the *On Tap* beer guidebooks and brewspaper columnist

BUSINESS AND GENERAL REFERENCE BOOK SERIES FROM IDG

Beer For Dummies™

Quick Reference Card

Ten Useful Beer Taste Descriptors

Aggressive: Boldly assertive aroma and/or taste

Crisp: Highly carbonated; effervescent

Complex: Multidimensional; many flavors and sensations on the palate

Estery: Fruity aromas

Fruity: Flavors reminiscent of various fruits

Hoppy: Herbal or spicy aromas and bitter flavors of hops

Malty: Grainy, caramel-like; can be sweet or dry

Roasty/toasty: Malt (roasted grain) flavors

Robust: Rich and full-bodied

Diacetyl: Buttery or butterscotchy aroma or flavor

Two other terms are commonly used to describe a beer, but they don't describe taste: *mouthfeel* and *body*. *Mouthfeel* is the tactile sensory experience of the whole inside of the mouth and throat — warmth (alcohol) in the throat, dryness, carbonation, and so on — and it includes a sense of body. *Body* describes the sensation of fullness, or viscosity, of a beer on the palate, ranging from watery to creamy; beer is generally described as thin-, light-, medium-, or full-bodied.

Five Most Common Ales

Barleywine	Complex, caramelly/toasty and fruity flavors; extra alcohol
Pale ale	Mild malt flavor accented with firm hop edge
Porter	Medium-bodied dark beer with pleasant grain astringency
Stout	Dark, rich, roasty, coffeelike
Wheat beer	Faintly malty; sometimes yeasty; refreshingly mild acidity

Quick Pronunciation Guide to Common Beer Styles

The stressed syllable in each word is capitalized; if no syllable is capitalized, all syllables carry equal weight.

Altbier	AHLT beer
Helles	HELL iss
Dubbel	DOO bl
Kölsch	kelsh
Dortmunder	dort MOON der
Lambic	lahm BEEK
Dunkel	DOON kl
Märzen	MARE tsen
Dunkelweizen	DOON kl VY tsen
Rauchbier	ROWK beer
Eisbock	ICE bock
Schwarzbier	SHVAHRTS beer
Faro	FAR oh
Wassail	WAHSS ul
Framboise	fram BWAZ
Weiss	vice
Gueuze	GURZ eh (barely pronounce the R)
Weizen	VY tsen
Hefeweizen	HAY feh VY tsen
Witbier	VIT beer

Ales and Lagers Defined

Beer is divided into two major classifications: ales and lagers. Ales, which are fermented at warm temperatures, are more robust; lagers, which are fermented and aged at cold temperatures, are more mellow.

. . .For Dummies: Bestselling Book Series for Beginners

Beer For Dummies™

Quick Reference Card

Five Beer Brands to Try at Least Once

E.K.U. Kulminator Urtyp Hell "28" (Germany): Incredibly malty-rich and spirited; a terrific Teutonic tipple

Guinness Stout (Ireland): Dark, dry, smooth, and roasty, with a creamy head; the perfect sipping pint

Pilsner Urquell (Czechoslovakia): Crisp and hoppy with a touch of malty sweetness; the original, classic Pilsner beer

Rodenbach Grand Cru (Belgium): Sharply sour but refreshing, with fresh fruity notes; beer masquerading as Burgundy wine

Samuel Adams Triple Bock (U.S.): Throat-warming malt complexity with hints of sherry and oak; the strongest beer in the world — sip it like a brandy

Five Most Common Lagers

American pale lager	Light, thin, crisp, and thirst-quenching
Bock	Medium-bodied, strong; chocolaty, malty richness
Munchener helles	Rich malt flavor with balanced spicy bittering
Oktoberfest (Märzen)	Medium-bodied and malty, literally made for a party
Pilsner	Crisp, pale, malty, and hoppy

Five Unusual Beer Styles to Try at Least Once

Belgian fruit lambic: Well-aged ale with surprising, effusive fruit aroma and taste; intoxicating fragrance

Doppelbock: Strong, dark, and caramelly bock beer with two times the flavor and body of bock (doppel your pleasure, doppel your fun)

Imperial stout: Dark, rich, and creamy stout with complex grain flavors; a brew to chew

Rauchbier: Oktoberfest beer made with a portion of beechwood-smoked malt; delicious and unique but takes somewhat of an acquired taste (great with smoked cheese or sausage)

Witbier: Perfumy Belgian wheat beer made with orange rind and coriander seed; like nothing else in the beer world

...For Dummies: Bestselling Book Series for Beginners

 ™

BUSINESS AND GENERAL REFERENCE BOOK SERIES FROM IDG

References for the Rest of Us!™

Do you find that traditional reference books are overloaded with technical details and advice you'll never use? Do you postpone important life decisions because you just don't want to deal with them? Then our *...For Dummies*™ business and general reference book series is for you.

...For Dummies business and general reference books are written for those frustrated and hard-working souls who know they aren't dumb, but find that the myriad of personal and business issues and the accompanying horror stories make them feel helpless. *...For Dummies* books use a lighthearted approach, a down-to-earth style, and even cartoons and humorous icons to diffuse fears and build confidence. Lighthearted but not lightweight, these books are perfect survival guides to solve your everyday personal and business problems.

> *"More than a publishing phenomenon, 'Dummies' is a sign of the times."*
> — **The New York Times**

> *"A world of detailed and authoritative information is packed into them..."*
> — **U.S. News and World Report**

> *"... you won't go wrong buying them."*
> — **Walter Mossberg, Wall Street Journal, on IDG's ...For Dummies™ books**

Already, hundreds of thousands of satisfied readers agree. They have made *...For Dummies* the #1 introductory level computer book series and a best-selling business book series. They have written asking for more. So, if you're looking for the best and easiest way to learn about business and other general reference topics, look to *...For Dummies* to give you a helping hand.

BEER FOR DUMMIES™

by Marty Nachel with Steve Ettlinger

Foreword by Jim Koch
Brewer, Samuel Adams Boston Lager Beer

IDG Books Worldwide, Inc.
An International Data Group Company

Foster City, CA ♦ Chicago, IL ♦ Indianapolis, IN ♦ Southlake, TX

Beer For Dummies ™

Published by
IDG Books Worldwide, Inc.
An International Data Group Company
919 E. Hillsdale Blvd.
Suite 400
Foster City, CA 94404

www.idgbooks.com (IDG Books Worldwide Web Site)
http://www.dummies.com (Dummies Press Web Site)

Developed and produced by Ettlinger Editorial Projects, New York.

Library of Congress Catalog Card No.: 96-77270

ISBN: 1-56884-865-X

Printed in the United States of America

10 9 8 7 6 5 4 3 2 1

1B/RW/QY/ZW/IN

Distributed in the United States by IDG Books Worldwide, Inc.

Distributed by Macmillan Canada for Canada; by Contemporanea de Ediciones for Venezuela; by Distribuidora Cuspide for Argentina; by CITEC for Brazil; by Ediciones ZETA S.C.R. Ltda. for Peru; by Editorial Limusa SA for Mexico; by Transworld Publishers Limited in the United Kingdom and Europe; by Academic Bookshop for Egypt; by Levant Distributors S.A.R.L. for Lebanon; by Al Jassim for Saudi Arabia; by Simron Pty. Ltd. for South Africa; by Pustak Mahal for India; by The Computer Bookshop for India; by Toppan Company Ltd. for Japan; by Addison Wesley Publishing Company for Korea; by Longman Singapore Publishers Ltd. for Singapore, Malaysia, Thailand, and Indonesia; by Unalis Corporation for Taiwan; by WS Computer Publishing Company, Inc. for the Philippines; by WoodsLane Pty. Ltd. for Australia; by WoodsLane Enterprises Ltd. for New Zealand. Authorized Sales Agent: Anthony Rudkin Associates for the Middle East and North Africa.

For general information on IDG Books Worldwide's books in the U.S., please call our Consumer Customer Service department at 800-762-2974. For reseller information, including discounts and premium sales, please call our Reseller Customer Service department at 800-434-3422.

For information on where to purchase IDG Books Worldwide's books outside the U.S., contact IDG Books Worldwide's International Sales department at 415-655-3172 or fax 415-655-3295.

For information on foreign language translations, contact IDG Books Worldwide's Foreign & Subsidiary Rights department at 415-655-3021 or fax 415-655-3281.

For sales inquiries and special prices for bulk quantities, contact IDG Books Worldwide's Sales department at 415-655-3200 or write to the address above.

For information on using IDG Books Worldwide's books in the classroom or for ordering examination copies, contact IDG Books Worldwide's Educational Sales department at 800-434-2086 or fax 817-251-8174.

For authorization to photocopy items for corporate, personal, or educational use, please contact Copyright Clearance Center, 222 Rosewood Drive, Danvers, MA 01923, or fax 508-750-4470.

is a trademark under exclusive license to IDG Books Worldwide, Inc., from International Data Group, Inc.

IDG BOOKS WORLDWIDE

About the Authors

Marty Nachel

A former welder and steel fabricator, Marty Nachel is a freelance writer on beer and brewing, an award-winning homebrewer, a Certified Beer Judge, and a beer evaluator for the Beverage Testing Institute. He is also a member of the North American Guild of Beer Writers, former president of the Chicago Beer Society, and founding member of the Brewers Of South Suburbia (B.O.S.S.) homebrew and beer appreciation club.

His first book, *Beer Across America: A Regional Guide to Brewpubs and Microbreweries,* was published in July 1995.

Marty has been the lead writer and editor for the newsletters that accompany monthly shipments of microbrewed beer from Beer Across America since October 1992. His articles have also appeared in *All About Beer, Beer & Tavern Chronicle, Brew Magazine, Brew Your Own, Fine Cooking, Heads Up, Midwest Beer Notes, On Tap* newsletter, and *Zymurgy.*

Travel in search of good beer has taken Marty to over 150 breweries and brewpubs and assorted beer festivals and shrines in Europe and North America. When he can find the time, he likes to collect breweriana.

Steve Ettlinger

Steve Ettlinger has been the book producer, author, or coauthor of over 20 consumer-oriented books since 1985 (he produced Marty's first book). He is president of Ettlinger Editorial Projects, an idea-developing and book-producing firm, and was president of the American Book Producers Association, a trade group, from 1991 to 1995.

Among his own titles are *The Restaurant Lover's Companion* and *The Complete Illustrated Guide to Everything Sold in Hardware Stores.* He also covers dining-related subjects for national magazines and Web sites.

Authors' Acknowledgments

Acknowledgments are the least I can extend to a team of dedicated people at IDG Books Worldwide who have given so much to this project, not the least of which was their overwhelming support and infectious enthusiasm. That team includes Sarah Kennedy, Kathy Welton, Stacy Collins, Melba Hopper, Diane Giangrossi, and many others behind the scenes.

I consider myself fortunate to be one of the . . .*For Dummies* authors and for not having to knock down doors to become one. Book producer, cowriter, and editor *extraordinaire* Steve Ettlinger created this opportunity for me, and for that I am most grateful. Steve's focus and attention to detail helped make this book complete. Thanks also to Steve's managing editor, Tim Smith, for his diligence and enthusiasm in research and manuscript preparation.

Grateful acknowledgments go to Candy Schermerhorn, beer gourmand *par excellence*. Candy's contribution of recipes in Chapter 16 of this book is invaluable, especially because her inclusion came late in the process of putting this book together. A huge thanks to her for stepping in and lending her talent and credentials to this effort. Not to be overlooked are the many contributions and verifications of Karen Barela and the staff at the Association of Brewers and the American Homebrewers Association in Boulder, Colorado.

Finally, the road that led to this book was long and enjoyable, and I had lots of company along the way. I'd like to acknowledge those individuals and organizations that have inspired, supported, or otherwise contributed to my passion for the malted beverage. They include Michael Jackson; Charlie Papazian; Steve Johnson; Randy Mosher, Ray Daniels, and all the beer geeks of the Chicago Beer Society; Steve Kamp, Dick Van Dyke, Mike Pezan, and the boys of B.O.S.S.; Robin Wilson; and all the neighbors, friends, and relatives who ever shared time with me in the pursuit and praise of good beer.

— Marty Nachel

First of all, I am eternally grateful to Marty Nachel for becoming my personal beer trainer, patiently explaining over and over again the intricate differences between the various beer styles. He taught me all I know about beer (my father taught me to appreciate it). I'm also in awe of Marty's sublime homebrewed beer.

Thanks to all those brewers and beverage salespeople who took time to answer my endless questions; to my sister, Betsy, and her pals for advice on beer appreciation; to my mother, Marge, for her editing as well as her testing of the beer/food recipes.

Special thanks go to CAMRA, in England, for research assistance and to Tim Smith, my managing editor, for constant, patient revisions and fact-checking.

Thanks also to freelance editor Ted Scheffler, as well as the knowledgeable Hercules Dimitratos, of Fancy Grocery in New York City — my retail beer supplier.

Above all, I am grateful to Dylan and Gusty (Chelsea, too) for their support and enthusiasm, especially when it came to extended deadlines and my having to burn so much midnight oil away from home.

Beer may be fun, but it took a lot of work to get here. I won't forget your help, all of you.

— Steve Ettlinger

Publisher's Acknowledgments

We're proud of this book; please send us your comments about it by using the Reader Response Card at the back of the book or by e-mailing us at feedback/dummies@idgbooks.com. Some of the people who helped bring this book to market include the following:

Acquisitions, Development, and Editorial

Project Editor: Melba Hopper

Acquisitions Editor: Sarah Kennedy, Executive Editor

Permissions Editor: Joyce Pepple

Copy Editor: Diane L. Giangrossi

Technical Editor: James L. Spence

Editorial Manager: Mary C. Corder

Editorial Assistants: Ann Miller, Chris H. Collins

Production

Project Coordinator: Debbie Sharpe

Layout and Graphics: Brett Black, Angela F. Hunckler, Todd Klemme, Jane E. Martin, Drew R. Moore, Patricia R. Reynolds, Anna Rohrer, Brent Savage, Gina Scott, Kate Snell, Michael Sullivan

Proofreaders: Michael Bolinger, Nancy Price, Robert Springer, Carrie Voorhis, Karen York

Indexer: Richard T. Evans

Special Help

Tamara S. Castleman, copy editor; Stephanie Koutek, proof editor; Sarah Layden and Shari Parks, fact checkers

General & Administrative

IDG Books Worldwide, Inc.: John Kilcullen, President and CEO; Steven Berkowitz, COO and Publisher

Dummies, Inc.: Milissa Koloski, Executive Vice President and Publisher

Dummies Technology Press and Dummies Editorial: Diane Graves Steele, Associate Publisher; Judith A. Taylor, Brand Manager

Dummies Trade Press: Kathleen A. Welton, Vice President and Publisher; Stacy S. Collins, Brand Manager

IDG Books Production for Dummies Press: Beth Jenkins, Production Director; Cindy L. Phipps, Supervisor of Project Coordination; Kathie S. Schutte, Supervisor of Page Layout; Shelley Lea, Supervisor of Graphics and Design; Debbie J. Gates, Production Systems Specialist

Dummies Packaging and Book Design: Erin McDermit, Packaging Coordinator; Patti Sandez, Packaging Assistant; Kavish+Kavish, Cover Design

♦

The publisher would like to give special thanks to Patrick J. McGovern, without whom this book would not have been possible.

Dedication

I am happy to dedicate this book to my wife, Patti, and my children, Drew and Jill, who contribute to my work in ways they will never know. Without their patience and support, none of this would be possible.

And to lovers of good beer everywhere. Life's short — drink well!

— Marty Nachel

Contents at a Glance

Cartoons at a Glance

By Rich Tennant • Fax: 508-546-7747 • E-mail: the5wave@tiac.net

page 249

page 183

page 45

page 95

page 219

page 7

page 121

Table of Contents

Foreword

I love beer. My dad was a brewmaster, so I grew up in breweries and came to appreciate the kettles, the tanks, and the smell of a brewery. As a kid, I read the family beer recipes, which had been handed down over six generations.

In 1984, when I brewed my first batch of Samuel Adams beer, there was no need for a basic guide book like *Beer For Dummies,* especially in the U.S. Mass-produced beers had undergone 40 years of becoming lighter and blander. And beers from abroad, then the only widely available alternative, were often stale because of their long, transoceanic crossing and lengthy warehousing.

But today, beer lovers are in heaven. We are in the midst of a genuine renaissance in what's known as craft brewing. Literally hundreds of new brands and styles are crowding the shelves and the bar backs — pretty intimidating for the uninitiated unless they have a copy of *Beer For Dummies* with them. Personally, I love walking into a bar and seeing a dozen tap handles for great, interesting beer styles.

I grew up knowing that beer can have all the nobility and complexity of a fine wine, and it's fun to see more and more people acknowledging that today. I think it has to do with education. The more you know about beer — its ingredients, its history, its brewing — the more respect you have for it. That's why I applaud Marty Nachel and Steve Ettlinger for writing *Beer For Dummies.*

In this book, Marty and Steve tell you what good beer is and how to find and enjoy it. I appreciate the opportunity to endorse *Beer For Dummies* and am sure it will entertain you, educate you, and make you thirsty for a really great beer.

Cheers,

Jim Koch
Brewer, Samuel Adams Beers

Jim Koch is credited by many as the leader in the current craft-brewing renaissance. As a brewmaster, he continues a family tradition — six first-born sons in his family have become brewmasters. Jim's own experience with brewing started at the age of four, when he tasted his first beer. He loved it.

In 1984, armed with his great-great-grandfather's original recipe for Samuel Adams beer, Jim started the highly successful Boston Beer Company. At the time, he didn't dream that there'd be a market for more than one style of Samuel Adams. Today, the Samuel Adams family of beers comprises 15 different brews.

Introduction

· ·

There once was a man named Stu —
About beer, he hadn't a clue.
At the behest of his chummies,
He read Beer For Dummies,
And now he's the Master of Brew!

*L*ike many people, I first discovered beer sitting on my father's knee. My
earliest recollections of the beer that Dad drank were that it was always ice
cold and foamed like soapsuds — probably an accurate taste descriptor as well.
Too bad Dad bought the cheap stuff.

After years of unconsciously buying the cheapest beer, like my father did, I
found that my regular beer started to become regularly boring and less appealing in many ways. By chance, a tour of a famous brewery — Molson's, in
Toronto — that made fresh, tasty beer in a number of the traditional styles
opened my unknowing eyes to an undiscovered world of beery possibilities
unavailable then in the U.S. Beer drinking for me would never be the same
again, because I had discovered the secrets to true beer happiness: freshness
and variety. From that point on, I went in search of all good beer and an education in the difference from mediocre beer.

Learning this difference was not only easy but fun — so much fun, in fact, that I
now make a living doing it! But even for the casual beer drinker, a little beer
knowledge can turn a possibly daunting experience into an enjoyable one. Good
beer, unlike fine wine, is widely available and generally inexpensive, but choosing among all the various styles can be a little confusing without some help. If
you've fallen in love with beer, you have plenty of ways to increase your beer
appreciation. This book should be of help to neophyte and beer nut alike. And
the best news is that even in the U.S., good beer is being offered by more
brewers every day (luckily, it didn't really ever go out of style elsewhere).

After water, beer is the most popular drink in the world. I'll drink to that!

How to Use This Book

The first parts of this book are for people who have just discovered the world of quality beer and who may want to get a little background or check out some specific information about beer — or carry on an intelligent conversation with someone who happens to be a beer nut. The latter parts are more oriented toward those of you who have caught the beer bug or have gone completely nuts about beer. Ultimately, this book is a guide to increasing your drinking pleasure, from broadening your choices among the many styles of beer to opening your eyes to beer-related fun, like homebrewing or collecting beer things.

Part I: Defining Beer: Style and Substance

These three chapters are meant to answer the first questions that most people who are new to the world of beer tend to ask.

Chapter 1 describes the most popular beer styles and defines the basic terms you see or hear used around beer. This chapter should help you make your first choices without being intimidated. It's really essential reading.

Chapters 2 and **3** try to answer the basic questions about how beer is made. Many drinkers are just plain curious, but you may want to know this stuff because beer labels and menus often mention the brewing process or ingredients.

Part II: Enjoying Beer: Tasting, Serving, and Cooking

Some beer lovers come dangerously close to being snobby about beer, almost like (shudder!) wine snobs, but this section helps you sort out the really important stuff to know about the enjoyment of beer (which is actually a very complex subject).

Chapter 4 is probably the most serious because tasting jargon is serious. Tasting beer is not serious business, though. The bottom line: If you like it, it's good.

Chapters 5 and **6** cover the best places to find beer and the best ways to serve it, because if you're looking for good beer, you want it sold and served right.

Chapter 7 opens your eyes to the world of beer and food, a world that's easily enjoyed. Beer and wine comparisons and substitutions are covered in detail here.

Part III: Buying Beer: Becoming an Informed Consumer

Here's where I make sure you get what you pay for. Beer is a perishable food and has to be shipped, stored, and sold as such. Often it isn't, making your life as a beer consumer fraught with perils — until you find the answers in this section.

Chapter 8 gets into the specifics of labeling laws and mysterious label lingo, while **Chapter 9** gives you the tools you need to shop with confidence.

Part IV: Making Beer: Homebrewing

You don't have to be a complete beer nut to want to read about homebrewing beer. Though it is a fairly lengthy process, any beer lover who reads this part will come away with an increased appreciation for commercial brews and a more complete understanding of beer talk.

Chapter 10 leads you by the hand as you brew your very first batch of beer, made from a "just-add-water" kit. As it happens, the same steps form the basis for brewing on the intermediate level with more ingredients and directions — covered in **Chapter 11**.

Chapter 12 gives you an idea of what else you can do with your increased passion for homebrewing — places to go, things to see, beers to try.

Part V: Going Nuts over Beer: Travel and Collecting

This part is for people who like to move around a bit. Your own local bars and homes are not the only places to enjoy beer — this part gives you plenty of ideas for places around the world to explore and enjoy.

Chapter 13 gives you detailed ideas for beer touring in Europe and elsewhere, noting famous beer halls, breweries, museums, and festivals. Family fun!

Chapter 14 lists some of the more popular U.S. beer festivals and museums, with hints and tips for festival-goers.

Chapter 15 tells how you can get started collecting breweriana — coasters, tap handles, and the like — and meet up with fellow beer enthusiasts.

Part VI: The Part of Tens

The Part of Tens is a . . .*For Dummies* series tradition, and this part is where you can find recipes for cooking with beer, statistics to wow your friends with, basic information that will calm beginners who have the usual questions, and some brewpubs to try out.

Part VII: Appendixes

This part is the basic resource for all beer enthusiasts, loaded with phone numbers, addresses, World Wide Web sites, publications, and above all, lists of both specific beer brands to try (make a copy so you're ready for any beer emergencies!) and important beer styles. With this information, you're all set.

Icons Used in This Book

 Tells funny, intriguing, or just plain interesting beer trivia or lore. Entertaining but also maybe educational. Excellent material for beer-bar banter, if you're into that kind of thing.

 Signals really important facts that are essential to know if you want to be sure you understand beer.

 Points out where tasting and brewing terms are explained, except where the whole section is devoted to explaining terms — that seems obvious enough.

 Shows pointers, suggestions, recommendations, and things to do yourself.

 Means "Don't do this!" or "Pay attention and do this right the first time!" You'll harm your beer or beer experience if you blow it.

 Explains technical subjects that are important only if you're really getting into beer or you're really into technical stuff. The rest of you can easily skip these sections.

A Last First Word

Partly because beer is so widely available and partly because so many different people make beer, beer styles are not always consistent from brand to brand.

What I've tried to do in this book is define the most important styles in everyday language, but you'll no doubt find other descriptions elsewhere that are stated differently. Descriptions mostly reflect an individual writer's perception, as a good many of the style descriptions are not really definitive. I've followed the American Homebrewers Association guidelines as a base and added my own twist to make them more easily understood by the average reader.

If you're confused, don't worry. It's just beer, after all. Please go have one now!

Part I
Defining Beer: Style and Substance

The 5th Wave   By Rich Tennant

"OK—We got one cherry lager with bitters and a pineapple slice, and one honey malt ale with cinnamon and an orange twist. You want these in steins or parfait glasses?"

In this part . . .

This part gives you the basics you need to be comfortable when making choices among the many styles of beer available today.

Because choosing a beer from the huge selections now at many bars and stores can be pretty intimidating, I put the descriptions of the various styles right up front, in Chapter 1. If you're *still* intimidated after reading this chapter, just start ordering from the top until you find one you like.

Nearly everyone seems to want to know how beer is made, and labels and menus often refer to the ingredients or the processes involved, so I put that information in Chapters 2 and 3. Although you can certainly skip the technical stuff in these chapters, my guess is that many of you will find the details there helpful and interesting.

On the other hand, if you're already familiar with the world beyond the heavily advertised commercial brands, then you may want to just skip right ahead to the next part.

Chapter 1

Beer Basics: Which Brew's for You?

*N*ot long ago (well, okay, before the '80s), you had few choices when ordering a beer in a North American bar. Those beers were fairly light in color, tended to be bland, and were generally not too different from one another.

But today, a real beer renaissance is going on in the U.S. More and more small, local breweries — *microbreweries,* or micros, and *brewpubs* — are opening their doors and offering a variety of superbly made craft beers. (*Craft brewing* uses traditional, complex recipes and costly ingredients to brew the many classic styles of beer.) Now over 1,000 assorted brands and types of beer are brewed in the U.S. alone, making it the world leader in beer variety. Amazing!

Even in England, where neighborhood pubs and local breweries are part of the culture, a movement is afoot to encourage serving well-made, tasty, traditional brews instead of the mass-produced, blander stuff.

Big beer numbers

Belgium, famous for offering about 600 different beers, led the world in producing the greatest varieties of beer for years. In case you wonder about Germany, although that country suppos-edly has over 1,200 breweries, they don't brew in a wide variety of styles. In 1980, the U.S. had only 4 microbrewers and no brewpubs. In 1996, there are 900 of both; by the year 2000, there may be close to 3,000 of them. That's a veritable movement!

In some U.S. beer bars, you can now easily find 20 to as many as 100 different kinds of bottled beers "on the wall" (you wondered where the song came from?) and a dozen on tap. U.S. supermarkets may have even more choices, including some special, regionally distributed domestic brands and imports. And liquor stores can offer as many as 700 different beers. Many wine lists in upscale restaurants include beers, too.

Today's offerings include a wide range of styles, flavors, ingredients, and colors — from pale straw to opaque black. Many of the beers have a unique character and are full of flavor, far from the usual innocuous stuff of yore. These choices — not to mention the new vocabulary used to describe them — can be intimidating. But don't worry: *Beer For Dummies* explains all you need to know to embark on your journey of becoming a beer connoisseur.

Introducing Beer's Building Blocks

What is beer — that is, what is it made of — is probably the question most commonly asked of bartenders in beer bars. Two other common questions are "What do you have that's really light?" and "How 'bout those Mets?"

I can't help with the last two questions, but for the first, try this: Beer is a fermented drink made from grain (usually barley, but also wheat, oats, corn, rice, or rye), water, yeast, and hops.

Barley (or a similar grain) is wetted until the kernels just start to sprout (germinate). The kernels are then dried or roasted, producing *barleymalt.* The malt is steeped in hot water; the water is drained into and boiled in a brew kettle, seasoned with *hops,* transferred to yet another vessel, and then fermented with *yeast.*

I've highly simplified the process, of course (see more in Chapters 2 and 3), and left out the different pieces of equipment — all those big tanks you see in breweries — that make the process happen. Everything depends on the recipe: the choice of ingredients and the "cooking" times and temperatures. The important thing to know is that any beer style can be fairly closely duplicated by any talented brewer who has the recipe.

The ancient beverage

Beer is believed to be over 10,000 years old, several millennia older than recorded history — the oldest alcoholic beverage known. Some anthropologists have speculated that Neolithic people made the transition from the nomadic lifestyle of the hunter-gatherer to the relatively sedentary lifestyle of an agriculturist in order to grow the grain needed to brew beer. Not the first time that beer has encouraged settling down.

Ale versus Lager: Not a Family Fight

If you're new to the world beyond Budweiser, you may be asking, "What's an ale?" and "What's a lager?" — as well as the obvious sequel, "What's the difference?"

All beers are made as ales or lagers; *ale* and *lager* are the two branches (classifications) of the beer family, and closely related branches at that. However, as in many families, some beers have mixed parentage *(hybrids)*, and others have been altered with unusual flavorings *(specialty beers)*. See "Style Is Everything (And You Thought Beer Was Simple!)" later in this chapter.

Ales are the older, distinguished, traditional brews of the world, predating lagers by thousands of years, whereas lagers are a relatively modern invention, dating from the mid–19th century.

Yeast makes the beer

The branch of the beer family — ale or lager — corresponds to the type of yeast used. You have ale yeast and lager yeast, and these yeast in turn dictate what other ingredients and techniques will work in a given recipe. Beer is not just "beer," and yeast makes the beer whatever type it is.

The cold fermentation and aging temperatures used with lager yeast slow down the yeast activity and require a longer maturation time. The cold environment inhibits the production of fruitiness (called *esters*) and other fermentation byproducts common in ales. This process creates lagers' cleaner taste. Long aging (or *lagering*) also acts to mellow the beer.

Gimme a beer — no, an ale!

When the lager beer style was fully commercialized in the late 1800s, it was an instant hit in Germany and most of Europe, but lagers never caught on in Belgium, Britain, and Ireland. In those countries, if you ask for a beer, you will be served an ale, unless you specifically ask for a lager.

Lagers quickly became "the beer" in North America, where the brewers were mostly German. Until recently, if you asked for a beer in North America, you would be served a lager.

(Some places still go so far as to categorize the brews on their menu as "Beers" and "Ales" — even though this division is completely inaccurate; the division is ales and lagers, as both are beers).

But the beer renaissance is changing that. Even in the remote villages of the hinterlands, beer drinkers can choose from among most, if not all, of the world's beer types and styles — ales, lagers, hybrids, and specialty brews of every hue, strength, and flavor.

You can taste the difference, sometimes

Taste — ah, yes. Every beginner wants to know how ales taste different than lagers. If only it were that easy! This is sort of like asking how red wines taste different than white wines. (Shameless plug: See the wonderful sister book from IDG Books Worldwide, Inc., *Wine For Dummies,* by Ed McCarthy and Mary Ewing-Mulligan).

Ironically, you can find beer styles called *red beer* and *white beer,* but that's another story altogether, and you can be sure that it doesn't involve grape skins.

Ales share many characteristics, as do lagers, but the two groups overlap so much that any absolutes about either class are usually wrong. This overlap creates some confusion and the need for experts (here I am!) to explain them, but it also creates the great fun of beer exploration. Didn't you always want to be an explorer? Now's your chance.

You could say that *ales* usually

- ✔ Include more robust-tasting beers
- ✔ Tend to be fruity
- ✔ Include more bitter beers
- ✔ Have a pronounced, complex taste and aroma
- ✔ Are drunk not too cool (50 to 55 degrees F, 10 to 13 degrees C)

And you could say that *lagers* usually

- ✔ Include lighter-tasting beers
- ✔ Tend to be highly carbonated or crisp
- ✔ Tend to be smooth and mellow
- ✔ Have a subtle, clean, balanced taste and aroma
- ✔ Are drunk fairly cool (40 to 45 degrees F, 4 to 7 degrees C)

If someone says, "I don't like ales," or "lagers give me headaches," respond that there's simply too much variety for that kind of distinction to hold water (or beer, for that matter). Beer exploration is called for!

Style Is Everything (And You Thought Beer Was Simple!)

You don't ask for "just beer" any more than you ask for "just food." With beer, ya gotta have *style*.

If you were to use fruits as a metaphor for all the beer styles in the world, the beer styles would be kind of like apples, bananas, grapefruit, pineapples, or kiwis: all with quite different colors, textures, flavors, aromas, and prices.

In that case, the U.S. national-brand beers might be apples. Sure, you have some variety, what with, to name a few, Golden Delicious, Jonathan, Granny Smith, and McIntosh (not named after the computer, by the way). Good, but still apples. Without tasting anything but apples, your concept of fruit would be rather narrow. Such is the concept of beer held by many consumers, alas! If beer grew on trees, there would be lots of new farmers.

What is so good about good beer?

Taste and style. Variety.

These words are not abstract concepts, like quality, but a combination of straightforward, measurable, easily described aspects of flavor, aroma, body, and color.

To use another food analogy, the craft brewmaster is like a great chef. Just as gourmet bakers turn out bread in astonishing but now familiar varieties, from breadsticks to bagels (with pumpernickel, jalapeño rye, and hot dog buns in between), brewers can come up with an almost infinite number of variations on the classic, traditional styles noted later in this chapter. Craft brewers tend to use more expensive ingredients (all malted grains, and lots more of them per barrel) than the big commercial brewers.

Craft brewers are gourmet brewers who all together brewed just under 4 million barrels in the U.S. in 1995 (about 2 percent of all beer sales).

Although gourmet beer is not inherently better than mass-market beer, it generally has more taste and comes in a wider range of styles. The well-known, heavily advertised mass-market brands brewed by the world's largest brewers are generally top-quality products that represent a fairly narrow range of taste and style in order to appeal to the largest number of consumers. They are famed for an excellent quality control and consistency not always found in gourmet beers.

So while the megabrewers such as Heineken and Anheuser-Busch are producing the beer equivalent to Wonder Bread, smaller craft brewers are making a wide range of beer styles, and you can taste the difference. Same basic ingredients, vastly different approach. That's the difference. For examples of a few American craft brewers, see the labels in Figure 1-1.

To order! To order!: a list of ales and lagers

If you ask a bartender to suggest a good beer, he or she will probably reply, "What do you want? Strong? Mild? Malty? Dark? Light?" The information in this section about the more common beer styles should help you make sense of a friend's or bartender's queries and recommendations; the beers themselves can, no doubt, help you answer life's most vexing questions.

The beer lists and descriptions that follow are based on classic bottled brands. The fun thing about beer exploring is that your local brewpubs (and friendly local homebrewers, natch) usually offer their own versions of these standard styles. For the best examples of bottled beers of these styles, check out Appendix A. And for all the various and wonderful substyles, see Appendix B.

Remember: Beer nuts can have heated arguments over the subject of beer styles. I've stuck to traditional, historically accepted styles in this section (and in this book, for that matter).

Though the following beer styles are referred to as international or world styles, they are all originally from Europe and North America. Please don't think of me as being thoughtlessly Eurocentric — that's just the way the beer world is. Although other styles exist elsewhere, they are often not available outside their local areas. Check out the unusual beers listed in the "Unusual beer" sidebar later in this chapter for some of the really exotic stuff that you won't find at your local grocery.

Describing beer

Many tasting terms are examined in Chapter 4 and listed on the Cheat Sheet, but you need to know at least the following ones in order to understand beer styles. Knowing these terms may also encourage you to explore and experiment (and also give you something to talk about with any hophead you may encounter at the bar).

✔ **Body:** Sensation of fullness, or viscosity, of a beer on the palate, ranging from watery to creamy; beer is generally described as thin-, light-, medium-, or full-bodied (*strong* simply refers to volume of alcohol)

✔ **Complex:** Multidimensional; involving many flavors and sensations on the palate

✔ **Crisp:** Highly carbonated; effervescent

✔ **Hoppy:** Herbal or spicy aromas and bitter flavors of hops

✔ **Malty:** Caramel-like flavors derived from the malted grain

✔ **Mouthfeel:** Tactile sensations of alcoholic warmth, carbonation, dryness, and the like

✔ **Roasty/toasty:** Malt (roasted grain) flavors

Figure 1-1:
This random sampling shows that American craft-brew beer labels are an art form that reflects an artisan pride in the craft-brewing renaissance.

Ales

Ales, the beers of antiquity, come in a wide range of flavors and styles.

- **Barleywine:** Hefty ale with fruity and caramelly aromas, complex malt flavors, and as much alcohol as wine — one of the few beer styles that are noticeably stronger than other beers. Often served in a wine glass or brandy snifter (after all, it is often called the beer version of cognac; it ages well, too). Usually produced in limited quantities for winter's holiday celebrations.

- **Belgian beers:** Often considered a specialty brew group, or separate styles, or even a class by themselves (listed as substyles in Appendixes A and B). These unusual and never-subtle ales cover a wide spectrum of strong aromas and flavors, including the fruity and intense Belgian ale; the complex, aptly named Belgian strong ale; the intensely sour but refreshing Flanders brown and red ales; the tart and fruity lambics; the sweet and sour faro (lambic); the extremely sour gueuze (blended lambic); the spicy saison; the dark, complex Trappist dubbel; the spicier, sweeter Trappist tripel; and last but not least, the spicy witbier.

- **Bitters:** This style isn't really bitter — it's betrayed by the name given it centuries ago when hops were first used by English brewers. A very common, popular beer in British pubs. Bitters come in a range of substyles, from subtle to robust.

- **Brown ales:** *English* and *American* versions. Good beginner beers for timid beer drinkers looking to try something beyond the ordinary (not bad for old-timers, either). Not too malty, not too thin, with subdued fruity and caramelly flavors. Mellow but flavorful.

- **Pale ales:** Rather fruity beers with nutty and toasty malt flavors and a pleasantly dry and often bitter aftertaste. Despite their name, they're generally golden to amber in color. Some U.S. brewers' versions are labeled *amber ale*. See the sidebar "Out in the colonies" for more about India pale ales (IPAs).

- **Porter:** Dark but not imposing ale. Light malt sweetness and pleasant dark grain flavors; makes for a wonderful sipping beer. May range from medium-bodied and mild to big-bodied and robust. Porter and its cousin, *stout*, are quite distinct from other beers.

- **Stout:** Porter's close cousin, brewed in five distinct substyles. More roasty-flavored and coffeelike than porter; one of life's little luxuries. Great for nursing (beers, not babies, though in the past, it was often recommended for nursing mothers!).

- **Strong ales:** Fruity and malty with a variety of buttery, nutty, and toasty flavors. These heavyweight sippers are great for casual after-dinner or late-night imbibing. The two types of strong ale are of English (the more bitter old ale) and Scottish (the maltier and subtly smoky Scotch ale) descent.

- **Wheat beers:** The ultimate summer quenchers. Their fruity-perfumy aromas, citrusy tanginess, and spritzy effervescence make these ales especially easy to enjoy when the weather is hot. Brewed in six substyles.

Out in the colonies

A particular style of pale ale known as *India pale ale,* or *IPA,* gets its name from Britain's colonial presence in India during the 1800s. British royal subjects living in India demanded to have their favorite ales shipped to them, but the month-long journey on the open sea devastated the average cask of beer.

A British brewer named Hodgson recognized this problem and decided to brew an ale of greater alcoholic strength that could more easily withstand the rigors of oceanic transit. The antiseptic properties of the increased alcohol volume, coupled with a high concentration of hop acids, assured the colonialists of a palatable, if potent, product at journey's end.

A surprising dividend was also realized upon receipt of the beer: The gentle rocking motion of the ship on water caused the beer within the casks to pick up some of the oaky character, much like barrel-aged wine. Some brewers today maintain that link with the past by employing oak barrels or using oak chips for the aging process of IPA.

Lagers

The name *lager* is taken from the German word meaning "to store." Most of the mass-produced beers of the world are lagers, but a wider range of styles exists than those commercial brands may lead you to believe.

- ✓ **American pale lagers:** Although these beers differ greatly from brand to brand in the mind of the unknowing consumer, thanks to advertising campaigns, they are for the most part identical in taste and strength (about 4 to 5 percent alcohol by volume). All the *light, standard,* and *premium* brands were originally based on the classic Pilsner style, but they are now much different from that style. They are light-colored, gassy, and watery, with a delicate sweetness and an *adjuncty* (corn or rice is the adjunct grain mixed with the barley) aroma and flavor (light versions have almost no taste or aroma). Primarily thirst quenchers, they should be served ice cold.

- ✓ **American dark lagers:** Like their pale counterparts, these lagers are timid versions of European exemplars. They lack the fullness and rich chocolaty flavor of the German dark lager style; more bark than bite — which is why they can easily be man's best friend. Not widely available.

- ✓ **Bock beers:** Traditional bock beers are generally dark, strong, and pretty malty, but with a chocolate-accented flavor that lasts long into the after-taste. Six very distinct substyles.

- **German pale lagers:** Mainstream examples of high-quality everyday beers; mildly malty and suitably bittered. Many regional brands are exported to the U.S., where they are nationally known.

- **German dark lagers:** Ebony brethren of the German pale lagers, but slightly richer tasting.

- **Märzen/Oktoberfest beers:** Much like bock beers (malty and medium-bodied), but without the chocolate flavor and burnt amber color. Easily consumed in quantity, especially at festivals.

- **Pilsner (also spelled Pils, Pilsener, and in the Czech Republic, Plzensky):** The authentic beer from Czechoslovakia that many American brand-name beers aspire to be: an aromatic, subtly malty, crisp, and refreshingly bittered (hoppy) lager. A real classic, brewed since 1842 by the folks who originated it (Pilsner Urquell was the first golden, clear beer); the most imitated style throughout the world.

- **Rauchbier — German smoked lager:** Can range from a friendly campfirelike smokiness to an intense and acrid pungency. Definitely an acquired taste, but you haven't lived till you've tasted one with smoked ham or sausage. This beer is for sipping, not inhaling!

- **Vienna lager:** Malty, medium-bodied cousin of Märzen beer.

Hybrid styles

Some beer styles don't fit perfectly into the ale and lager categories because brewers mix the ingredients and processes of both categories into one beer. For example, a brewer may use an ale yeast but a lager fermentation temperature.

Where do hybrids fit into the beer family tree? Think of an exotic, mysterious, well-traveled uncle: a bit off the chart, not to everyone's liking, but with a definite appeal for some of us.

- **Alt or altbier:** A German ale (a rare bird, indeed). *Alt* means "old," referring to the fact that the beer is fermented the "old" way — with top-fermenting ale yeast strains. Modern altbiers are fermented warm, like ales, but aged cold, like lagers. The typical altbier is malty with an assertive palate and a fair amount of hop bitterness, though the hop blend, because it's complex, tends to differ from one brewery to the next.

  Note: The terms *top-fermenting* yeast and *bottom-fermenting* yeast are based on where the yeast choose to feed in the unfermented beer.

- **California common beer, formerly known as Steam beer:** Like its Steam predecessor, this beer features a medium body, a toasty/malty palate, and a fairly aggressive hop presence in aroma, flavor, and bitterness.

- **Cream ale:** A light-bodied, thoroughly American invention. As American brewers continued to produce light-bodied ales, they tried making them with longer and colder fermentations, as was being done with lager beer (these ales weren't spared the introduction of adjunct grains, either). The resulting beer is similar to American lagers and is often noted for its obvious corny aroma and flavor, along with a mild, perfumy-sweet grain palate. Pale and highly carbonated.

- **Kölsch:** Pronounced *kelsh*. Named after the city of Köln (Cologne), Germany, and indicates that the beer was brewed in the traditional style of that city. In Germany, only members of the Köln Brewer's Union may call their beer a Kölsch. Noticeably pale and hazy, partly due to the addition of wheat, but mostly the result of being unfiltered. Clean on the palate, with a slight lactic (milky) sourness. Relatively thin-bodied and not very strong. Medium hop bitterness has a drying effect; overall, a refreshing, summery type of beer.

Whereas ales are typically fermented at warm temperatures, cream ale, Kölsch, and altbier are brewed as ales (with top-fermenting yeast strains) but undergo a cold fermentation or aging period. California common beer, on the other hand, is fermented warm, like an ale, but with a lager (bottom-fermenting) yeast.

Specialty beers

The *specialty beer* category is more or less a catch-all for the beer styles that don't fit elsewhere. When it comes to specialty beers' place on the beer family tree, the wild artiste cousin is the model: bold, loud, experimental, often goofy, always controversial. Usually quite memorable. Lovable despite having flouted convention.

Specialty beers are typically regular beers brewed to a classic style (porter, stout, pale ale) but with some new flavor added; others are made from unusual foods that are fermented. The addition of fruits, herbs and spices, miscellaneous flavorings (such as licorice, smoke, and hot pepper), and odd fermentables (such as honey, maple syrup, and molasses) turn an ordinary beer into a specialty beer. In many ways, specialty beers are the most fun to try.

People who are new to beer drinking or perhaps those who claim not to be beer fans seem especially surprised and pleased when they try these exotic brews, especially fruit-flavored beers, for the first time. This fact is not lost on brewers, for whom creating new beers with broad appeal is now a high priority. Urge them on!

Brewmasters take a great deal of pleasure and artistic liberties when creating specialty beers. Everything but the kitchen sink can be added to a beer, and I'm not so sure how long it will be until someone tries the sink, too. After all, people have tried garlic beer (very, very bad idea) and even hot chili pepper beer (it's sort of like drinking liquid heartburn). *Caveat emptor.* Some of the more subtle blends are often the most outstanding — a blackberry porter comes to mind.

✔ **Fruit beers:** Generally light- to medium-bodied lagers or ales that have been given a fruity flavor by way of real fruit or fruit extract. Tend to have a sweeter finish than other beers. Cherry, raspberry, and blueberry are the popular flavors, but a beer that tastes of apricot, peach, or merionberry isn't unusual.

Note: Belgian lambic beers are also fruited, but they are in a class by themselves (see the ale descriptions in the previous section).

✔ **Herb and spice beers:** May include anything from cinnamon to tarragon; any beer style can be made with any herbs or spices. Summer and winter seasonal brews are typical.

Although pumpkin beers have been made with real pumpkin, the big-name commercial versions are generally just laced with the spices that are reminiscent of pumpkin pie (cinnamon, nutmeg, and allspice).

✔ **Smoked beer:** Any beer style that has been given a smoky character, though one style in particular lends itself well to a smoky aroma and taste: porter. The flavor profile of the underlying beer should always show through the smoke.

✔ **Wassail:** A very traditional style of spiced beer that is brewed for Christmas and the holiday season. Wassail is often called by other names, like *holiday beer, yule ale, winter warmer,* and if it contains fruit, *mulled ale.* (Wassail can be grouped with the fruit or the spice beers — it's hard to plug neatly into a slot — but as an old standard, it merits its own listing.)

The word *wassail* (rhymes with *fossil*) comes from the Old English *waes hael* — "be hale" or "be whole," both of which meant "be of good health." This was considered the proper toast when presenting someone with a libation. The drink of choice back then was usually mulled ale, a warmed-up strong ale laden with spices like nutmeg and ginger and sweetened with sugar or pieces of fruit, usually roasted crab apple.

Red and amber beer: Neither is clear

One consequence of the craft-brewing renaissance has been the creation of new, nontraditional "styles," such as red beer and amber beer.

In my opinion, *red beer* exists only because of marketing creativity. Before the profusion of red ales and lagers (mostly brewed by megabrewers or their subsidiaries) recently hit the store shelves, no such style existed. The parameters for red beer are hard to outline; red beers are pretty much whatever the brewer or marketing genius wants them to be, though these beers tend to be light- to medium-bodied, fairly well malted, with a distinct nutty or toasty flavor directly attributable to the grain used to infuse the beer with a reddish-brown color.

You may also see the word *amber* on labels and think that it designates a style. Amber is just a vague description of a beer's color, as in *amber ale, amber lager,* or *amber beer* (amber ales are usually some imitation of a pale ale). However, no matter how the brewers put it, amber is just a color, not a true style.

Where to Start

Deciding what to order actually gets harder when you discover how many different styles you have to choose from. Want some help? Make your next beer purchase an occasion-based decision. Consider when, where, and with whom you will be drinking the beer. What goes well with something sizzling on a grill on a hot August afternoon is unlikely to inspire the same praises if served with something fresh from the oven on a frosty winter evening. Beer does have its seasons.

If ten of your nail-pounding construction crew buddies are coming over to watch the Super Bowl, well, you may want to just buy whatever's on sale, considering you'll need a lot of it. However, if you're having a special someone over to share a nightcap by the fire, a gassy, watery beer won't enhance your chance for romance. Or perhaps you're planning the ultimate impressive gourmet repast for your boss or colleagues and want something unusual and memorable.

The wide range of colors, aromas, flavors, textures and strengths allow beer to be bought and consumed at any time of day, with or without food, at occasions grand or informal, intimate or riotous (that last one you already knew).

Buying according to season

One way to decide on a choice of beer is to take the season into account. Some beers are made only at certain times of the year, while others, available year-round, just have a natural taste link to a particular season. Table 1-1 offers some suggestions.

Table 1-1	Seasonal Beers
Season and Description	***Beers***
Summer quenchers: Should be light-colored, light- to medium-bodied, and spritzy. Can be served cold but not cold enough to numb the palate. Some brews are lemon-enhanced just for the summer.	Wheat beer Witbier Pilsner Pale ale Cream ale American premium lagers Kölsch Saison

(continued)

Table 1-1 *(continued)*

Season and Description	Beers
The "shoulder" seasons — spring and fall: The brewing industry has traditionally created its maltier beers for these two seasons. These beers are good mid-range ones, neither light nor dark, neither light-bodied nor heavy-duty. Alcohol content is only a percent or two higher than in the summer beers.	Bock beer (Maibock, helles bock, standard bock, weizenbock) Märzen Oktoberfest Vienna lager
Winter treats: These tend to be darker, medium- to full-bodied; tend to contain higher levels of alcohol. With their spices, fruits, and herbs, they add to the celebratory spirit of this time of year. They also make good gifts.	Barleywine Doppelbock Triple Bock Old ale Scotch ale Stout (oatmeal, cream, Russian Imperial) Belgian strong ale Trappist/abbey ales Medium- to full-bodied, spiced ales/wassails (winter warmers or winter brews)

Candlelight, a glass of beer, and thou: wine/beer substitutions

Next time you're about "go grape" out of habit, consider a brew instead. Table 1-2 offers a few good ideas.

Table 1-2	Beer Substitutions for Wine
Wine	**Suggested Beer Substitute**
Dry red wine	Fruit lambic or other fruited Belgian specialty beer
Champagne	Light and spritzy wheat or witbier
Brandy	Spirituous barleywine or old ale; Triple Bock (good gifts, too!)
Port wine	Russian Imperial stout

Keep in mind that these suggested substitutions are not trading taste for taste, but style for style. In other words, don't expect the Imperial Stout to *taste* like a port wine; it will serve the same enjoyable purpose as a rich and spirited after-dinner libation. I talk more about matching beer with food in Chapter 7.

Unusual beer

To broaden your perspective of beer, take a look at some of the more unusual cereal grain beverages made around the world that rightfully qualify as beer.

✔ The traditional Japanese sake, which is made with rice, has for years been mislabeled "rice wine." Because rice is a cereal grain, sake is really a form of beer.

✔ In South America, indigenous tribes still make a communal drink called *chicha*. Chicha is made of corn that is chewed by the tribal women, spat into a wide bowl, and allowed to ferment for two or three days before being consumed by the whole tribe. Doncha just love home cookin'?

✔ The Finnish uncarbonated beer *sahti* dates back to the 9th century. It is made primarily from barley but also uses rye, oats, and juniper for flavoring. Rumor has it that years ago, sahti was occasionally fermented with the saliva of a wild boar in heat. Cool!

✔ Until the latter half of this century, a beer of sorts had been produced in Egypt for over 5,000 years. Made with partially baked bread, *bouza* also used mandrake root, skirret weed (a licorice-flavored plant), and an Assyrian radish grown only in the area. Because bouza was unfiltered, long straws were needed to penetrate the thick layer of solids floating on the surface of the liquid.

Bouza is believed to be the etymological root of *booze,* the slang word Americans use to describe distilled spirits.

✔ In Russia, a mildly alcoholic, rye-based brew called *kvass* dates back over 2,000 years. Kvass starts with mixed bread crumbs and hot water, which is mixed with a sugar solution and yeast. The brew is flavored with raisins, honey, absinthe, mint, or juniper.

✔ In sub-Saharan Africa, tribeswomen make a thick, opaque, sour, and gruel-like beer called *Joala,* using a combination of grains, including sorghum, millet, and maize. It is said to have a flavor resembling yogurt (all you need now is for the yogurt companies to make a yogurt that tastes like beer).

✔ In the Tibetan Himalayas, a brew called *chang* is part of the local culture. Chang starts with partially fermented, moist yeast cakes made with rice or barley, called *phap.* The dried cakes are crushed and mixed with rice flour, softened grain, and water, and then fermentation begins again.

✔ Anyone looking for information on Zima has gotta look elsewhere. This malt-based beverage is just not a beer. Zorry.

You'll probably never again look at your "Olde Foamy" the same way.

Chapter 2

From the Sublime to the Ridiculous: Beer Ingredients

In This Chapter

▶ Getting to know beer's building blocks

▶ Becoming hip to hops

▶ Adding other grains, licorice, and who-knows-what

*B*eer is made almost entirely of water. Expensive water. Water that has been steeped, boiled, cooled, flavored, aged, pumped into a bunch of places, and finally shipped to you. As you're about to see, the beermaking process is not as simple as you might think. Is anything that tastes so good simple?

The taste and style of beer are profoundly affected by the individual ingredients, even though only four ingredients are absolutely necessary to make good beer.

The fab four are

- Barley
- Hops
- Yeast
- Water

These four together form the basic foundation of beer, and most fine beers are made *only* from these ingredients.

Barley: Cereal for Beer, Not for Breakfast

What comes to mind when you think of cereal grains? Rice Krispies, Corn Flakes, Wheat Chex, Quaker Oatmeal? You may be surprised to know that cereal grains (not the flakes, the grains) and many other grains can be used to make different kinds of beer. The cereal grain that lends itself best to beermaking is barley (shown in Figure 2-1); unlike most other grains, barley has a low gluten content, which, conversely, makes it a lousy choice for making bread. Before barley grain can be used to make beer, it must undergo a process known as *malting* (see Chapter 3 for more about beer processes).

Barley has been cultivated for thousands of years, and the thought that it may have been among the first domesticated grains because of its role in beermaking is kind of nice.

What malted barley introduces to beer are color, malty sweet flavor, body, protein to form a good head, and perhaps most important, the natural sugars needed for fermentation. Barley's role in beermaking is equivalent to grapes' role in winemaking: fundamental. Malted barley comes in a variety of colors, flavors, and degrees of roastiness that profoundly affect the color and taste of the beer (roastiness is covered in Chapter 4).

While barley is the most commonly used grain in beermaking, many brewers use additional grains, such as wheat, oats, or rye, to imbue their beer with different flavors. These *specialty* grains all serve the purpose of creating different flavors and levels of complexity in the beer (and perplexity in the beer critic). The principal difference between these grains and cheaper, adjunct grains like rice or corn (see "Wing of Bat, Eye of Newt: Adjuncts You May Love or Hate" in this chapter) is that specialty grains enhance the barley, not replace it.

Barley basics

Barley — the kind good for beer, anyway — is grown in two forms: two-row and six-row, so called for the number of rows of barley kernels as viewed from the top of the barley stalk. Two-row barley is generally used for brewing ales, and six-row barley is generally used for brewing lagers.

The six-row variety offers higher yields, making it less expensive to use. Two-row barley, which costs more, is the stuff brewers brag about using, though that's largely hype.

Barley is grown wherever other grains are grown: cool, temperate regions, such as the U.S. Pacific Northwest, Canada, Bohemia, Bavaria, Britain, Ireland, and Tasmania.

Figure 2-1:
Barley, a cereal grain, has natural sugars that feed the yeast during the fermentation of beer.

Hops: Not Just for Bunnies

Hops are the pinecone-like flowers of a female climbing plant in the cannabis family of plants (see Figure 2-2). They are grown on enormous trellises as tall as 18 feet (5.5 meters) and are often hand-picked because they are so delicate.

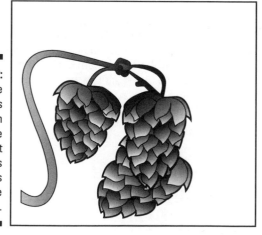

Figure 2-2:
Hops are vining plants with conelike flowers that give beer its bitterness and unique aroma.

Hops contain pinhead-sized glands of *lupulin,* a sticky substance that is secreted when boiled. Lupulin contains the essential oils, bitter acids, and resins that do the following four big jobs — a lot of work for a tiny flower:

- ✔ Counterbalance the sweetness of the barley with bitterness
- ✔ Add flavor
- ✔ Provide aroma
- ✔ Help preserve the beer

Hops' unmistakably pungent aromatics (sometimes described as spicy, herbal, floral, piney, citrusy, or even cheesy if the hops are old or oxidized) are unique, though prior to the common usage of hops in the Middle Ages, bitter herbs and spices like juniper berries (which are now used to make gin) were used. Beers with strong hop aroma and flavor are said to be *hoppy,* and beer fans who crave this kind of beer are said to be hopheads.

Hops' fourth benefit to beer — natural preservation — was realized several centuries after the advent of regular hop usage. These same resins and acids that flavor the beer have been found to counteract and delay the inevitable effects of bacterial spoilage, thereby giving beer a longer shelf life. Who needs chemical preservatives? (Answer: Brewers who are shipping beer around the world, where temperature and time reach extremes.)

Before anyone panics, I should point out that nothing that occurs naturally in the beermaking process is pathogenic, or virally harmful to your health. (Note the use of the word *naturally. . . .*)

Hop hits

More than 50 hop varieties are grown in five major hop-growing regions throughout the world. You'll often see these names on labels and menus. Many of the various hop varieties have been dubbed with names that hint at their origins in these regions:

- ✔ East Kent Goldings (England)
- ✔ Saaz (Bohemia, Czech Republic)
- ✔ Hallertau (Germany)
- ✔ Pride of Ringwood (Tasmania)
- ✔ Mt. Hood (U.S. Pacific Northwest)

Hop history

In 8th-century, central Europe, hops were cultivated for the first time rather than picked in the wild. Records show that hop growing flourished in Bohemia in 859. Prior to hop usage in beermaking, brewers bittered their beer with flowers, leaves, berries, spices, and a host of odd and unpalatable ingredients, many of which failed miserably. By the 16th century, hops had become the most widely accepted spice for beer.

Most of the North American hops are grown in the Pacific Northwest. North American hops are considered pretty assertive; Cluster, a bittering hop, and Cascade, an aroma hop, are the best known (see "Bitter news" in this chapter for more on bittering and aroma hops).

The vast majority of the hop varieties (or *cultivars*) are hybrids of original varieties, cross-bred to capitalize on specific genetic qualities, such as high yields and resistance to disease. An amazing amount of effort has gone into cultivating hops, considering that they are used so sparingly in the beermaking process (only a few ounces are used in a 5-gallon batch of homebrew), almost like herbs in cooking. Each kind of hop is distinctive in its bittering, aroma, and flavor. The differences among them are so subtle that even the most experienced beer judges are hard put to recognize the use of different hops in a given brew. (If you're the kind of persnickety reader who insists on knowing everything, see Chapter 11 for the varieties and their characteristics.)

Bitter news

Each hop variety is more or less bitter, just like rejected lovers. Only instead of being measured in the number of forlorn letters and pleading phone calls, hop bitterness is measured scientifically and expressed by alpha acid content.

Brewers learn these numbers so they can judge what they call the *bittering potential* of each hop variety, which allows them to substitute different types of hops (because of availability or price) and to determine the exact quantity of hops needed for a particular brew recipe. They also learn each variety's unique aromatic properties (those hops used primarily in brewing are called *bittering* hops, and those used for aroma are called *finishing* hops). And the brewers generally are not bitter with their lovers (or so I'm told), though they may love their "bitters."

The distinctive aroma of each type of hop comes from the essential oils that are destroyed during the boiling part of brewing, so some hops are added after that stage in order to get their aroma into the beer, in a step known as *dry hopping*.

Brewers take into account all these variables — bitterness, aroma, the need for dry hopping — when designing a recipe for a beer. That's why you'll see hops mentioned on some beer menus. People actually know and appreciate this stuff!

Yeast: There's a Fungus Amongus

Yeast works hard but really enjoys itself (like me, most of the time). This little single-cell organism, one of the simplest forms of plant life, is responsible for carrying out the fermentation process in beermaking, thereby providing one of life's simplest forms of pleasure.

Yeast is in the fungus family (yikes — mushrooms in beer!) and because of its cell-splitting capabilities, is self-reproducing. Yeast has a voracious appetite for sweet liquids and produces abundant quantities of alcohol (ethanol) and carbon dioxide in exchange for a good meal (which means that yeast is also responsible for producing brain-splitting headaches if you drink too much).

The vast majority of beer contains between 4 and 5 percent alcohol, but occasionally, brewers make beer with higher alcohol contents. In these beers, after a level of 8 or 9 percent alcohol by volume is reached, the beer yeast falls into a stupor, and fermentation is effectively over. When the brewmaster wants higher alcohol levels, hardy champagne or sherry yeast may be brought in to do the job.

Note: Yeast is responsible for fermenting not only beer but wine as well, and because it produces carbon dioxide, it's what causes bread dough to rise.

The story on yeast

Ale yeast has a lineage that reaches into antiquity — wild, airborne strains did the trick. Yeast was not even considered an ingredient in beer until its role in fermentation was discovered and understood. (This discovery began with the invention of the microscope in the early 1700s and was furthered by Louis Pasteur nearly a century later when Pasteur proved that a rapid heating process would kill bacteria and other microorganisms. Pasteur was more interested in beer than milk, by the way, as am I.) The genetically engineered lager yeast variety was only perfected in the mid-1800s. This factoid is not all that important, except that before this discovery, brewers could not make what is now called a lager by plan. They had to brew ale, ferment and store it at cold temperatures, and hope for the best.

Yeast genus and genius

For all you biology fans out there, here's the scoop on yeast. I'm talking about two different species of the genus *Saccharomyces:* ale yeast, s. *cerevisiae,* and lager yeast, s. *uvarum* (sometimes called s. *Carlsbergensis*). And bread (or baker) yeast is part of the same genus, in case you wondered.

Do you recognize a familiar root word in the lager yeast strain Latin name? s. *Carlsbergensis* is named for the giant Danish brewery, Carlsberg. The founder's son, Jacob Christian Jacobsen,

who counted Louis Pasteur among his friends and colleagues, set up a company laboratory in 1875. In this lab in 1883, the first single-cell yeast culture was definitively isolated. Emil Hansen set the stage for modern lager brewing by giving the brewmaster the ability to choose a specific strain of yeast that produced good beer and thereby establish brand consistency.

Just think: If you're a homebrewer with a serious lab, maybe you could do the same thing. Someday.

In the early days, knowing only that the frothy, sludgy substance that accumulated on the top of a vat of fermenting beer was somehow responsible for turning raw, sweet stuff into finished beer, English-speaking brewers spoke from the heart when they christened it "Godisgood," and when warm-weather fermentations went sour, they blamed it on "beer witches."

Nowadays, brewers can order yeast strains from a catalog, by number: "Mailorderisgood." (If it doesn't arrive, blame it on "mail witches.")

Since the late 1800s, numerous pure yeast strains — over 500 different types — have been isolated, identified, and cultured. Commercial yeast banks inventory these strains in the form of sterile *slants* (test tubes), and individual breweries keep their own sterile cultures on hand for future brews. Many brewers consider their yeast to be their most secret ingredient and often guard its identity jealously.

Yeast sets the style

Yeast can also take credit for the classification of the beer style. Brewmasters pick a yeast according to the recipe or the style of beer that they want to make. As mentioned in Chapter 1, yeast is identified as either a *top-fermenting* or *bottom-fermenting* strain, based on where it chooses to feed in the unfermented beer.

> ✔ Ale yeast, which is a top-fermenting strain, works best in warm temperatures (60 to 75 degrees F, 15 to 24 degrees C).
>
> ✔ Lager yeast, which is a bottom-fermenting strain, performs best in cold temperatures (38 to 52 degrees F, 3 to 11 degrees C).

Because of the temperature differential, each strain produces the vastly different flavor and aroma characteristics that in turn create the different beer styles you know and love (and drink). Yeast, in combination with different fermentation processes, can also contribute a certain fruitiness and other flavors characteristic to the beer. The brewmaster tries to keep these flavors in check.

H₂OH!

Considering that it constitutes up to 95 percent of a beer's total ingredient profile, water can certainly have a tremendous influence on the finished product. Today's brewers are fortunate to have the ability to alter and adjust the chemical makeup of a given water source to suit their brewing needs by adding calcium carbonate, magnesium, gypsum, and the like.

Some of the classic world styles of beer became classics because of the water used to make the brew. The famed Pilsner beers of Bohemia, such as Pilsner Urquell, are considered premier examples. These crisp, hoppy lagers are made with extremely soft water pumped from the aquifers below the brewery. By contrast, the legendary British ales of Burton-upon-Trent, such as Bass Ale, are made with particularly hard water. Brewers attempting to emulate these British beers simply add minerals called *Burton salts* to the brewing water in a process named *Burtonizing.*

You've heard ads for beer "from the land of sky-blue waters," or "brewed with Rocky Mountain spring water." Breweries like to gloat about the purity of the local water used in their beer. But any given water source can be, and usually is, chemically manipulated to match another source — some of the traditional sources are treated anyway. The water is just one of many variables that affect the final taste of the beer.

Wing of Bat, Eye of Newt: Adjuncts You May Love or Hate

Although the four ingredients of barley, hops, yeast, and water are all that's needed to make beer, they are by no means all the ingredients that are used. Additional grains, natural sugars, and flavorings are often added, for either of two reasons:

- ✔ To create unique flavors
- ✔ To cut costs

Brewing artistes like to use a wide variety of nontraditional ingredients, including spices, fruits, and grains, to give their beers unique and unusual flavors. Big beer factories, on the other hand, tend to use adjuncts to cut costs rather than to create different or innovative brews.

Many industrial brewers use some unmalted cereal grains such as corn and rice just to save money, as barley is a relatively expensive grain. Using corn and rice as adjuncts also produces lighter and less malty beers. While some European brewers use between 10 and 20 percent adjuncts in their beers, some large U.S. brewers are notorious for using as much as 30 to 40 percent adjuncts (which is why some people call these "add-junk" beers!). In Germany, the use of adjuncts — or anything other than malt, hops, yeast, or water — in lagers is prohibited by the famed German Purity Law (see Chapter 8 for information on this law).

Non-grain adjuncts may include honey, maple syrup, dextrose, brown sugar, and molasses. And then you have the chemical additives and preservatives, including over 50 antioxidants, foam enhancers, and miscellaneous enzymes. All these are permitted under U.S. law, but most small brewers, especially those in the U.S. microbrewer renaissance, pride themselves on their voluntary exclusion of these nontraditional ingredients.

That some brewers put rather odd ingredients into their beers is no longer unusual, though perhaps a bit unsettling to beer drinkers. These days, adventurous beer lovers can find beers with fruits and fruit flavorings, licorice, herbs and spices, even whole jalapeño peppers right in the bottle! And as long as the market can stand it, brewers will continue to introduce beers with new and unique ingredients. Why not?

Early American brewing

On his fourth voyage to the New World (circa 1502), Christopher Columbus partook of a beer-like beverage made by the natives of Central America. After throwing a handful of maize (corn) and a dollop of black birch tree sap into an earthenware jug, the people filled the jug with water and allowed natural fermentation to do the rest. Researchers have since found that a variety of beers were made by the people of both North and South America for hundreds of years prior to Columbus's arrival.

Chapter 3

Brewing Beer

In This Chapter

▶ Identifying equipment at a brewery

▶ Adjusting the brewing process to fine-tune a beer's taste

*B*eer brewing is fairly complex and involves a lot of equipment, especially when compared to winemaking. Things are roasted, ground, heated, cooled, boiled, stirred, and so on. Brewmasters have plenty of room to assert their taste and demonstrate their talent, but brewing takes a lot of work and skill. The brewmaster's symbol is the same as the alchemist's symbol, a six-pointed star. Small wonder.

A visit to any brewery will show you that while all breweries are in the business of brewing beer, no two breweries are alike in terms of their equipment and the processes they follow. Refer to Figure 3-1 for a schematic of the brewing process used in most breweries. Brewpub owners usually like to show off their breweries. *Brewpubs* — restaurants/taverns with small breweries attached — are less automated than the big breweries, and everything is on a smaller scale. Be sure to ask for an impromptu tour the next time you visit a brewpub.

See Chapter 2 for a rundown on beer ingredients. Chapter 1 goes into the styles of beer.

Tuns, Kettles, and Tanks: Equipment

Although the equipment needed to brew beer traditionally was fairly simple, large commercial breweries today use equipment that does everything from cracking the grain to sealing the boxes, and a multitude of chores in between.

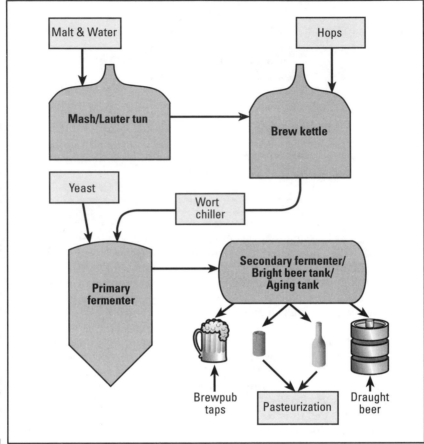

Figure 3-1:
Although the
actual
size and
complexity
of the
brewing
equipment
and process
vary among
breweries,
this
schematic
shows the
basic
brewing
process
from raw
materials to
bar or keg.

Most folks visiting a brewery would immediately recognize the large, round brew kettle that usually dominates the brewhouse. (Please don't call it a still! Distill beer, and you get whiskey, a good subject for another book altogether.) Somewhere nearby is usually a second, sometimes smaller, kettle called a *mash tun,* and if the place is big and brews lagers, it has yet another one, called a *lauter tun.*

These vessels are vented through stacks that carry the steam out of the brewhouse, consequently treating the whole neighborhood to the intoxicating, malty-sweet aroma of beer in the making.

Traditionally, these vessels were made of copper and were often referred to simply as the *coppers* (which always reminds me of Edward G. Robinson in a black fedora, but he was no brewer). Nowadays, the term has fallen out of use; modern brewing equipment is fabricated from the relatively cheaper and easier-to-obtain stainless steel.

BEER LINGO

Mega, micro, and money

It takes all kinds to make the world work, especially in the world of beer. Brewers tend to fall into categories by size, with some correlation to styles brewed. You often hear these terms:

✔ **Megabrewers:** The biggest brewers. For example, Anheuser-Busch, the company that brews Budweiser, makes about 80 *million* barrels of beer each year (44 percent of the U.S. market). Runner-up Miller brews only half that, European giant Heineken about the same as Miller, and Coors and Stroh/ Heileman about 20 million barrels a year. That's why they're called megabrewers. The big four in the U.S. tend to make similar pale lagers.

✔ **Regional brewers:** These guys fall between the big and the small. They distribute mostly on the regional level and may produce either gourmet or mass-market beer under their own or other labels.

✔ **Contract brewers:** Anyone with a good recipe and a ton of cash for marketing can have a commercial brewery (usually a regional one) make beer for them, perhaps at several locations. Only one contract brewer has broken the million-barrel-a-year mark.

✔ **Microbrewers:** Small entrepreneurs with breweries that make less than 15,000 barrels a year. Some people disregard the quantity qualifier — and the dictionary — and simply associate microbrews (also called *micros*) with good, flavorful beer.

✔ **Brewpubs:** The folks who brew on the premises of their own bar (or restaurant). They rarely brew more than several thousand barrels a year.

After these first three vessels are used, the beer is pumped (and cooled at the same time) into a big tank called a *fermenter*. For sanitation purposes, these fermenters are usually airtight and allow only for the escape of the carbon dioxide pressure built up inside. However, some traditionalists in the industry, particularly in Britain and Belgium, still allow their beer to ferment in open vessels, and some even encourage spontaneous fermentations caused by wild, airborne yeast (Belgian lambic brewers, for example).

At this point, each brewery uses different kinds of tanks and does different things to its beer. Most breweries allow beer to go through a short aging process following the initial fermentation, using additional vessels cleverly named *aging tanks* for this purpose. Next: You've heard of finishing school? Well, breweries transfer the aged beer from aging tanks into *finishing tanks* to prepare them for their introduction into society. Because the beer must be regularly transferred from one vessel to another throughout the brewing and aging processes and because everything has to be super-clean, various pumps and hoses are scattered throughout the brewery, making some setups look like a Rube Goldberg device. Watch your step!

In case you're actually taking this stuff seriously and walking about a brewery with this book as a guide, please note (before you bang your head against the stainless steel in confusion) that brewers tend to use these tank terms loosely and interchangeably. Aging tanks are often called *secondary fermentation tanks* (because the primary fermentation took place in the previous tank), while finishing tanks are alternatively called *conditioning tanks* by packaging breweries or *serving, holding,* or *bright beer* tanks by brewpubs ("bright" because the beer has clarified by this point). Is that clear?

Note: After the brewery tour, a simple "Tanks a lot" will do.

So if you're itching to start your own brewery, you'll only need, oh, about a million dollars to get all the basic equipment.

Ale Alchemy: Brewing Processes

 Explaining the usual sequential steps to making beer on the commercial level gets a bit technical — you have my permission to skip this section and move on. If you're sticking around, grab a brew and get comfortable.

Malting

The first step of brewing is malting, in which raw barley (or sometimes wheat) is converted to malted barley (also known as *barleymalt* or just plain *malt*). If you want to get technical, the malting process involves converting the starchy insides of the kernel (the *endosperm*) into soluble sugars called *maltose* by stimulating the natural germination process with moisture. Most often, professional maltsters with large malting plants handle the whole process and sell the malt to the breweries; the megabrewers often do their own malting.

Thinking that it's in a moist springtime meadow and not on the floor of some enormous factory, the seedling begins to grow. When this little shoot reaches a certain length, hot air is blown through the bed of grain, stopping the germination cold (sorry — hot!) and turning the grain into malted barley. Who said it's not nice to fool Mother Nature?

Once dried, some of the malt is further roasted in a kiln to bring out various colors and roasty or toasty flavors that are used to create different colors and flavors in the beer, much as with coffee beans and coffee. Some malts, slyly called *crystal malt, black malt,* or *chocolate malt,* are roasted to the point of becoming crystallized, charred, or deeply browned, respectively. Crystal malt is a bit crunchy and fun to eat at this stage (ask a brewer for a handful), and it may be used to make other products, like malted milk (which is not as much fun as beer).

Brewing through the ages

A team of Yale archaeologists excavated the remains of a 4,500-year-old bakery and brewery outside Cairo. They believe that the remains are from a village that housed pyramid laborers on the Giza Plateau. In addition to earthenware pots and petrified grain stores, they discovered tombs and clay tablets with hieroglyphics. One of these tablets describes the brewing processes and sings the praises of a Sumerian beer goddess. The "Hymn to Ninkasi" has been studied not only by students of ancient history but more recently by brewers wishing to learn more about brewing in the past.

Milling

Before brewers can put the grain into the mash tun and begin brewing, they have to mill the grain. *Milling* is relative here; the intent is not to make flour — just to crack open the husk of the barley kernel.

The cracked grain, now called *grist,* can then be dropped through an opening in the floor down into the mash tun. If it has to be moved up or around, the grain must be moved by machine or (ouch) carried by hand to its destination. Makes you thirsty just thinking about it. I wonder what they quaff to quench their thirst with in those dry, dusty parts of the brewery? Hmmm.

Mashing

Once in the mash tun, the cracked grain is infused with hot water, just like making a couple thousand pots of tea. Quite often, several different kinds of malt or specialty grains (see Chapter 2) are blended to achieve unique colors and tastes. The water's pH (measure of its acidity and alkalinity) is adjusted as necessary. Together, the grist and the water create a thick porridge called the *mash.* Strict time and temperature controls help to effectively convert the starches to natural sugars within the kernels of grain. At this stage, even a small error can spell disaster for the batch.

Once the brewer determines that the mash is complete, the thick, sweet, sticky *wort* (as the malt juice is now called) is transferred over to the brew kettle for the *boil.* Depending on the mashing method, the brewer either drains the liquid through a false bottom that keeps the grain in the mash tun or transfers it first to a lauter tun, which is built like a giant kitchen colander. Who knows — maybe some brewpubs use the lauter tun for pasta, too.

The grain, now called *spent grain,* is no longer of use to the brewer and is often sold to local farmers to be used as hog slop. Some brewpubs use the spent grain to bake a high-fiber bread — usually sold to go!

Extract brewing

Certain brewers, mostly in the microbrewing industry, are able to circumvent all the mashing procedures by using a dehydrated wort called *malt extract. Extract brewers,* as people who use this stuff are called, need only to pour these extracts into their brew kettle and rehydrate them with boiling water.

Although this shortcut may sound like a tremendous time, money, and energy saver, malt extracts are considerably more expensive than raw grain, and extract beers are often inferior to *all-grain beers* (beers made with freshly milled grain). There's no such thing as a free lunch, or even a free beer, for that matter.

Boiling

After the mashing process comes the boil in the brew kettle — usually one to two hours. The boil accomplishes many things, not the least of which is the complete sterilization of the liquid and any other ingredients added to it.

The brew kettle is also where the brewer goes about balancing the cloyingly sweet wort with the pleasant bittering effects of the hops. By choosing a measured amount of a certain hop variety or a blend of several varieties and adding them at precisely prescribed times (*bittering hops* at the start, *flavoring hops* late in the boil, and *finishing hops* at the very end), the brewer gives the beer its indelible hop signature.

When added skillfully and evenhandedly, the hops' bittering, flavoring, and aromatic attributes are in perfect contrast and balance to the flavor and complexity of the malt. That's the brewer's art.

Additional aromatic hop character can be infused by a method called *dry hopping,* where the brewer puts aromatic hops directly into the secondary fermenter along with the beer after it has undergone primary fermentation.

Out with the hops, into the whirlpool

After an hour or two of boiling time, the heat is shut off, and the beer, now called *bitter wort,* is prepared for transfer to the fermentation tank. The hops can be removed by a *hop extractor,* which functions much like the false bottom of a mash tun, or by a *whirlpool,* in which all solid matter is forced to the center of the vessel by centrifugal force as the now-clarified wort is drawn off from the side.

Kissin' cousins (but not in this crowd)

The Scotch-whisky–making process starts out somewhat similarly to that of beer, its barleymalt-family cousin. Malt whisky is made from malted barley (which gets its smoky character from being kilned with peat), which is also milled and mashed. It is also fermented with yeast, but the similarity stops there: Malt whisky uses no hops. Whisky makers sometimes call the result of this fermentation the *beer!* Beer (the regular kind) and whisky (especially unblended, single-malt whisky) share a scent of malt and as you can thus expect, many fans. In fact, at least one magazine, *The Malt Advocate,* covers both subjects, along with some coverage of cigars. However, at last report, cigars were not known to be distilled or hopped, but like whisky malt, they *are* smoked. (You had to see that one coming.)

Chilling out

The wort is pumped from the kettle through a *wort chiller* (refer to Figure 3-1). Now rid of unwanted solids, the hot wort needs to be cooled down quickly for two reasons:

- Warm, sweet liquid is the perfect medium for bacterial growth.
- The wort has to be made ready for yeast, which is killed by any temperature over 100 degrees F or 38 degrees C (even levels above 80 degrees F or 27 degrees C can cause off flavors and yeast cell mutations).

Fermenting

After it's boiled and subsequently cooled, the wort is pumped into the fermentation tank, and a slurry of fresh, aerated yeast is *pitched,* or added to the tank. Commercial brewers use about a liter for each barrel (approximately 31 gallons) of beer that they are making, while homebrewers need only a ¼-ounce packet of dry yeast for a 5-gallon batch. That little bit of yeast packs a wallop.

At this point, the fermenter is either sealed or left open to nature's way, depending on the recipe, for the *primary fermentation*. Within 24 hours of the yeast pitching, vigorous fermentation should take place. If the fermentation tank is sealed, the mounting carbon dioxide pressure must be vented. If it is not sealed, a thick layer of dense foam appears on top of the turbid liquid, and the carbon dioxide gasses are released into the air. This process goes on for five to ten days, depending on the yeast strain as well as the fermentation temperature — determined, again, by the recipe. (The cooler the fermentation temperature, the slower the action of the yeast.)

Getting kraeusened

Some brewers boast of using an old-fashioned, traditional German method of conditioning beer called *kraeusening*. To kraeusen a beer, the brewer adds a small amount of a young fermenting wort to a fully fermented one in order to induce a secondary fermentation. Though it sounds novel, this method is not unique among the larger brewers — especially in Germany, where the procedure was developed. The modern, industrial alternative is to merely pump in carbon dioxide.

Aging

Beer ages quickly, compared to wine and people (especially people who drink beer, of course). As I mention earlier in this chapter, after primary fermentation is complete, the beer is transferred to an aging tank called a *secondary fermentation vessel* for — guess what — secondary fermentation and a period of aging and maturation that ranges from a couple of weeks (for ales) to a couple of months (for lagers), depending on the beer style. A small brewpub may skip aging and send the beer straight to the bright beer tank for the final stage and sale as draught beer.

Packaging

After the beer has been given the appropriate amount of conditioning, it's ready to be packaged for you to drink.

In brewpubs, where the beer is meant to be served on the premises, the finished beer is transferred to the finishing tank, which, in this case, is often called the *serving, holding,* or *bright beer tank.* The tank is usually connected directly to the tap standards at the bar where the beer is drawn.

In most packaging breweries, where the beer is packaged and shipped, the beer is drawn from the tank, after the appropriate amount of conditioning, to be filtered and kegged (under pressure) and bottled or canned. Bottled or canned beer is pasteurized to kill any rogue yeast cells or bacteria that may have slipped through the system.

Kegged beer that is not being shipped abroad is rarely pasteurized, a big distinction to some drinkers. Why? The downside to pasteurization is that while it creates a more stable product, it also damages the product, killing off as much of the beer's taste as bad microorganisms.

The pasteurizing process stabilizes the beer by heating it up to relatively high temperatures. *Tunnel* pasteurization, favored by megabrewers, sprays hot water over the bottles and cans for up to an hour. A less effective but gentler method, favored by microbrewers, is called *flash* pasteurization, which may use extremely hot water or even steam, but for no more than a minute or so.

In Germany, only draught beer that is scheduled for export is pasteurized. In other parts of the world, the chances are 50-50 that draught beer for export has been pasteurized. Remember, unpasteurized beer usually tastes better, but only if it's fresh; unpasteurized beer is likely to go bad faster.

Cleaning up

Brewers say that more water ends up on the floor of the brewery than in the brew kettle. This is true because of all the cleaning and rinsing that must take place before and after each brew (be sure to wear your boots when you visit). Sanitizing the brewing equipment is as critical to making good beer as cleaning the kitchen is to cooking good food (most gourmet kitchens are spotless). It's an integral part of the brewing process.

Brewing in the bottle and cask

In England, brewers of traditional, *cask-conditioned* ale (affectionately called *Real Ale* by its passionate fans) do not filter their beer and use only oak casks for kegging. They also never use gas to push the beer from the cask, always hand-pumping instead. Not complying with any of these standards is considered untraditional and not worthy of the title of Real Ale. Die-hard fans consider Real Ale part of England's heritage (it is rarely found elsewhere).

Traditional cask-conditioned ale is considered "live" beer. Cask ales (a *cask* is traditionally a wooden keg) get a small dose of sugar and a clarifying agent in the cask at the brewery (and sometimes some hops, too, for dry-hopped beers) and then spend two or three days in the pubs' cellars at a temperature of about 55 degrees F (13 degrees C), where they are allowed to *condition* (working up natural carbon dioxide, which the pub manager releases slowly) before the beer is served to discerning customers.

Cask-conditioned ale is served the traditional way, pulled on a vacuum hand-pump rather than pushed from the cask with carbon dioxide from pressurized tanks. Hand-pumping makes for a superb head and a smoother, more traditional drink with less carbonation than other beers. Cask-conditioning demands more care and talent from the pubkeeper and brewer. Big commercial brewers prefer to package their product in pressurized kegs that require gas for dispensing.

Bottle-conditioned beers get a dose of live yeast (not unlike homebrewed beer or champagne) just before bottling. Some English ales, many Belgian beers, and a few German styles are bottle-conditioned. German hefeweizen is probably the best-known bottle-conditioned style of beer. All feature a hefty amount of bubbles.

All That Just for a Brewski?

Now you can appreciate how hard a brewmaster must work to achieve a balance of all the flavors, aromas, and textures that the various ingredients and processes contribute to this complex beverage. The struggle to balance the final aroma, palate, and finish of the recipe when all the variables are taken into account is well worth the price of a pint when it works. And just so you can recognize when it works, check out Chapter 4 for the nuances of appreciating beer.

No, you can't age beer like you do wine

In 1911, excavators in Alzey, Germany, found an earthen jug within the ruins of a Roman dwelling. Chemical analyses of the dark brown substance within proved it to be an unfinished beer mash. It was estimated to be over 1,600 years old.

I wonder whether the excavators finished making the beer....

Part II
Enjoying Beer: Tasting, Serving and Cooking

The 5th Wave   By Rich Tennant

BILL AND IRWIN'S LAST VISIT TO THE LOGGER'S BAR

BOY, THE LAGERS IN THIS PLACE REEEALLY STINK! AND THEY'RE WEAK! WEAK AND PUTRID! I MEAN IF THIS WERE MY BAR, I WOULDN'T EVEN SERVE WEAK GIRLY-LAGERS LIKE THIS!!

In this part . . .

Though it comes as a surprise to some folks, beer merits as much attention in terms of serving and tasting as does wine. Beer even substitutes very nicely for wine in the kitchen and at the table. Like wine, beer has a vocabulary and set of techniques that can really increase your understanding and enjoyment of beer.

Of course, if you're merely thirsty, just go pop a cold one!

Chapter 4

Tasting and Evaluating Beer: Making Your Buds Wiser

*Y*ou've tasted beer before. How complicated can formal beer tasting be? You open the beer, pour it into a glass (or not), lift it to your lips, sip, swallow, and you're done. Right?

Not so fast! What did you see? What did you smell? What did you taste? Can you still taste it? Was it good? Or bad? Or neither? Was it what you expected or what it was advertised to be? Would you recommend it to friends or buy it again for yourself? You can go way beyond just plain "tastes great — less filling!"

You want to pay attention to how you taste beer for plenty of reasons. Here are just a few:

✔ Knowledge and familiarity increase your drinking pleasure.

✔ You may be interested in homebrewing and its focus on beer styles.

✔ Someone you're crazy about is crazier about beer than you (are), and knowledge is power.

Remember, you're on your way to becoming a beer connoisseur of sorts. Your old style of beer tasting was undoubtedly to pop the tab, gulp the brew down, belch (well, some of you, perhaps), and maybe toss the beer can over your left shoulder (in that order). Your new, enlightened approach, however, involves a slightly different sequence to evaluating beer. Don't worry — the steps are completely natural and quite easy. If you can open a bottle of beer, you can evaluate the beer.

If you've tasted only megabrewed, U.S.-style pale lagers, your beer-evaluating tools have been mostly dormant. But now that you're giving beer the respect it deserves and sampling a wide range of beer styles, you want to get as many of your senses involved as possible.

How? Fetch a beer, sit down, and read on.

However, if you don't want to formalize your beer tasting, that's cool, too. Beer should be simply enjoyed! That's rule number one, and don't forget it.

Tasting 1-2-3 (Actually, 1-2-3-4-5)

Drinking beer is a sensual experience. Oh, all right, maybe it's not as exciting as a date, but it had better be more fun than doing your taxes. Consuming beer (or any food, for that matter) should be a full sensory experience; the more senses involved, the more you'll remember about the experience — positive or not.

When barbecuing a steak, you don't just see the meat cooking on the grill; you hear the sizzle and pop of its juices and smell its tantalizing aromas wafting through the air. When you taste the steak, you not only savor the flavor but also describe it in a tactile manner — you might say that it's moist and tender, or if you're eating at my house, probably that it's as dry and tough as shoe leather.

"Its noble bouquet belies its plebeian origins"

The exchange of information on any specific subject generally requires a special language, and — just your luck — beer tasting has its own jargon as well.

This little-known language is the basis for menu and label descriptions, as well as being absolutely necessary for professional brewers and homebrewers, judges, and critics as a quality-control vocabulary. More important, you'll hear these words bandied about at any popular beer bar. Good terms to know are interspersed throughout this chapter. If you want more lingo, jargon, and geeky vocabulary, see the Cheat Sheet, Chapter 1, and the chapters on homebrewing (Chapters 10 through 12).

But the existence of serious beer words brings up the issue of beer snobbery. Please, beer lovers, do not bring wine snobbery into the beer arena. If you can't fathom how someone else is able to drink a particular beer that tastes awful to you, please go ahead and say, "This beer stinks!" If you can't figure out what to say about a brew, don't try to fake it with an "Ah, er, a very complex beer indeed — reminds me of my days abroad" or the artsy phrase at the head of this sidebar when all you really want to say is "Damn, this tastes good!"

It's just beer, after all. For pleasure, remember?

Transfer these mental notes to tasting beer. When pouring a beer into a (clean) glass, *listen* for the plop-plop of the liquid and the fizzing of the escaping carbonation. But wait — don't drink it yet! *See* the tiny bubbles race upward only to get lost in a layer of dense foam. *Watch* the head rise and swell up over the lip of the glass. *Breathe* in the full bouquet of aromas emanating from the beer. *Taste* the many flavors of the grains, hops, and other ingredients. *Feel* the viscosity of the beer and the prickly effervescence of the carbonation on your tongue and palate. *Savor* the lingering flavors of the aftertaste.

You don't want any distractions when you are seriously tasting beer. Use a glass large enough to hold a whole bottle, and follow the pouring and cleaning guidelines in Chapter 6. And no frosted mugs, please!

There's a particular order for beer tasting. I suggest doing the following steps in the order shown. Note that Steps 1 and 2 happen separately, as does Step 5, but Steps 3 and 4 really happen together. Some of the most important tasting work is done before you even drink!

1. **Smell: Check aroma and bouquet.**

2. **Look: Check appearance.**

3. **Taste: Check flavor.**

4. **Touch: Check body and mouthfeel.**

5. **Reflect: Check final judgment.**

Of course, you can just skip all this and go ahead and drink, noting only whether you like the beer. But if you ever want to tell someone about a beer you like, you'll find all this discussion helpful. As Mom says, it always helps to talk.

Following from the steps of the five senses, you can easily see that you evaluate beer in five corresponding areas. Each beer style (see Chapter 1 for more on beer styles) should have certain characteristics in each area, and that's what beer judges look for in beer competitions; on the other hand, as a consumer, you need only note the characteristics for comparison, except, of course, for affection or rejection.

Plop plop, fizz fizz

Although the eyes, nose, and mouth are the key players, the ears can give you some important information as well. "Hearing" beer is pretty much limited to its carbonation (fizzzzt) upon opening the bottle or the sound of breaking glass when you drop one. If the beer doesn't fizz when you open it, be prepared for a flat beer. If it doesn't fizz when you drop it, no loss (though it's a mess to clean up — time for another beer).

Smell: The Nose Knows

Beer aromas are fleeting, so start with a sniff even before you take a look. Also, flavor is partly based on aroma — a full third of your ability to taste is directly related to smell, so don't skip this step.

Like wine and whiskey critics, beer critics use the term *nose* two ways: to describe aroma and bouquet (if aroma were a sound, bouquet would be the volume) as well as the action. You could say, "While nosing his porter, he commented on its robust licorice nose." You could also say, "While nosing around the pub, he commented on its robust clientele," but that has nothing to do with this discussion.

The most prominent aromas associated with beer's nose usually come first from malt and second from hops:

- **Malt:** *Malty* aromas can run from perfumy-sweet to rich and caramelly and are fairly obvious. Depending on how dark the beer is, *roasty, toasty,* or *chocolaty* aromas may come from the specialty grains added to the beer.

- **Hops:** This aroma depends on the variety and amount of hops added to the boiling beer and on whether aromatic hops were added to the beer during the fermentation or aging phases (see the discussion of dry hopping in Chapter 3). Hop aromas may be described as *herbal, perfumy,* spicy, *grassy, floral, piney, citrusy,* and occasionally *cheesy* (and Sleepy, Sneezy, Dopey, Grumpy, and Doc, too, no?).

Other aromas, such as fruit and alcohol aromas, come from fermentations. Some ales have a *buttery* or *butterscotchy* smell *(diacetyl)* that is the result of warm fermentations and certain yeast strains. If you smell or taste creamed corn in your lager, it may be something called DMS (di-methyl sulfide). *Plastic, cooked vegetable, rotten eggs, skunky (catty),* and *wet dog* smells are common signs of — guess what — badly made or stored beer.

Look: You Can't Judge a Bock by Its Cover

What should you look for in a beer? Your eyes can discern color, clarity, and head retention (as well as price, of course, and maybe even the meaning of life).

Every color in the rainbrew

The colors that make up the various beer styles run the spectrum from pale straw to golden, amber, copper, orange, red, brown, black, and everything in between. One color is not necessarily better than the others, and none indicates directly how the beer will taste — color is dictated by style (see Figure 4-1).

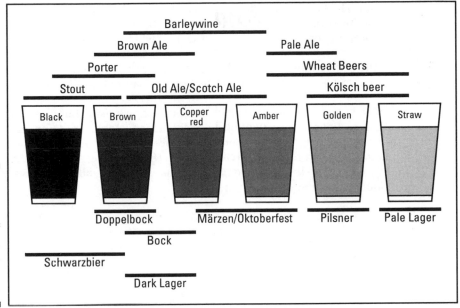

Figure 4-1:
Beer styles
come in a
full range of
colors,
regardless
of taste and
strength.

However, I recommend avoiding any beer that's blue! Colorless malt beverages don't count — clear malt beverages are *not* beer — and you get five minutes in the penalty box for being caught drinking one.

On a clear day

Many beer drinkers are obsessed with beer clarity. If their beer isn't crystal clear, they won't drink it. Fair enough, but beer is transparent only as a consequence of modern filtering techniques. Not all beers are intended to be clear. Most brews throughout history have been anywhere from hazy to murky (no, *hazy* and *murky* aren't two long-lost Disney dwarfs) due to the organic ingredients used in the beermaking process, mostly the yeast. These particles that clouded the beer were also what helped to make the beer the nutritious drink it was. Today, a cloudy appearance is appropriate for at least a half-dozen beer styles, such as witbier, hefeweizen, and any other unfiltered beer styles.

A head in the hand

Head retention can tell a short story about the beer at hand.

When a beer is poured, a head of foam should both form and stay (with some styles more than others, of course); the latter quality is as important as the former. The bubbles should be small and should quickly form a tightly knit head. The beer's head may also take on a "rocky" appearance if sufficient proteins (from the grain) are present. If a beer can't form a head, either it's improperly carbonated or the vessel into which it is being poured is dirty.

If the beer bubbles stick to the sides of your beer glass and don't get to the top, you may want to check out the section in Chapter 6 on cleaning beer glasses.

If the head forms but dissipates into big, soapy-looking bubbles, chances are that the beer has been charged up with a foam stabilizer (some foam stabilizers are made from a seaweed derivative). Most of the large breweries use foam stabilizers — a necessary evil, thanks to the clarifying process. Microfilters also remove all the head-coagulating proteins. The finest, all-malt brews have small bubbles and dense, creamy heads.

Finally, at least some of the head should remain atop the beer until the glass is empty. Along the way, some of the head's residue should leave what is commonly called *Belgian lace* on the sides of the glass.

Taste: Nuts and Bolts, Malt and Hops

After the first two steps in the beer-tasting process, you can at last get down to the nuts and bolts of beer. Regardless of how a beer looks and smells, if it doesn't taste good, it hasn't fulfilled its promise.

Beer as nutrition

Beer used to be considered nutritious — a concept far removed from today's stereotype of the beer drinker as a pot-bellied couch potato.

"Stone Age" beer, though probably crude, may have been an important source of nutrients in the diet. While this same grain was also used in the baking of bread, it probably became more nutritious after undergoing the beermaking process in which the starchy insides of the kernel were transformed into proteins and soluble sugars not otherwise available. And it surely kept longer.

And jumping forward in time a bit, Martin Luther, founder of the Lutheran church, reportedly preserved his health while he fasted by drinking copious amounts of strong beer.

For true beer nuts, a beer's overall flavor intensity can be thought of as a pyramid of taste, with slight but notable fluctuations from level to level. Related terms run through the following range:

lacking → faint → mild → slight → moderate → definite → strong → intense

Use all the taste zones on your tongue (sweet, sour, bitter, and salt). Try to distinguish between the first taste sensation experienced by the tip of the tongue (foretaste) and the midtaste or *true taste,* in which the beer displays its taste attractions completely. Swish the beer around gently. If everything goes according to Hoyle, the foretaste and midtaste should blend harmoniously and make you want more. Good beer is complex: You find a wide range of flavors in a single taste.

As with aroma, flavor comes from malt, hops, and fermentation, all of which are balanced in a good beer. A related but more subtle sensation is the *aftertaste,* where alcohol asserts its throat-warming ability in the strong, high-octane brews, much as it does in brandy.

Marvelous malt taste

The foretaste you encounter is the *sweetness* of the malt. With most industrial brews, the sweetness is delicate and perfumy and only vaguely tastes of true malt flavor, due to the lightening effect of the adjunct grain used, usually corn or rice (see Chapter 2). The fewer adjuncts used, the more the rich, caramel maltiness of the barley comes through. *All-malt* beers (those without adjuncts) are appropriately referred to as having a *malty* character.

The more specialty grains that are used, roasted (kilned) ones in particular, the more "layered" or complex the beer's flavor becomes. These specialty grains rarely add sweetness — only the flavors of the individual grain. Kilned malts create a mosaic of *toasty, roasty, nutty, toffeelike,* and *coffeelike* flavors that meld into the brew. A lot of these flavors are registered in the middle and at the back of the tongue. Some of the more highly roasted malts add a dry *astringent* taste that is perceived by the tongue as being bitter, much like strong coffee or tea. Misuse of the grain by the brewer can also lead to a *grainy* or *husky* astringent flavor in the beer. Certain beers exhibit a slight *tartness* that is detected at midtaste.

Normally, *sour* flavors are considered a flaw in beer, but for several well-known Belgian beers, sourness is actually a prerequisite, as it is for a few odd ales. Lagers definitely should not be sour.

Heavenly hops taste

The primary purpose of hops is to offset the malt sweetness with a pleasant and refreshing bitterness. Hop flavors are described with pretty much the same terms as used for aroma, but hop bitterness uses some new terms.

- **Hop flavor:** Distinctive, usually tasting much like its aroma: grassy, piney, floral, citrusy, herbal, cheesy, and so on; normally experienced at midtaste. Expressed as *mild, normal, definite, pronounced,* or *aggressive.* The latter terms would describe a *hoppy* beer.

- **Hop bitterness:** Rather one-dimensional; experienced at the back of the tongue, as an aftertaste. Expressed as *delicate, fine, coarse,* or *clinging.*

Hopheads are passionate beer nuts who crave the hop aspect of beer over all other aspects. If you drink with such a person, be sure to refrain from making any inflammatory antihop statements. Just hunker down and share the experience. You've been warned.

Fabulous fermentation

The fermentation process is responsible for some of beer's more appealing tastes, like fruit, butter, butterscotch *(diacetyl),* and alcohol tastes. Ales have more of the fruity and buttery flavors; lagers should not have any of these tastes. Alcohol should be evident in only the strongest of beers.

On the negative side of the ledger, fermentation can stimulate a long list of unpleasant flavors: the rubbery taste of autolyzed (deteriorated) yeast, cidery aldehydes, medicinal phenolics, bloody metallics, poopy enterics, and dozens of other equally unappetizing off tastes that brewers and beer drinkers alike need to be on the lookout for. Yuck!

Other flavors you may encounter are the *yeasty* or *bready* "odors" of bottle-conditioned beers (see Chapter 3) and the *winey* or *alcoholic* flavors of stronger beers.

After you've honed in on the various flavors, try to gauge their intensity. Most beer styles share common flavors, but the intensity of each is different according to each beer style (see Chapter 1).

Aftertaste: Let it linger

Beer's aftertaste, also called the *finish,* is one of the most essential and enjoyable aspects of the total beer-drinking experience, one that chiefly affects the decision about whether to take another sip. And yet many corporate megabrewers, with their advocacy and marketing of beers with little or no aftertaste (as in *light, dry,* and *ice* beer), have made aftertaste a *perspectiva non grata.* They would have you believe that beer is not supposed to have an aftertaste and that those with an aftertaste are bad.

Why is aftertaste desirable? Imagine dining on succulent Maine lobster dipped in pure, drawn butter, only to have the flavor disappear from your mouth the second you swallow. That lingering flavor "memory" is what aftertaste is all about. Don't let advertising campaigns condemning "bitter beer face" deter you from expecting and enjoying the aftertaste of quality brews.

Many facets of a beer become more obvious in the aftertaste in a sort of harmonic convergence (of course, the beer's faults, if any, are also magnified there). Certain beer styles are designed to accentuate malt over hops and vice versa, but no one ingredient should be allowed to completely dominate the other. There's no room for a bully here.

Gravity and Plato: weighty, nonphilosophical issues

Some fairly technical terms, *gravity* (as in *original gravity* and *final* or *terminal gravity*) and *attenuation,* find their way into beer enthusiasts' evaluations and written reviews, but these terms are not directly related to taste.

These more technical terms are brewers' measurements of fermentation and are not an indication of quality, even though some labels or ads may boast about a beer's gravity.

What does gravity mean to the beer drinker? A beer's gravity is used to calculate its volume of alcohol. The specific gravity scale is based on water at 60 degrees F (15 degrees C). Some brewers prefer to note gravity on the Balling scale, measured in degrees Plato, which

indicates the same information as the specific gravity scale, just on a different scale (see Figure 10-2 in Chapter 10).

Higher original gravities of beer — about 1.060 to 1.100 — usually mean stronger and creamier beers (sometimes called "big beers"). Above 1.090 is rare indeed. Lower original gravities — about 1.032 to 1.044 — mean lower alcohol contents and thinner, lighter-bodied beers. The vast majority of beers fall in the middle ground — about 1.044 to 1.060 or 11.5 to 15 degrees Plato.

More details on this kind of stuff are tucked safely in the chapters on homebrewing (Chapters 10 through 12) and in Appendix F.

Touch: Mouthfeel and Body

The tactile aspects of beer evaluation are *mouthfeel* and *body*. You can literally *feel* the beer in your mouth and describe it in familiar physical terms (such as *thick* and *thin*).

Mouthfeel is the sensory experience of the whole inside of the mouth and throat. You don't *taste* cold; you *feel* it. Finely carbonated beers (with their small bubbles) tend to have a creamy mouthfeel. So a continental lager beer might be *effervescent,* while a stout is *soft* and *chewy,* but none of these descriptions has anything to do with how the beer tastes. It's how the beer feels (to you — this is not about the beer's self-esteem).

In beer competitions, judges use the term *body* to refer to the "weight" or thickness of a beer. A "light" beer is described as *light-bodied,* an India Pale Ale is considered *medium-bodied,* and a doppelbock is *full-bodied.* Higher carbonation levels help to clear the palate and create the impression of a lighter-bodied beer.

Colorful descriptors such as *wimpy, voluptuous, massive, robust,* and *chewy* are effective at getting the point across. Obviously, just as with people, one body type isn't necessarily better than another — thin folks, heavy folks, and every-one in between make the world an interesting place.

Win friends and influence people by using some of the other mouthfeel terms that pros use, such as *astringent, crisp, flat, full, gassy, light, sharp, smooth, thin, thick, vinous (winey), viscous,* and *watery.* Phew!

Reflect: Time for Analysis of the Gestalt

Not to get too philosophical on you, but didn't someone say that the unexamined life is a life not worth living? Well, so it goes with beer. Reflection doesn't mean trying to see your image in a beer glass (though I imagine some of us have tried that); it's about your overall impression of the beer. The difference here is that all the previous assessments — smell, look, taste, touch — are, or should be, made as *objectively* as possible. Reflection is a time to take into account all those objective observations and then form a *subjective* opinion about the beer.

The aftertaste is also the time to evaluate the harmony and balance of the various taste components of the beer and to reach some sort of conclusion, like "Hey, I'll have another one of those!" Bottom line — would you like another one?

If you like it, it's good

Professionals have consultants analyze their brews all the time for consumer feedback. You hedonists out there will be happy to know that the Beverage Testing Institute (BTI), the largest and only full-time independent product testing service specializing in beverages in the U.S., employs a *hedonic* scoring method, which addresses the simple question at the root of consumerism: "Does this bring me pleasure?" The hedonic method suggests that tasting good is more important than tasting correct or typical. It allows for subjective observations in an objective environment.

The BTI hands out the annual World Beer Championship awards to winners from more than 300 breweries in 28 countries. Results are posted on the Food & Drink Network on America Online (see Appendix D) and in various magazines — and in the winners' advertisements, you can be sure.

Because of the wide availability and reasonable pricing of beer, you may want to keep a record of the beers you taste and your reaction to them. Following the points just explained in this chapter, you can write down a full profile of a beer in only a few sentences.

You can also use a book created expressly for this purpose — *The Beer Explorer's Logbook* (Passport to Adventure Press, Colorado, U.S.) — or use the form prepared by the American Homebrewers Association (shown in Figure 4-2). Or you can easily organize your own notes on plain paper.

Figure 4-2:
The American Homebrewers Association evaluation sheet provides a good format for beer tastings.

EASY STEPS FOR EVALUATING BEER

FIRST: Smell the beer for hop and malt **aroma** characteristics.
SECOND: Look at the beer to determine its **color** and clarity.
THIRD: Taste the beer to determine its **flavors** and **mouthfeel.** (Is it light, medium or full bodied?)
LAST: Rate your **overall impression** based on these four characteristics: aroma, color, flavor and mouthfeel.
HAVE A GOOD TIME.

American Homebrewers Association
PO Box 1679 / 736 Pearl St., Boulder, CO 80306-1679
(303) 447-0816; FAX (303) 447-2825

BEER NAME/STYLE		BEER NAME/STYLE	
hoppy — AROMA — malty		hoppy — AROMA — malty	
pale — golden — COLOR amber — brown — black		pale — golden — COLOR amber — brown — black	
bitter — FLAVOR — sweet		bitter — FLAVOR — sweet	
light/thin — MOUTHFEEL — full/thick		light/thin — MOUTHFEEL — full/thick	
can't stand it — OVERALL IMPRESSION — can't get enough		can't stand it — OVERALL IMPRESSION — can't get enough	

Copyright © American Homebrewers Association. Reprinted with written permission from the American Homebrewers Association, Boulder, Colorado.

Remember, while all the details are interesting, it's the bottom line that counts. Is the beer good, or is it not?

So it's good — but how does it rate?

Beer has its figure-skating equivalent, where the art and science and rules all come together: competitions. Various commercial and homebrew competitions take place at major festivals, such as the widely acclaimed annual Great American Beer Festival in Denver, Colorado (strictly commercial), and the Great British Beer Festival, in London (see Chapters 13 and 14).

Like wine, beer needs to be judged according to its style. Just as you can't fairly judge a fine, hearty cabernet sauvignon against a field of fruity Beaujolais wines, you can't compare a bock beer to a brown ale. Each wine and each beer should be judged on its own merits and compared to wines and beers of like style; published guidelines specify all the taste components that homebrewers and commercial brewers must match, style by style, in great detail. Check out the American Homebrewers Association (Appendix C) for an example.

In the days before filtering . . .

The early Egyptians, like many people of the time, chose to drink their beer through reeds or tubes so they would not choke on the barley husks left in the unfiltered brew. The University of Pennsylvania Museum displays a golden straw used by Queen Shubad of Mesopotamia for sipping beer.

Chapter 5

Beer Exploring

• •

• •

*T*here's no time like the present to have the beer bug. With so many styles out there to choose from and so many talented brewers making such wonderful brews, you have more opportunities than ever before for beer tasting.

With the profusion of tasty traditional and original brews now available throughout the world (more than at any other time in history), avoiding good beer is becoming more and more difficult. And you can enjoy beer in a wide variety of places both traditional and nontraditional — like brewpubs and beer bars, or the newest trend in the U.S.: the teaming of minor-league ballparks with microbreweries — and, of course, your own home. For more ideas on U.S. beer travel, check out Chapter 14.

Checking Out Brewpubs, Beer Bars, and Beer Dinners

Although you can simply pick up some bottled beers at the local store, the more common — and adventurous — way to taste a variety of beers is in a bar of some kind. The advantage of bars is in the beer (or maybe televised sports, romance, or games, but none of those advantages figure in this book). Explorers know that bars come in two shapes: brewpubs and beer bars.

Growlers to go

U.S. brewpubs offer beer-to-go poured directly from the tap into glass jugs (typically in half-gallon sizes) called *growlers.* This bizarre name dates back to pre-Prohibition time, when factory workers regularly drank beer with their lunches. Local children were paid as much as a nickel to run to the local brewery or bar to fill the workers' pails with beer. These metal pails — usually not larger than a few quarts' capacity — were named after the growling stomachs of the waiting customers. The kids were trained to be good at "rushing the growler." Much more picturesque than picking up a six-pack, yes?

Brewpub basics

The best place to taste different beers is often at a *brewpub* — a pub, usually with a restaurant, that serves its own beer made in a small brewery on the premises, kind of like a restaurant with its own pastry shop or bakery.

By definition, a brewpub does not distribute more than 50 percent of its beer outside the pub — and most brewpubs don't distribute any — though you can usually get it "to go" in kegs and small containers.

Even with the 600 or so brewpubs now operating in the U.S. and new ones opening there and in Europe (especially the U.K.), brewpubs still aren't "local" to the majority of people. But brewpubs are opening with mushroomlike frequency in every kind of place — especially urban areas, but also suburban and rural vacation areas.

Chains of brewpubs have even appeared in the U.S. and U.K. (dubbed "Brewer Kings" by skeptical wags). The jury is still out on whether the art and science of brewing, so often harmoniously (deliriously?) accompanied by personal passion, can be franchised.

Standout brewpubs make great travel destinations, and guidebooks are ideal companions for traveling beer nuts. One in particular — a book, not a beer nut — is a favorite of mine: *Beer Across America,* by yours truly. Check it out! (A shameless plug, I admit.) If you feel like denying my children their oatmeal, check out the free brewspapers stacked by the door of just about any brewpub for a listing of other brewpubs in the area or see the guides listed in Appendix D.

Brewpubs come in all sizes, from an innkeeper's hobby with an annual output of a couple hundred gallons to huge commercial operations that brew thousands of barrels a year. The Wynkoop Brewing Company of Denver is the biggest in the U.S., and probably the world: It brewed 5,008 barrels in 1995. (At 33,000 square feet, you could say it's pretty big physically, too.)

Beer lovers treasure brewpubs for a number of very good reasons:

- ✔ **Fresh beer:** Brewpub beer is about as fresh a product as you are going to find anywhere (brewpubs routinely boast that while commercial megabrews may travel hundreds of miles before it gets to your glass, their brewpub beer travels only a few yards from the serving tanks to the tap). With beer, freshness is *paramount* for preserving taste.

- ✔ **Variety:** Brewpubs offer beer in a variety of regular major styles, one or two seasonal specials, and a brew or two in exotic styles, normally for a very limited run (keeps you coming back to see what's new). Brewers like to test the scope of their skills as much as they like to please your palate. Imported or "guest" beers are often featured alongside the house brews, for fun.

- ✔ **Serving know-how:** Brewpubs know how to serve beer. For example, no serious beer drinker wants a frosted mug, and I've yet to encounter one at a brewpub. Most brewpubs serve beer at proper ambient temperatures and in the appropriate glasses (see Chapter 6 for more about proper glasses).

- ✔ **Elementary education:** The curious and the inquisitive can see the brewing equipment and get the chance to watch the brewmaster at work and ask questions. With luck, a tour may be offered. What's really cool is when dedicated brewers offer a particularly intrigued customer the opportunity to spend a day working alongside them.

- ✔ **Postgraduate work:** Brewpubs may sponsor weekend beer and brewing seminars or tasting clubs. The Goose Island Brewing Company in Chicago was among the first to do so. This company offers its Master of Beer Appreciation (MBA) program, which encourages customers to sample a "curriculum" of styles throughout the year and earn points toward premiums such as MBA T-shirts and free beer (you expected parchment?).

- ✔ **Camaraderie:** Not the sporting, testosterone-laced kind — the beer-aficionado kind, the beer-geek kind, the hophead kind, the gourmet-beer-fan kind. Striking up conversations about the beer is pretty easy in these places (many brewpub owners are former homebrewers). The weather and sports come up, too, of course, but beer-as-topic is special.

- ✔ **Food:** And oh, yes, the food. Good brewpub folks generally like to cook up recipes that feature their beers, and they are glad to suggest beer and food matches. But food is secondary to good beer (pity the rare brewpub with bad brews). When the food is imaginative and excellent, the experience is blissful.

A good brewpub is defined by good beer, of course (and *consistently* good, too), but also by evidence of the brewer's passion, even reverence and respect, for beer. These qualities are what make a brewer take the time to talk beer with you, to show you around the brewery, to train the waiters and waitresses. Gotta have the passion, or else it's just another bar.

TIP

Prepare to board your flight

Most brewpubs offer small glasses for tasting, sometimes in sets of four or more (called a *flight* or some similar term — be sure to ask about them, as they are not always listed on the menu). Flights are probably the most interesting way to sample the various beers.

Some brewpubs provide special place mats for flights of beer to help you keep track of what you are tasting. The Capitol City Brewing Company (Springfield, Ill.) uses the place mat shown in the following figure.

Pilsner

Red Ale

Australian Lager

Once drawn, our Pale Lager Pilsner releases a rich, fresh and malty aroma. With its golden color and frothed head, this is a very tasty, drinkable beer. Here the pilsner tradition of heavily hopping the pale lagers has been adhered to, resulting in a smooth finish to a mildly complex, light-bodied beer. There's a decidedly sour aftertaste, but with less bitterness than most pale lagers. An enhanced aroma bespeaks the regionality of the Bohemian and North Coast hops. Traditional "Noble" hops production is honored, with hops grown under near-perfect conditions of soil, climate, altitude, and small growing areas . . . guaranteeing a smooth, spicy draught and the promised clean bite.
Grains: Pale and dextrin malts, lightly caramelized.
Hops: Washington State and Saaz

A full bodied Red-Amber Ale brewed with a combination of pale and crystal malts. A flavorful and aromatic beer with caramel and chocolate malts added to balance hops and bitterness, resulting in a hint of malt sweetness.

Rich and amber colored, you first taste the barley malt, then you'll sense the aroma and smooth finish, both wonderfully hops-scented. This is a seductive lager, reflecting the complexities of three hops varieties, the likes of which are the hallmark of "down-under" draughts. The color is richly ruddy, with a frothy head, sharp aroma of hops, and malty richness. A quaffery's brew, not sweet or cloying, this Australian has a bright, quaffable, dry finish with a charming flavor, especially if it is slightly warmed in the glass to a European room temperature of between 45° and 50°. You'll be looking for Mr. Dundee when you and your mates finish one of these.
Grains: Roasted barley malts.
Hops: Mild Bittenger, blended with Hallertau & Cascades

Pale Ale

Springfield, Illinois
Capitol City Brewing Co.
Brewers of Fine Ales and Lagers
Established 1993

Winterfest

An amber ale with a complex aroma redolent of malt, hops, and fruity elements of the classic ale yeast. A dark caramel malt enhances both the flavor and color, while the barley, due to traditional "flaking," leaves a smooth, pleasant to the palate, grainy finish to this ale. Characteristically, the balance of flavor leans to the more bitter hops influence, rather than the sweeter, malty body found in stouts.
Grains: Pale and Dark caramelized malts with flaked barley
Hops: Yakima and Williamette

A medium hued, bittersweet stout, in which the heavy roasting of the barley imparts a rich, aromatic, coffee-like flavor. To balance the natural hops bitterness, caramel malt is intensified in the recipe, building smoothness and adding to the stout's robust body. The finished product shows very little hops aroma. Instead the flavor of the grains and the fruitiness of the ale yeasts predominate.
Grains: Pale and Dark caramelized Belgium malt: roasted barley
Hops: Cascade and Yakima

Beer bars

In Ireland, the U.K., and most of western and central Europe, the pub culture is still intact. Many pubs and taverns are quaint, quiet places to enjoy a comfortable drink with the local folk where just about everybody knows one another (Norm!). Women and children are traditionally part of the daytime crowd. More often than not, the beer on tap is a local delicacy; it is served and drunk with pride and respect. See Chapter 13 for more on European bars.

Pardon me, but what kind of water are you serving tonight?

Although some label lingo has merely passed through the creative minds of marketing folks, beer menus are the products of entrepreneurial folks at brewpubs and bars who often prove to be quite poetic — or anal-retentive. For example, many beer listings indicate all the various exotic-sounding ingredients, like three different types of hops, maybe four different types of malts, or the various brewing techniques used.

Such detailed menus may be appetizing, but can you imagine a local pizza parlor listing the kind of oregano that's on a pizza? What's important is the beer, not the ingredients or the technique. Unless you are a super-brewer yourself, feel free to ignore the technical hyperbole.

Despite the history of Prohibition, the beer-can culture, and the lack of beer variety, some of that Old World–style pride and respect is returning to the U.S. in the form of dedicated beer bars. Of course, this trend is not without its extremes: Some U.S. beer bars endeavor to be grand Germanic beer halls, others to be old-fashioned Celtic pubs; still others aspire to the brewpub concept, going as far as installing fake or inoperable brewing equipment in order to affect the ambience of a pub-brewery.

The beer police report that beer snobbery is on the rise by people who have just discovered that beer is cool and have become "beer experts" overnight. And as more everyday bars with good beer selections enter this expanding and competitive market, beer is forced to take a back seat to live bands, the clang and crash of pinball machines, rowdy crowds, and beer ignoramuses. Choose your destinations carefully: See Appendix D for some books that list beer bars.

500 bottles of beer on the wall

Many beer bars stake their reputation on the length and breadth of their bottled beer list. Offering three, four, and even five *hundred* different brands of beer is not unusual for these places — and is not necessarily a good thing.

First of all, stocking that many different brands in any quantity at all is a near physical impossibility, so your choice is likely to be sold out. Second, not only is stocking that much difficult, but storing it at the proper cool temperature is probably out of the question. Third, when a bar offers such a mind-boggling number of beers, stocks of particular beers can't possibly sell quickly.

I'm a former patron of a bar that boasted more than 600 different beers. I say "former" because my first and often second choices were rarely in stock. The third or fifth choice that was finally located after 15 minutes of searching was dust-covered on the outside and flaky on the inside. Needless to say, I would take a pass and just order something fresh from the tap.

What's on tap?

Fresh from the tap are the new buzz words in beer bars. Instead of stocking hundreds of aging and breakable bottles of beer, wise bar owners have invested in dozens of draught lines and tap handles and now offer as many beers on draught as space allows. You can find bars that offer 10, 20, or 30 different brews on tap, much of it as fresh as just-picked hops.

In the U.S., craft-brewed beers occupy most of the tap space, but imported beers are experiencing a resurgence in draught sales; as a result, availability of imported kegged beer is on the rise. A few bars have even made arrangements with local craft brewers to receive a regular supply of beer to be sold under the bar brand name.

To most beer drinkers, draught beer is better than bottled beer. Why? Because draught beer

✔ Is fresher (the beer is delivered quickly, sometimes directly from the brewery)

✔ Is unpasteurized (the taste hasn't been killed along with the microbes)

The art of pouring the perfect pint — of Guinness

The folks at the famed Dublin brewery Guinness know they have a special product that deserves special attention, and their millions of loyal fans demand that the bartender give the beer special attention.

One aspect of serving Guinness correctly is pouring carefully, and Guinness headquarters provides special taps and a seven-point directive that specifies, among other things, that the carbonization mix be 75 percent nitrogen and 25 percent carbon dioxide, that the glass be held at a 90-degree angle at first, and that the beer must be allowed to settle so a ³/₄-inch head can form (you are supposed to chat with the bartender while waiting for the head to form). This process

can take several minutes. (Inspired bartenders gently touch the head of the spout and create a four-leaf clover impression in the soft foam.)

Guinness aficionados often compare notes as to which pub in a certain town pours the best pint. A pub can screw up the process in plenty of ways, so the debate is seemingly valid. How valid is anyone's guess, but valid nonetheless, at least to Guinness devotees.

Another bit of Guinness lore is the tale of the seven rings: Devotees of Guinness Stout say that downing a standard (16-ounce) pint of the "black gold" should take exactly seven sips — each sip leaving behind a perfect ring of foam on the side of the glass.

Hail, Caesar! Bring us more beer!

Julius Caesar considered beer a "high and mighty liquor." He toasted his troops with beer when they crossed the Rubicon River in northern Italy, beginning his conquest of Europe. Caesar customarily served beer to his guests in golden goblets. By the end of the Roman Empire, beer was well established in Europe. During the 350 years that the Romans occupied Britain, the conquerors built many roads to connect the early outposts of civilization. Among the first amenities on these roads were *tabernae* (taverns), where beer was among the alcoholic beverages sold.

✔ Has probably been stored properly (people who order by the keg are probably more interested in beer quality than those who don't)

✔ Has smaller bubbles and a creamier texture than bottled beer, if poured right — especially with a *hand pull* tap (see the "Daft about draught" sidebar later in this chapter)

Beer dinners

Usually, a restaurant is an unlikely place to find a good beer. Wine has always been, and still is, the conceptual favorite for food and drink pairing. But there is now hope. You can expect more and more often to find an upscale eatery that either has decided to wake up and smell the barley or has received numerous requests for something other than Chateauneuf Dew Pop and Vin d'Pay d'ay (sorry, just couldn't resist the moment). Such a restaurant has a beer list, or at least a few decent craft brews to offer. Some are also starting to have occasional *beer dinners*.

The beer dinner is a phenomenon inspired by the plethora of available gourmet brews (all competing for attention). Beer dinners are hosted by restaurants, brewpubs, and beer bars across the country. These places may not necessarily be known for their lengthy beer menus, but their owners recognize the draw of good beer. Beer dinners are often a joint effort between the chef and a hired "beer celebrity" — a brewmaster, beer importer, beer magazine writer, or beer book author (or how about me — just joking, of course).

The newest wrinkle is doing beer dinners to promote something, much as wine tastings or fashion shows are often hosted by groups with something to celebrate or show off.

Daft about draught

The Old English word *draught* meant "to pull," like the draught horses that delivered beer kegs (*draft* is the U.S. spelling of the British term). Before pressurized carbon dioxide and nitrogen were used to push beer through beer lines to the taps at the bar, the beer had to be "pulled" with a *beer engine,* which has come to be called a *hand-pull.*

Hand-pulls are widely used in English pubs that serve cask-conditioned ale, or what connoisseurs call Real Ale (lagers usually don't figure in here). In the U.S., hand-pulls are becoming popular for serving craft-brewed beer, but these hand-pulls are rare and highly prized.

Hand-pulls work by suction/siphon, like a pump; filling a 16-ounce pint glass usually requires two or three vigorous pulls of the very large tap handle (at least 1 foot long). A wooden box at the base houses the pump works. At the end of the thin, curved spout is a special opening that diffuses the beer, creating a cloud of finely beaded bubbles that gives the beer a super-creamy head and texture for that wonderful draught-only mouthfeel. Mmm-mmm, good!

Beer dinners customarily feature several courses that spotlight certain beer and food combinations and often use beer as an ingredient in as many of the dishes as possible. These events are a real treat, but they usually don't come cheap. Look for special promotions and plan on making reservations way in advance.

A typical beer dinner menu lists the dishes along with the beer served with each course. Menus may also have a few lines of background about each beer.

Some dinners may be themed. For example, one dinner might feature only beers from France or Belgium, or maybe only stouts are served at a banquet that features oyster dishes (oysters and stout are a classic pairing). Themes can be food (such as game or fish), seasons, local specialties, or cooking styles.

A recent trend has been to offer cigars as well, a combination that works well and parallels the growing interest in single-malt-whisky-and-cigar dinners. No one said you had to stick to health food all the time.

Be It Ever So Humble, There's No Place like Home

Never underestimate the comfort and serenity of your own home and easy chair when it comes to appreciating beer. Given the advantage of homey ambience, some beers are just a La-Z-Boy away from greatness.

Eat, drink, and be merry — but don't drive

Remember, if you are drinking away from home, be sure to let a nondrinker drive. If you are the driver, limit your drinks to one or two beers (depending on your weight), eat hearty (high-protein and fatty foods eaten prior to drinking tend to slow alcohol absorption), and take your time leaving. This said, you're always better off not driving after drinking alcoholic beverages. And never, *ever* drive while under the influence. *Please.*

Tasting beer in your own home is the total do-it-yourself level. The downside is that you have to go out and buy the beer, serve yourself, and clean up after you are done (I can think of greater inconveniences). The upside is that you have total control over what you drink, when you drink, and how you drink it, and you won't have to drive (plus there's no waiting line to use the washroom). Home tasting is cheaper, too.

How much you are able to take advantage of this situation depends on your source of beer and your desire for help in the tasting experience. Beer lends itself well to socializing — and talking to yourself is not a good sign of progress along the road to beer knowledge.

Beer-of-the-month clubs

Even with the explosion of microbrewing in the U.S., many people in rural areas still don't have access to the best the market has to offer. For them and others who simply like the convenience of having good beer delivered to their doorsteps, beer-of-the-month clubs (BOMCs) were born. American craft-brewed beer was the impetus for this venture, but a few clubs deal in imported beer, too.

While wine-of-the-month clubs have existed for decades, the first BOMC was not in operation until 1992. The then-26-year-old guys who started Beer Across America were considering getting into the wine club business when they realized the potential of microbrewery beers. Four years later, their success has spawned dozens of copy-cat operations around the country, serving hundreds of thousands of beer nuts who want great beer.

Members of these clubs receive different bottled beers from craft breweries across the country. In most cases, two different six-packs from two different microbreweries (total of 12 bottles) are delivered to the member's home or business address each month. Some clubs have further split the 12-bottle allotment into 4 beers from three breweries or 3 bottles from four breweries. All BOMCs include some form of newsletter (some considerably more informative than others) with each shipment.

Note: Beer-of-the-month clubs are not without their problems. The interstate delivery of alcoholic beverages is stuck in a quagmire of laws. Several states still don't allow door-to-door delivery of beer, which is also why you don't see big beer mail-order houses. Because of this situation, some BOMCs operate within only a few states or sometimes only within their home state. Check before you order to see whether they can deliver to you.

For a listing of some beer-of-the-month clubs, see Appendix C.

Party time!

After you have mastered the finer points of beer etiquette, you may want to show off what you know by hosting an informal beer dinner or tasting. Or for that matter, why not host a *formal* tasting, black tie optional?

Attempting a tasting

For your first tasting, you may want to start small; invite a half-dozen people to begin with (you'll have a better time if you actually *like* these folks).

To make the selection surprising and interesting — and to help defray the cost of the tasting — you may want to ask your guests to bring their favorite brews or perhaps beers that they haven't tried before.

You may also want to plan the tasting with a beer theme — German ales, Belgian fruit beers, microbrewed hot-pepper beers, or Canadian smoked-doppel-hefe-Märzenbiers (I know there's a homebrewer somewhere who's tried making this). Of course, no harm comes from mixing and matching styles, but comparing apples with apples is always easiest.

Before dinner, you might try offering small servings of each beer for commentary (no need to formalize it — reactions will flow as naturally as beer down the side of a glass). During dinner, you may ferret out a few of the better beer-and-food matches. After dinner, just drink what's left — enough thinking, already!

If you feel a need for a beer-tasting vocabulary or want some basic guidelines for tasting and evaluating beer, turn to Chapter 4. I'm just setting the stage for you here.

Blind man's bluff

For educational purposes — I'll bet you weren't thinking of this as "higher learning" — as well as for fun, try a blind beer tasting.

No, this definitely doesn't mean drink until you're blind. You just don't divulge the beers' identities beforehand, in order to remove subjective observations and personal biases. Blind tasting also adds a touch of mystery and suspense — and couldn't you use a little mystery and suspense in your life?

In a blind tasting, store and pour the beers in a room separate from where the tasters are seated. Be sure to open only one or two bottles of each sample at a time and serve 2- or 3-ounce portions.

Why such small servings?

- ✔ Only a couple of ounces are needed to evaluate a beer.
- ✔ The tasting won't drag on interminably.
- ✔ The participants won't suffer "palate fatigue."
- ✔ This is meant to be a tasting, not a debauchery!

You can break out (not literally) the remaining bottles after the "official" tasting is over.

You may want to coordinate your points of judgment along these lines: aroma of malt and hops (aroma goes fast, so start here); color, clarity, and head retention (the visuals); flavor and mouthfeel; and overall assessment or reflection (was it wonderful, awful, or somewhere in between?). See Chapter 4 for more details on tasting and evaluating.

Tastings have their own little requirements

- ✔ **Scrupulously clean glasses:** See Chapter 6 for information on avoiding problems.

- ✔ **Plenty of palate cleansers:** Serve plain stuff, such as crackers or chunks of French bread, not chicken curry, so as not to compete with beer taste. Palate cleansers not only clear the palate between beers but also help soak up the beer in your stomach.

- ✔ **Pitchers of water:** Water serves the dual purpose of providing drinks to cleanse the palate and a convenient source of water for rinsing the tasting glasses if they are in short supply.

Chapter 6

Are You Being Served?

*T*he simple act of serving someone a beer doesn't need to be done with a flourish, but it should go a bit beyond sliding an ice-cold can of Yahoo Brew across the kitchen table. So let's talk serving beer.

If you're into good beer, you're into tasting it right, and that means paying attention to how it is poured, which glass to use, and the finer points of keeping glasses clean. Ensuring that the beer you serve tastes as good as it can to you and your guests takes only a little effort.

Pouring It On

Although chugging beer from a can is a common occurrence, drinking beer straight out of the bottle is about as classy as hoisting a bottle of wine to your face (okay, okay, I confess that I've done it, too). Don't chug it — pour it!

Can you believe that you're reading about how to pour a beer? Don't laugh — you'll learn something here, I promise. Life is truly full of surprises.

To tilt or not to tilt . . .

First of all, make sure you have a glass that can hold the contents of a whole bottle or can plus a head. That makes everything easier.

How to best pour a beer depends on the type of beer.

For most craft beers, the best way to pour is right down the middle of the glass — again, a glass big enough to hold the whole bottle of beer — and tilt it or slow the pouring only after a big head has formed. (See Figure 6-1.) Go ahead — be aggressive! Assertive! Macho! Macha!

Why pour so vigorously? To release the carbon dioxide. You want to do this for the following reasons:

- Unless it's released by pouring, the gas is trapped in the bottle or can and goes straight into your belly, where it struggles to release itself in an unwelcome burst. Ugh and urp.

- Unpoured beer has unappealing, gassy "bite."

- Releasing the gas by pouring into a glass forms a head and lets the beer's fragrance rise. (Sniff right after pouring because the aromas don't last long.)

Some types of beers require special techniques — these techniques aren't rocket science, but they are worthy of attention.

- **Wheat beers and corked-bottle beers:** Be a little less aggressive when pouring these types of beers, as they tend to throw a larger-than-normal head. A proper head should be at least 1 inch thick, or "two fingers" deep. (These same two fingers also come in handy for measuring tequila shots, but that's another story for another time.)

- **Bottle-conditioned beers:** You may want to pour these beers so that you leave the last $1/2$ inch or so of dregs in the bottle. Absolutely nothing is wrong with drinking the settled yeast sediment, except that it may cause excess flatulence — the live yeast continue the fermentation process within your digestive system! In addition, not everyone is fond of this concentrated yeast taste, though some beer aficionados swear by it. But then, some folks like anchovies, too.

- **American light lagers:** Beers such as Budweiser and Miller are best poured slowly down the side of a tilted glass, or else they produce a glass full of head. Because these beers have little protein, a big head dissipates quickly. Creating a big head slows the pouring process needlessly (and risks having a mess on the table).

Finding the right temperature

One of the finer points of beer enjoyment too often overlooked is proper serving temperature. In the U.S., most beers are served much too cold for serious appreciation. In fact, ice-cold beer tastes awful to a real beer nut.

Beer warms the soul

In centuries past, consuming ale very warm during cold weather was not at all unusual. Because all taverns had large fireplaces, small iron pokers were hung by the fire to be used for warming drinks. These red-hot pokers, called *loggerheads,* were sometimes brandished by inebriated patrons when tempers flared, giving rise to the phrase "to find yourself at loggerheads."

Figure 6-1: Pour craft-brewed beer to create a head. Use a straight shot, long drop, right down the middle of the glass.

Serving beers at their proper temperature may take a little extra effort or planning, but the rewards are significant. Drinking beers at the proper temperature allows you to really *taste* the beer.

The average refrigerator is set to keep things chilled at around 38 to 40 degrees F (about 4 degrees C), but serving beers at this temperature has several negatives, including the following:

✔ The colder the beer, the less carbonation that is released; the less carbonation that is released, the less aroma the beer gives off.

✔ The palate is numbed to the point that it cannot discern many of the beer's flavor nuances. (So this explains why some beers are best served just above the freezing mark!) Why bother drinking a beer if you can't taste it? May as well have a Slurpee.

✔ Most premium lagers should be served between 42 and 48 degrees F (6 to 9 degrees C), and quality ales between 44 and 52 degrees F (7 to 11 degrees C).

✔ Authentic stouts can be served as warm as 55 degrees F (13 degrees C), considered "British cellar temperature."

✔ Some high-gravity barleywines, old ales, and Triple Bocks should be served only very lightly chilled or at room temperature, like a snifter of brandy.

Cold temperatures = less carbonation released = less aroma = less taste = why bother? Save the really cold temps for "lawnmower" beer — the kind you chug down after mowing the lawn (taste? who cares?).

Choosing a Glass with Class

Beer should always be poured from its bottle or can before serving. Period. Any *clean* vessel will suffice, but transparent glass has a clear advantage over opaque cups and steins — you can appreciate the color and head of the beer. After all, "We drink first with our eyes," as the saying goes. A bright, bubbly beer capped by a dense and rocky head of foam is a sight for thirsty eyes.

Besides looking good, however, the various shapes and sizes of beer glassware play a meaningful role in your enjoyment. Glassware that is deep or that curves inward toward the top is very effective in capturing and concentrating the beer's aromas.

Beer garnishing: lemon-aid

Beer garnishing — adding something to a beer both for taste and for ornamentation — is pretty rare but not without its traditions.

One of the few examples that people may recall goes back to the mid-1980s, when Corona beer first became popular, served with a wedge of lime crammed down the neck of the bottle.

Though that may have seemed a purely U.S.-based schtick, it was probably based on the habit of people from Mexico who routinely rubbed a lime wedge around the rims of their cans of Tecate beer before drinking. Far from being a stylish affectation, this was seen as a way of disinfecting the can tops and openings.

Another example of beer garnishing that seems to be catching on quickly is the addition of a lemon slice to a towering, frothy glass of weizen (wheat) beer. Traditionally a summer thirst quencher, a slice of lemon adds a nice touch of citrusy tang to the beer.

Note: Some establishments position the lemon over the rim of the wheat beer glass, giving the customer the choice of removing it, while others toss the slice into the glass before the beer is poured. You may want to make your preference known as you order your wheat beer.

Mug and thistle, clean as a whistle: a short history of beer glassware

The ancient Sumerians were known to drink their beer directly from a communal bowl into which straws — hollow reeds — were dipped. Some later civilizations learned how to fashion rough earthenware vessels to hold their liquids, while others sewed animal hides together to create a *bottel* — much like the bota bag of today. As civilization progressed, wood, glass, and bronze were used to great effect.

That wooden bowls, clay steins, and pewter chalices were opaque mattered little to these people, whose ales were dark and murky. These turbid brews scored low on the scale of visual appeal and were just as well drunk from nontransparent vessels.

Glassware's fullest potential wasn't realized until the mid–19th century, when Czechoslovakian Pilsners and pale lagers from Germany first appeared. These brilliant golden beers were shown to their best advantage in tall, thin, footed glasses. The invention of the glass pressing machine just prior to these beers' entry into the world made possible the production of glasses in a variety of shapes and sizes. As the popularity of these beers spread, so did the use of style-specific glassware.

With modern society's heathenish return to drinking beer directly from its container, civilized beer drinking was set back several centuries.

Nowadays, a quiet revival of style-specific glassware is going on, likely an outgrowth of the microbrewing revolution, wherein brewpubs or beer bars may feature a range of glassware styles as extensive as the number of beer styles being served.

The concept of brew-specific glassware may be new to Americans, but it's old hat in many European nations. Beer-producing countries are generally more observant of this unwritten code of beer protocol — the Germans and the Belgians can be downright finicky about it. In some instances, Belgian and German brewers have commissioned world-famous glassmakers to design unique glasses for their brews.

One story tells of a foreign visitor to a Belgian beer bar who, upon placing his order, was told that all the glasses for that particular beer were in use and that he was welcome to order a second choice or wait until a glass for his first choice became available!

Some glasses are designed for specific beer styles. Using them is a sign of your high regard for great beer. Not using them is a sign of being a normal person without really cool glassware, so don't freak out if you lack a certain glass.

Traditionally, certain beers have had a specific glass style associated with them — read on for details. The nice thing about beer glassware, though, is that it doesn't involve hard-and-fast rules. Don't worry if you don't have the perfect glass — that Flintstones iced-tea glass in the cupboard has been known to serve the purpose.

Glass class

Simple beers can be served in simple glasses; well-aged and expensive beers should get the regal treatment. Table 6-1 describes which glass to use for which kind of beer.

Table 6-1	The Right Glasses for Select Beer Styles
Glass Description	*Beer*
Deep, tulip-shaped glasses	Strong beers, such as Belgian ales
Simple pint glass	Stouts
Small, brandy-snifter–type glasses or even cordials	Rich and spirituous barleywines, old ales, and Imperial stouts
Thin, stemmed flutes	Some aromatic Trappist ales and Belgian fruit beers
Tall, narrow glasses	Light, spritzy, and aromatic beers, such as Pilsners and witbiers
Tall, thick glasses, to keep the beer cooler longer	Wheat beers
Wide-bowled goblets	Aromatic beers, such as Berliner Weisse

You may run across some of the following glass styles in your beery journeys. Here are some definitions and explanations. Figure 6-2 shows some common glass styles. (See Chapter 16 for a basic metric-conversion table.)

- **Altbier glass:** Short, slim, cylindrical glass similar to a Tom Collins glass; a shorter and fatter version of a Kölsch beer glass.

- **Beer flute:** Rather thin and dainty with a stem and a base, used for Pilsners and similar beers but meant for beers that emulate wines, such as Belgian fruit beers. Emphasizes tart and vinous qualities.

- **Dimpled pint mug:** Used at one time as the standard drinking vessel in British pubs. Slowly and quietly replaced by the straight-sided pint glass, which was easier to store on crowded pub shelves. Well suited to English ales and bitters.

- **Goblet:** Used almost exclusively for Berliner Weisse and some Trappist ales. Chalicelike in appearance, with a wide and shallow bowl and a heavy stem and foot. Discourages excessive head formation and allows the drinker's nose inside the opening of the glass.

- **Halbe:** ("Half" in German, for half-liter.) Simple glass mug preferred by many Germans for everyday helles beers. Similar to a British pint glass with a handle.

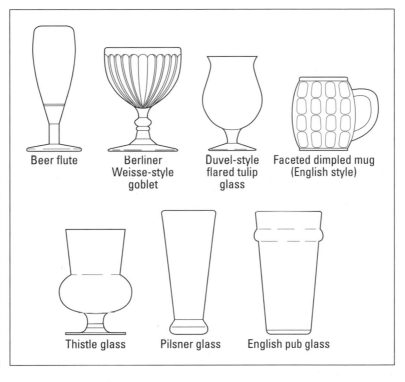

Beer flute

Berliner
Weisse-style
goblet

Duvel-style
flared tulip
glass

Faceted dimpled mug
(English style)

Thistle glass

Pilsner glass

English pub glass

Figure 6-2:
A wide
range of
beer
glasses
allows you
to choose
the right one
for a
particular
beer style.

- ✔ **Kölsch beer glass:** Tall, slim, cylindrical glass, similar to a Tom Collins glass; a taller version of the altbier glass.

- ✔ **Krug:** Literally means "mug" or "tankard" (may also refer to a jug or pitcher). Rather large; usually made of sturdy glass, making it safe for ceremonial clinking following a toast.

- ✔ **Mass:** (Pronounced "mahss," means "measure" in German.) Also called a Bavarian *masskrug*. Large and heavy dimpled glass mug with a liquid capacity of 1 liter (34 ounces, or the equivalent of $2\,^2/_3$ bottles of beer); also allows for 2 inches of head space. Stands about 8 inches tall and weighs about $2\,^1/_2$ pounds when empty (!). Standard serving size at Munich's Oktoberfest.

Sipping is for wimps

German quaffers say that when the large mass glass is in use, each sip (gulp) of beer should lower the liquid level to the next "dimple" in the glass. The glass has only four vertical dimples, so each "sip" is equivalent to 8 ounces of beer! *Ein, zwei, G'suffa!*

- **Middy:** Of Australian origin. Size depends on where you're drinking: In Sydney, a middy holds 10 ounces, but in Perth, only 7.

- **Pilsner:** Comes in a variety of styles. The more elegant ones are tall and footed and made of wafer-thin glass; they hold 10 or 12 ounces. The more ordinary versions are usually hourglass-shaped or slightly flared tumblers, holding between 8 and 12 ounces.

- **Pint glass:** Probably the most pedestrian and interchangeable of beer glasses, the standard pint glass is made of thick glass, tapers slowly outward toward the top, and holds 16 ounces of beer (before you say "duh," read on). The *imperial pint* glass holds 20 ounces of beer (not too common in the U.S.). Both may have "sleeves" — bulges near the top of the glass that protect the lip from nicks should the glass be tipped over (sleeves also allow the glasses to be stacked one inside the other without becoming stuck). Another variation is a slightly curvaceous version of the standard pint, simply called a *pub glass.*

- **Pony:** Australian liquid measure of $^1/_5$ pint. The actual glass may hold 4 or 5 ounces of beer, depending on whether you are in Victoria or New South Wales (no one knows why, though these territories were once quite independent of one another).

- **Schooner:** Typically a tall glass similar to a tumbler, measuring 15 ounces. In Australia, gets you anywhere from 9 to 15 ounces, depending on the bar. Laid-back types, those Aussies.

- **Schnelle:** Tall, slender, tapered earthenware tankard with a hinged lid.

- **Sham:** Generally of small proportions, ranging from 5 to 10 ounces, regardless of shape. The exact origin and definition of this beer glass is dubious (after all, the word *sham* is defined as "an impostor").

- **Stein:** ("Stone" in German.) Made of clay or ceramic; often features a hinged lid (usually made of pewter). A "glass stein" would be a contradiction in terms.

- **Thistle:** The silhouette of the thistle glass is exactly as the name implies. A uniquely shaped glass, almost exclusively used for strong Scottish ales (the thistle is the symbol of the Scottish Crown). However, the glass itself is attributed to the Belgians who developed a fondness for this style when Scottish soldiers stationed in Belgium during World War I brought their strong ale with them. Thistle glasses help to intensify the beer's aroma.

- **Tulip:** Shape closely resembles its name. Very effective in capturing the aromatic qualities of beer. Flared opening allows the drinker to sip the beer and the foam at the same time, creating a creamy mouthfeel. Favored for Belgian strong ales.

- **Tumbler:** Can be rather pedestrian, but beveled edges add some panache. Used for a wide variety of beer styles.

- **Weizen beer glass:** Tall, shapely, wide-rimmed, with a capacity usually exceeding 18 ounces — designed to hold a half-liter of wheat beer and its towering head.

What style of beer goes best in *that* glass?

This explanation of the word *skull* in the English language may not be etymologically correct, but it's a story worth repeating: The fierce Norse warriors, forever drunk on ale, had a particularly barbaric way of celebrating their conquests. They would drink strong ale from the boiled craniums of their foes, toasting their victory with the word *Skol* (skull)!

Sport drinking tools

Some non–style-specific glassware can provide the unsuspecting drinker with a challenging and often surprising outcome. Please don't try this at home!

- ✔ **Yard glass (or yard-of-ale or aleyard):** Holds about 2 ½ pints of beer. Three-foot-tall glass with a bell-shaped top, a ball-shaped bottom, and a long, skinny body (picture a coach horn or see Figure 6-3). Also comes in a half-yard size. The world record for emptying a yard glass is a scant 5 seconds; the previous record of 12 seconds was held by former Australian Prime Minister Bob Hawke, achieved while he was a student at Oxford. Ouch!

- ✔ **Stiefel (or boot):** Literally a glass in the shape of a boot. Can vary in size but commonly holds 4 to 5 pints of beer. Popular among young fraternal groups, as it's meant for communal drinking (and whoever takes the last gulp buys the next round). Drinking from a boot filled with beer presents a problem similar to that of a yard glass. The solution? Drink with the toe pointed horizontally.

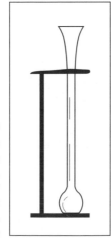

Figure 6-3:
Yard glass
and stand.
Not for
the faint
of heart.

Drinking by the yard can create quite a splash

The problem (the challenge? the sport?) with drinking out of a yard glass is that when the rising air bubble reaches the bulbous bottom of the glass, the remaining beer is released in a sudden gush, thereby usually drenching the unwary drinker. The trick to drinking out of a yard glass is actually pretty simple: Slowly rotate the glass as you drink, and the pressure won't build up in the bulb.

The supposed origin of the yard glass is interesting. The Napoleonic Code forbade aristocrats' coach drivers from descending from their coaches while passengers were seated inside, to avoid the risk of losing control of the horses. In order for the driver to get refreshment, a drink had to be handed up to him. An enterprising Belgian tavern keeper invented the yard glass to facilitate this transaction. The yard glass is still occasionally referred to as a *coachmen's horn*.

✔ **Kwak glass:** Another glassware oddity is a drinking receptacle made specially for a single brand. The Belgian brewer of the dark and richly herbal Kwak bier encourages bar owners to serve this beer in the famous Kwak glass. This glass stands about 1 foot high and is part weizen beer glass, part yard glass. Because of its shape and size, it cannot stand up without its own supportive wooden frame. Together, glass and frame represent a fair investment on the part of the brewer.

To keep customers from making the Kwak glass part of their personal collections, many Belgian bartenders require one of the customer's shoes as a security deposit on the glass.

Let's get practical

Does every budding beer connoisseur have to run out and buy two dozen different sets of beer glassware in order to consume "correctly"? Not at all. Beer drinking is meant to be enjoyable, and a great part of that enjoyment is comfort. Choose a beer glass style that is pleasing, and enjoy using it — often.

At minimum, however, I would recommend having a set of standard 16-ounce pint glasses on hand, matched by a set of more elegant footed beer flutes.

> ## The plimsoll line
>
> The interests of beer consumers are protected in many countries that require beer glasses to have a measure mark, called a *plimsoll line* (named for inventor Samuel Plimsoll, the brilliant guy who invented the way to mark hull-depth lines on the bows of ships). This line enables customers to see that they're getting full and proper servings. Drinkers in English pubs should be aware that the government has recently backed off from legal enforcement of this law.

Neatness Counts: Cleaning and Storing Glassware

After you've made your choice in glassware, make the commitment to keep your glasses clean. No matter which beer is poured into which glass, one thing is for sure: Keeping your beer glassware completely free of dust, oily fingerprints, lipstick, and soapy residue is absolutely crucial. These kinds of dirtiness can have a detrimental effect on your enjoyment of the beer, not to mention that your glasses look crummy.

Beer clean

A certain level of glassware cleanliness is known as *beer clean*. That's not just lip service — it's a reality. Beer glasses need to be spotlessly clean if they are to present the beer in its best light. Any shortcomings in cleansing and rinsing practices are betrayed by the beer.

Even though a glass looks clean, it may not be beer clean. Rinse water "sheets off" a glass that is beer clean; on a dirty glass, water breaks up, streaks, or spots. Bubbles that appear on the bottom or sides of the glass below the head indicate invisible fats — like soap residue, food, or makeup grease — or dust. Cracks, chips, and general wear and tear also attract bubbles. These contaminants can cause a beer to go flat quickly because the presence of fats (emulsifiers) breaks down the surface of the head and destroys it.

The most reliable way you can check that a glass is "beer clean" is to pour a craft-brewed beer into the glass, allowing a good head to form. After the beer stands for a few minutes, the head should remain firm and compact. If the glass was not correctly cleaned, the foam breaks up, leaving large, fish-eye bubbles.

Depending on your level of seriousness — and I sure hope you're not taking this *too* seriously — you have various ways to properly clean beer glassware. The first and best way is to rinse it thoroughly right after using. A bit compulsive, maybe, but very effective at keeping your glasses from becoming fouled. For some people, a hot-water rinse is as far as they want to go, partially because of the belief that you should not clean beer glasses in soapy water. This argument has two sides: One camp says that household dishwashing detergents are scented and can be hard to rinse off. The other camp (Camp Marty) says that if you use very small amounts of *unscented* dishwashing liquids and follow up immediately with a hot-water rinse, no damage is done.

Officially speaking, there is a better (and even more compulsive) strategy: Draw a sink full of hot water and add a couple of heaping tablespoons of baking soda. Use a nylon bristle brush to scrub the deepest recesses of the glass. Pay particular attention to the rim, being sure to remove any lipstick or lip balm. Follow with a good hot rinse and air dry only in a dish drain or empty dishwasher (the dishwasher itself can't do a better job).

Never towel-dry beer glasses. The towel can leave traces of soap, body oil, and especially lint on the glasses.

If you want to clean a yard glass, just use a long brush, which is usually sold with the glass.

At the professional/commercial level, where governmental regulations apply, health departments require chemical sanitizers or sterilizers, including products made with tri-sodium phosphate. Commercial establishments generally use a glass-cleaning compound that is odorless, sudless, of a nonfat base, and free-rinsing.

Putting it all away

Storing your glassware is only slightly less critical than cleaning it. A poor storage location could make your cleaning efforts all for naught. Be sure to store air-dried glasses away from the unpleasant odors, grease, and smoke that are emitted from kitchens, washrooms, and ashtrays. If possible, store the glasses upside-down in a breakfront, credenza, or enclosed cabinet that is relatively dust free. Of course, if you're a real beer geek, you'll keep them in your safe.

Freezin' fingers

Do not store glassware in the freezer or refrigerator. The glasses can pick up food odors, and frozen glasses are uncomfortable to hold (they also leave a nasty water ring wherever you set them). Some misguided bars serve beer in iced mugs, but these mugs are terrible to use. The primary effect that iced mugs have on beer is to water it down. If that's what you're looking for, just opt for a "lite" beer. Or go ahead and stick your fingers directly in the freezer to duplicate the sensation of holding onto one of these aberrations. Yikes!

Chapter 7

Cooking and Dining with Beer

. . . .

In This Chapter

▶ Using beer in recipes

▶ Matching up food with the right beer

▶ Serving the right beer for the occasion

. . . .

Certain beers fit certain foods like a hand fits a glove — they're made to go together. Unlike hands, however, beer is made to be consumed. On second thought, what about finger sandwiches?

Beer is not only a great beverage at mealtime but a terrific, low-cost, low-fat, versatile, easy-to-use ingredient in the cooking process. Compared to wine, beer comes out ahead (and *with* a head) in many different ways. Beer is easy and fun and has no fat or cholesterol (noted!). Most of its calories come from the alcohol, which is cooked off when you use it in a recipe — something that doesn't happen with most other foods.

In fact, wine no longer holds the patent as the alcoholic beverage of choice as either an ingredient in or an accompaniment to food. Beer is the perfect food partner in many, many instances. You could even say that it is inherently superior, but there's no need to be judgmental. Thanks to the wide availability of high-quality, additive- and preservative-free, flavorful hand-crafted beers, a new gustatory door has opened.

Cooking with Beer

Cooking with beer is nothing new. Beer has been used in the kitchen almost as long as food has — not surprising, given that beer was probably one of the first elements of civilization (see Chapter 1 and Appendix G). Back when beer was first discovered, it was more often the base material to which other things were added than the other way around. Beer back then was also more foodlike, with all the ingredient solids suspended within the liquid.

Nowadays, brewpub chefs are taking the lead in developing new and unusual recipes to incorporate the house brews into the food menu. Beer brings a whole new palette of flavors to the cooking pot or skillet. Chefs are even using it in the three Cs of good nutrition: cakes, caramel sauce, and candy!

Beer cheese dips and soups, chili with beer, baked beans with beer, beer bread, beer gravy, anything with beer batter, and bratwurst boiled in beer and onions (a Legion Hall favorite) — these are the traditional beer food recipes. Classic cuisine has often included beery Belgian dishes, such as carbonnade Flamande (beef stew). With some imagination, you have thousands of other possibilities — you can start with the ten really beery and easy recipes from Chapter 16.

If you want to go further, most of the beer magazines listed in Appendix D usually have a recipe or two in each issue, and most of the books listed have many more. You also have beer cookbooks, such as Candy Schermerhorn's *The Great American Beer Cookbook.* (She developed the recipes in Chapter 16 especially for *Beer For Dummies.*)

When cooking with beer, don't worry about your kids and nondrinking friends — alcohol has a lower boiling point than water (173 degree F or 79 degrees C) and evaporates quickly in the presence of heat. Unless beer goes unheated or is added to a dish just before serving, none of the alcohol ever gets to the table.

By the way, if you want to try some really interesting recipes to serve *with* beer, be sure to read *Cooking For Dummies,* by Brian Miller and Marie Rama (published by IDG Books Worldwide, Inc.).

Getting started

Anywhere wine, broth, or water is called for in a recipe, beer usually offers a unique, and often improved, alternative. Imaginative cooks can have a field day experimenting with beer as a substitute for at least part of the other common cooking liquids. In general, a pale lager can substitute for half the liquid in any bread recipe and a quarter to a fifth of the liquid in a soup recipe. More elaborately prepared recipes call for more measurement and practice. In all cases, cook the beer long enough for it to impart its flavor.

Good news for vegetarians: Flavorful beer, such as Scottish ale, is a terrific substitute for chicken or beef stock. Beer is made from grain, so it has a natural affinity for grain-based dishes.

The easiest place to start fooling around (with cooking and beer, that is) is with steamed food, soups, stews, marinades, glazes, and bastes. Just pour it on or in, following some of the guidelines coming up in this chapter. On the other extreme, you can try chocolate stout ice cream, definitely an exercise in open-mindedness: Try it as a float (with stout, not root beer). What's next — beer peanut butter? I wouldn't be surprised.

If you are new to beer and want to experiment with your own recipes, try using the following:

- ✔ Pale lager for thinning a batter
- ✔ A lighter ale or lager (and some water) for steaming mussels
- ✔ Pale lager mixed with water (and spices) for steaming shrimp
- ✔ Light- to medium-bodied lagers for lighter marinades
- ✔ Full-bodied lagers or ales for stronger marinades (such as Chinese-inspired ones)

Beer mixes easily with oil or soy sauce and various seasonings for marinades.

One of the simplest ways to start cooking with beer is with a roast chicken: Simply pour one bottle of a flavorful beer, such as Märzen or porter, under the baking rack and let it mix with the pan drippings; add corn starch or flour and fresh beer when done, for a wonderful, lumpless gravy (the rest is up to you).

Don't automatically assume that beer is a complementary ingredient in every recipe. After all, of the four basic flavors (sweet, sour, salty, bitter), beer contributes only sweet and bitter. Sometimes beer just won't work, usually because its natural bitterness or sweetness gets concentrated by cooking. (Wine is not normally bitter, and sweet wines are fairly rare.)

Recipe for disaster

Beware of the many recipes floating around out there that call for just plain "beer" as an ingredient, without specifying a particular brand or style (see Chapter 1 for information about beer styles). This is evidence of the simplistic and uninformed mentality that a beer is a beer is a beer. I mean, come on, would any writer call for just plain "vegetable" or "meat"?

Given the great diversity in beer today, using the wrong style can be a recipe for a disastrous meal. On the other hand, if the errant recipe author is from the U.S., you can probably assume that a pale, commercial lager is the intended style.

Choosing the right beer

With the wide array of styles available, you need to make a choice about which beer to use in a recipe. Although the everyday, light-bodied, commercial lagers generally do fine, they obviously don't add as much flavor as other styles. Consider the following factors when choosing a cooking beer:

- ✔ **Color:** Beers that are brewed with a large percentage of dark grain, such as stout and porter, are likely to transpose their color to your meal — not an appetizing hue for fettucine Alfredo or scrambled eggs.

- ✔ **Level of sweetness (maltiness) versus level of bitterness (hoppiness and grain astringency):** Malt is by far the predominant beer taste in a recipe, but bitterness can take over easily because beer's bitterness increases with *reduction* (that is, the decrease in volume caused by boiling). Add bitter beer later in a recipe, or if a beer is being cooked for a while, choose a maltier beer style. In general, go with a mild beer rather than a bold one and avoid highly hopped beers, such as some pale ales. Sweeter, heavier beers should be reserved for dessert mixes and glazes.

    Remember: As the water and alcohol boil off, both the sweet and bitter flavors in the beer are concentrated, so choose your cooking beers carefully.

Unless you are well versed in beer styles and know what to expect from each, you'll find the light but tasty Munchener Helles (pale Munich-style lager) well suited to cross-culinary usage.

Recipe: beer in haute cuisine

Okay, so beer nuts are a tad defensive about beer versus wine. In order to truly trump the doubters, hoity-toity wine snobs who wouldn't even *think* of cooking with beer instead of wine, try this: André Soltner, the great chef of the famous, fancy French restaurant Lutèce, the restaurant that has served for years as the model of classic French cuisine, cooks with beer! He says that cooking with beer has become fashionable in France and that as an Alsatian, using beer in recipes is natural to him (half of French beer comes from Alsace, mostly in a pale lager style such as he uses in the following recipe). Following is one of his favorite recipes.

By the way, you may want to refer to Chapter 16 for a basic metric-conversion table.

Coq Sauté à la Bière d'Alsace (Sautéed Chicken in Beer)

salt

pepper, fresh ground

1 chicken, about 4 pounds, cut in 8 serving pieces

3 tablespoons (³/₈ stick) unsalted butter

1 onion, peeled and chopped

1 garlic clove, peeled, green germ removed, chopped

1 bay leaf

2 cloves

3 cups beer (light-colored)

1 tablespoon flour

1 pinch grated nutmeg

3 egg yolks, beaten

1 cup heavy cream

1 Salt and pepper the chicken. In a large skillet, melt 2 tablespoons of the butter over medium heat. Sauté the chicken until the pieces are golden brown on all sides.

2 Add the onion, garlic, bay leaf, cloves, and beer. Bring to a boil; simmer until the drumsticks are tender to the fork — about 40 minutes. Remove the chicken from the skillet, set it aside, and keep it warm.

3 Over medium heat, cook the liquid in the skillet until it is reduced by a third. Strain this bouillon through a sieve and set it aside.

4 In a saucepan, melt the remaining tablespoon of butter. Stir in the flour and cook for 2 minutes. Then gradually stir in the bouillon and the nutmeg. Cook gently for 10 more minutes.

5 Put the egg yolks and cream in a bowl. Whisking constantly, *slowly* add 1 cup of the bouillon. Then, still whisking, pour in the rest of the bouillon. Return this sauce to the saucepan and, whisking constantly, slowly reheat it. *Do not boil.*

6 Pour the sauce over the chicken and serve hot.

Note: *Nouilles à l'Alsacienne (Alsatian Noodles) are the right accompaniment to this dish (see* The Lutèce Cookbook*).*

From The Lutèce Cookbook by André Soltner and Seymour Britchky. Copyright © 1995 André Soltner and Seymour Britchky. Reprinted by permission of Alfred A. Knopf, Inc.

Just for more perspective, M. Soltner's book also includes a recipe for beer soup, made with 1 ¼ sticks of sweet butter, chicken stock, and a cup of heavy cream. (Hold the parsley — I'm watching my weight.)

On the other hand, don't ignore the ridiculous. Just for fun: The recipe for Dancing Chicken in *John Willingham's World Champion Bar-B-Q* calls for grilling a whole chicken with a half-full can of beer jammed into the cavity. That's different, man. I wonder, does the delicate hop aroma come through intact?

Dining with Beer: Beer/Food Matchmaking

There's a world of possibilities beyond pretzels and beer. Even more than nachos and popcorn and beer. Even more than barbecue and beer. Even more than. . . . You get the idea. Lotsa possibilities.

"Unsophisticated" is one of the more polite adjectives that have been used by elitists to describe beer. Unfortunately, some folks see the average beer drinker as unsophisticated, too; this goes a long way toward explaining the almost complete absence of beer in the typical fine-dining experience. Boy, are those restaurateurs and gourmets missing something! Actually, beer is considered to be the world's most popular beverage.

Restaurants that do stock beer often do so with an after-the-fact attitude; for as much attention as it is given, beer may as well be served in water pitchers. It seems unfair — while some upper-crust clientele yap on about their brochette of lamb au chanterelles pairing wondrously with an early vintage Chateau Haut-Brion, beer drinkers are expected to wash down blue-plate specials with mugs

Using leftover malt and wort in recipes (for homebrewers)

If you are a homebrewer or have access to homebrew supplies, you may want to throw some steeped (spent) malt into bread dough along with some beer. The malt gives the bread an interesting sweetness and coarseness and increases the dietary fiber (so you can throw away the laxatives).

You can also try malt extract or wort (the unfermented, unhopped syrupy stuff that is produced in the middle of the brewing process — see Chapter 3) as a base for sauces. Brewpubs and serious restaurants connected to breweries have gone this route with intriguing results.

full of cold and homogeneous light beer. Although vintage wines and aged spirits can boast of a long companionship with haute cuisine, beer, until recently in some places, seemed destined to be relegated to the backyard barbecue.

Well, that's wrong. Beer is only for thirst quenching as much as computers are only for number crunching and sports are only for boys. Get with it, folks! Beer is for dining, too.

After far too many years, I'm happy to say that the outlook for beer drinkers is rosé — oops, rosy. Thanks to the enthusiasm of brewers, restaurateurs, and consumers of flavorful craft-brewed beer, it has reclaimed its rightful place on our dinner tables.

Good craft-brewed beer can be much more interesting than wine — it's cool and refreshing and, depending on the style, can be much richer, more complex, and more flavorful than wine. Plus, if you have an average person's budget and capacity, you'll find tasting several different beers during a meal is preferable to tasting several different wines.

One of the best — hey, the most amazing — ways to experience beer as a dinner beverage is to attend a beer dinner (see Chapter 5), where the chef has teamed up with a brewmaster to develop and pair food and beer recipes that call for the perfect beer as either ingredient or beverage. If you are even moderately intrigued by the concept, go for it. You'll find it unlike anything you've ever experienced.

Go ahead — pour that beer into a wine glass!

The idea isn't to do a straightforward substitution of beer for wine, but when you do replace your wine with beer, you get some intriguing side effects (see Chapter 1 for some beer/wine substitutions).

✔ You tend to need less beer than wine with a meal. Split a bottle with friends and use tulip-shaped wineglasses.

✔ Dining alone? One 12-ounce bottle usually suffices (try to justify having a full bottle of wine just for yourself).

✔ You're imbibing less alcohol and fewer calories.

✔ Ultimately, gourmet beer is cheaper than wine.

Neat, huh? A four-way winner.

European models (the best and the wurst)

Europeans seem to have no qualms about drinking beer with their meals, including an occasional breakfast nip. This is particularly true of those nations with dynamic brewing industries: Great Britain, Germany, and Belgium.

While the island countries of Ireland and Britain may not be renowned for their upper-crust culinary traditions, their everyday national cuisines are great in the pubs. "Pub grub," as the food is modestly referred to, is hearty (though maybe uninspired), well portioned, and best of all, inexpensive.

In Germany and most of the other northern European countries, the national cuisines were built around beer. This is stick-to-your-ribs food, and beer is always within reach in case you want to unstick it. Just about anything that these folks throw on a plate begs for a beer. Here, *wine* is the afterthought, not beer.

In Belgium, which is known for its gastronomic gusto as well as for its diverse beers, restaurants regularly feature *Cuisine à la bière*. It is not at all unusual for chefs to both prepare dishes with beer and serve each course with yet another beer in accompaniment.

Guessing at guidelines

Within the sometimes intimidating world of wine and food, even the amateurs can lean on the old "red meat–red wine" axiom in a pinch. But beer drinkers have no such axiomatic, general guideline to fall back on, because none exists. And few people have a good enough grasp on the various beer styles and flavor profiles to make choices easily.

Actually, you'll find it hard to go wrong when matching beer and food. What's fun is trying to do better than not going wrong.

Every kind of food conceivably has an appropriate beer to accompany it. The beauty of beer is in its versatility. You can usually find a beer style that's a natural match for a given food. Beer even works better than wine with some dishes, such as especially spicy or sour ones. And slightly acidic beers are great foils for rich foods.

People like general guidelines, so here they are. But please don't follow them slavishly. For simplicity's sake, I borrowed from wine's example to describe the two major beer categories and how to match them with particular foods.

The lager beer category is the white wine equivalent. When compared to ales, lagers have the following characteristics:

- ✔ Generally lighter in body and color
- ✔ Narrower flavor profile and a high degree of drinkability (that is, tend to appeal to a wider audience)

The ale category is the red wine equivalent. When compared to lagers, ales have these qualities:

- ✔ Darker
- ✔ Rounder, more robust and expressive
- ✔ Wider flavor profile and thus a lower drinkability (that is, tend to appeal to those with a more experienced beer palate)

Just to keep you on your toes, remember that these guidelines are really general — dark and full-bodied lagers exist just as surely as do light and mild ales.

"Red wine with red meat, white wine with fish" is already fraught with loopholes for wine; no iron-clad beer equivalent exists. Sorry!

The general guideline for matching is to save the heartier beers, such as characterful ales, for the heartier dishes and try the lighter-bodied, mildly malty lagers with more subtly flavored dishes. Table 7-1 offers just a few examples of matching beer with various styles of cuisine.

Table 7-1 Suggestions for Matching Beer and Cuisine Styles

Cuisine	Dish	Beer
Mediterranean	Pasta dishes with red or white sauces	Dortmunder or Munchener helles
	Pork or lamb	Hoppy pale ale
Seafood	Fresh fish	Crisp Pilsner or wheat beer
	Shellfish	Porter
	Salt-cured fish	Porter
	Oysters	Dry stout (a classic pairing)
Indian	Curry dishes	Premium pale lager
Asian	Vegetable dishes (with fish sauce)	Premium pale lager
French	Aged, herbed cheeses	Bière de Garde
	Rich sauces	Spicy, sharply refreshing saison
	Red meats	Earthy Belgian Trappist ales

(continued)

Table 7-1 *(continued)*

Cuisine	*Dish*	*Beer*
Continental	Cheeses	Altbier or rauchbier (smoked beer)
	Steak	German pale lagers or Porter (especially with Porterhouse steaks)
	Pork and chicken	Maibock or Munchener helles
	Pumpernickel or rye bread and butter	Munchener dunkel or schwarzbier
	Sausages	Bock or Märzen/Oktoberfest
	Pizza	Vienna lager
	Asparagus	Pale lager or Trappist tripel
Spicy hot foods	Buffalo wings	Märzen/Oktoberfest
	Five-alarm chili	Bock
	Mexican hot sauces	Vienna lager
	Thai cuisine	Dark wheat
Desserts	Heavy desserts	Double or Triple Bock or Imperial stout

Remember: Table 7-1 is only meant to give you some ideas of beer and food match-ups. The range of styles from light to dark, dry to sweet, and mild to robust presents an unlimited number of culinary combinations and lots of room for experimentation.

With spicy food, rather than try to extinguish the flames by rinsing the mouth with just anything that's cold and wet, coat the mouth with a creamy, malty, medium-bodied lager and don't serve it ice-cold. You want sweeter, not drier, beers to cut through the heat; the extra alcohol in stronger beers also knocks out the heat. Water stinks at putting out fires on your tongue.

As for specific dishes that go well with beer, or better with beer than with wine, check out *Jay Harlow's Beer Cuisine,* a book devoted to this delightful subject.

Contrast and conquer

Complementary flavors between beer and food are good, but contrasting tastes are not necessarily bad.

In meal preparation, involving as many as possible of the four flavor zones of the human tongue — sweet, salty, sour, and bitter — is the goal of many chefs. This effort rounds out the meal and makes it more complete and interesting. On the other hand, if one of these flavors completely dominates or is missing altogether, the meal's balance suffers. What beer brings to the dinner table is mostly sweet and bitter, so you can make choices accordingly.

Before and after dinner

Stretching out the party? Try these ideas for the beginning and end of dinner.

Aperitifs: Light- to medium-bodied, tart, and well-hopped (bitter) beers make good before-dinner drinks with their appetite-whetting capabilities. Here are some examples:

- A dry, well-hopped Pilsner (the beer equivalent to the ubiquitous dry white wine, Chardonnay)
- California common beer (Steam beer)
- India pale ale
- West Coast microbrewed pale ales
- Belgian beers, such as lambic (fruited beers, such as kriek or framboise, are only for those who like cranberry juice or other fruit juices as an aperitif)

After-dinner drinks: Postprandial beers should be lightly carbonated and light- to medium-bodied. Here are some examples:

- Brown ale/English mild
- Ordinary (not extra special) bitter
- Kölsch beer

Nightcaps: Nightcap beers are generally big bodied and robust, with fairly high alcohol contents — hence their suggested use with late-night samplings, on full stomachs. You can try these with dessert (or even in place of it):

- Barleywine
- Old ale
- Doppelbock

- Triple Bock
- Eisbock
- Belgian strong ale
- Russian Imperial stout
- Scotch ale
- Trappist/abbey ales

These sweet, dark, strong beers are what go best with chocolate. Highly, highly recommended, though not nightly, of course. Every other night, maybe.

Chasing the heat

Beer is also a terrific complementary beverage to other beverages. Unfortunately, acting as a chaser for vodka, gin, tequila, and various liqueurs, beer is demoted to the position of rinsing or flushing the mouth and throat of the heat of distilled alcohol. The most popular combination is the boilermaker: a shot of whiskey with a beer chaser.

In the case of single-malt Scotch, however, quality beer is more of a companion beverage than a subservient wash. With good reason: Scotch whisky starts out as a beer, without hop bittering, the difference being that it's distilled to its present form. The designation "single malt" refers to the fact that Scotch whisky is made from 100 percent barleymalt and is unblended, unlike U.S.-made whiskeys that are made from grains considered inferior for beermaking purposes, such as corn and rye (ever heard of "corn squeezin's"?).

Lasting delight

"The discovery of a new dish does more for human happiness than the discovery of a star." — Brillat-Savarin, in his 1825 book *The Physiology of Taste.* Amen, especially if it is made with beer.

Part III
Buying Beer: Becoming an Informed Consumer

The 5th Wave   By Rich Tennant

"I'm sure 'Viking's Pillage' is a very good beer, but do you have anything with a less violent label?"

In this part . . .

1n this part, I provide information that will make you an informed beer consumer — so that you don't go to all the trouble of tracking down and selecting an interesting beer only to discover that it's stale or just not at all what you expected. You find out what you need to know about labels and advertising claims. After all, you want to be certain that your beer money is smart money.

I'll drink to that!

Chapter 8

Label Lunacy and Marketing Mayhem

··

In This Chapter

▶ Looking at labeling laws

▶ Watching quality control

▶ Understanding beer advertising and marketing

··

Making an informed choice when buying packaged beer is a small challenge. Weird government regulations and, let's face it, brewer's poetic license have combined to make beer labeling and advertising less than helpful. Determining what you're buying, or paying extra for, is sometimes very hard to do.

The brewer's poetry is usually obvious (a rundown on the taste, which is helpful, and ingredients and brewing processes, which are mostly irrelevant to the average consumer). The words *malty* and *hoppy* can give you a good idea of the taste, but a list of the specific malts or hops doesn't mean much to most people, though it is appetizing and fun, even educational. Other information, like *finest grains,* is sometimes confusing. Do these things make the beer better? Should a beer fan understand the terms and make a choice based on that information? Mostly, the answer is no.

What's *not* listed on the label is of more concern and raises even more questions in the mind of the informed consumer. This chapter gives you some background on what's what so that you can consume with confidence.

Labeling Laws

In the U.S., the Bureau of Alcohol, Tobacco and Firearms (BATF), part of the Department of the Treasury, oversees the American brewing industry and thus beer labeling with some very archaic laws, some predating Prohibition (which was in effect from 1920 to 1933). The situation is similar in the U.K. and Europe. The bottom line is that despite their best intentions, governments may have managed to prevent useful information from reaching you — important information, like nutritional content and strength. A bizarre paradox.

Label must-haves

U.S. rules say that very little is required on beer labels — only the basics, and they can be woefully incomplete:

- ✔ The name and address of the bottler or packer, but not necessarily the actual brewer of the beer, is stated (the actual street address may be omitted).

- ✔ The class (ale or lager) *must* be stated, and the type (style — porter, bock, and so on) *may* be stated. Ironically, the type is the more important distinction of the two — bad news for consumers.

- ✔ The law spells out — often inaccurately — which beers can and cannot be called an ale, a porter, or a stout. At least one brewer has actually resorted to deliberately mislabeling an ale as a lager or as a nonexistent style in order to conform. Bigger bummer.

In the European Union (E.U.), laws are similar, with one important addition: Brewers exporting within the E.U. need to list the country of manufacture, alcohol content by volume (not done in the U.S.), and a "best before" date, something that some of the leading U.S. brewers do by choice to impress discerning fans.

Prohibited label practices

Plenty of other statements and representations may not be used on container labels by U.S. law, including any statement or representation relating to nutritional analysis, ingredients, standards, or tests and, until very recently, any indication of strength, including percentage of alcohol (unless the beer has no alcohol at all) — even though *all* other alcoholic beverages are *required* to clearly list alcohol content on their labels. For years, the government has been afraid that people might sell or buy beer based on strength alone (why didn't the same reasoning apply to wine or spirits?).

The vast majority of beers have alcohol contents of 4 to 5 percent alcohol by volume (for example, Budweiser has 5 percent). Many beers may contain as much as 7 or 8 percent, and a select few contain alcohol levels equivalent to quality wines, which are about 12 to 14 percent. The alcohol content of specific beer styles is addressed in Appendix F.

The weak, the strong, and the unintelligible

The more common method of listing alcohol content in beer is by actual percentage of volume, which is the law in the U.K. and Europe; in the U.S., the brewers' custom is to note alcohol by weight (why should this be easy?). Of these two methods, alcohol-by-volume is easier to understand because you buy beer by volume.

Why is the weight method used? Because alcohol weighs less than water, beer, and many other liquids and therefore appears to be lower when comparative measurements are made. In English measure, a pint of water, for example, weighs 1 pound (actually, a fraction of an ounce over). A pint of alcohol, on the other hand, weighs only 0.79 pound.

So a beer with an alcohol content of 3.2 percent by weight is actually 4 percent by volume. A beer that is 4 percent by weight is actually 5 percent by volume. To figure it out yourself, convert an alcohol-by-weight reading to alcohol-by-volume by multiplying by 1.25. To convert an alcohol-by-volume reading to alcohol-by-weight, multiply by 0.80. Fun, huh?

Some internationally published beer writers give both measurements in their beer reviews. Read labels and menus carefully. You may be consuming much more (or less) alcohol than you think. **Remember:** Figures for weight are *lower* than those for volume.

Europeans are accustomed to seeing some indication of alcohol content in their beers, whether or not accompanied by a figure:

- In Germany, beer bottle labels are likely to contain one of the following three legal strength designations: *schankbier* (light), *vollbier* (medium), or *starkbier* (strong).

- Belgium has four categories of beer strength, ranging from Catégorie III (weakest) and moving up through Catégories II and I, ending with Catégorie S, for *strong*.

- The French have to be different, of course. They invented their own strength measure, degrees Régie, which they use to measure beers ranging from bière petite (the lightest) through bière de table, bière bock, bière de luxe, bière de choix, and bière spéciale (the strongest).

If you want to know the strength and brewing details about a particular beer, you have to read a good review in a beer magazine or guidebook. Labels just don't cut the mustard. Check out Appendix F for information on the alcohol content of various beers.

Know-nothing labels: additives and preservatives

The U.S. brewing industry is one of the few consumable-producing industries not required by the government to list ingredients on product labels. Surprisingly, the consumer at large has not demanded that brewers do so, either.

Among the many allowable additives and preservatives are more than 50 antioxidants, foam enhancers, colorings, flavorings, and miscellaneous enzymes, such as aspergillus oryzae, propylene glycol, sodium bisulfite, benzaldehyde, ethyl acetate, and food coloring. And you thought beer was just nicely flavored water!

One of the hallmarks of craft-brewed beers is that they are made without chemical additives and preservatives. It's my opinion that the large corporate brewers are infamous for using cheaper ingredients (adjunct grains, such as corn and rice — see Chapter 2) to make beer, but to good-beer fans like me, far worse than their frugality is their use of additives and preservatives.

The Reinheitsgebot: the German beer purity law

Many beer labels boast some phrasing of the following: "Brewed in strict accordance with the German purity law of 1516." That's saying a lot: The beer has no adjuncts (sugar, rice, corn), additives, or preservatives and is brewed using only malted barley or wheat, hops, yeast, and water. The absence of such a claim doesn't necessarily mean the beer has adjuncts, although a weak equivalent is "all malt" — meaning no adjunct grains were used (only barley and wheat are malted).

The *Reinheitsgebot* (pronounced "rine HITES ga boat"), rooted in German political history, has become synonymous with U.S. craft brews. Why? Because the Reinheitsgebot stands for beer purity, and U.S. craft brewers have wholeheartedly embraced that idea; some even advertise the fact (see Figure 8-1).

Our hand crafted beer conforms to the Bavarian Reinheitsgebot purity laws enacted in 1516. Using only the finest malted barley, hops, water and yeast.

KEEP REFRIGERATED   22 FL. OZ.

SEABRIGHT BREWERY

SEABRIGHT BREWERY • 519 SEABRIGHT AVE. • SANTA CRUZ, CA

Figure 8-1: Some beer labels proudly claim adherence to the Reinheitsgebot.

Impure but good

The belief that today's German brewers are not allowed to make beer with anything other than the four basic ingredients is somewhat misleading. Brewers are allowed to use fruits and spices in their beer (even sauerkraut, if they choose); the stipulation is that they cannot call that beer a lager if it is being marketed in Germany — even though it might be one. Weird, no?

As a result, the distinction between ales and lagers is twisted, in what must be one of the first and most bizarre loopholes in a consumer protection law. Regardless, the Reinheitsgebot is still a universally recognized standard.

Of course, rules can be interpreted, not followed to the letter, and still be honored. For a brewer who breaks the confines of the Reinheitsgebot to develop an unusual taste — using unmalted barley, extra sugar for prolonging fermentation, or adding some fruit for flavor — there should be no shame (see Chapter 2, on ingredients). What is most important is for the brewer to continue to use high-quality ingredients and not rely on additives and preservatives to artificially enhance a product.

The first consumer protection law

Written in 1516 by Duke Wilhelm IV of Bavaria, the Reinheitsgebot guaranteed that a true Bavarian beer was made with nothing other than malted barley or wheat, hops, and water. This purity law was updated (to include yeast, for example, which people didn't know about in 1516) and became part of modern laws over time.

Actually, the question of allowable ingredients constituted only half of the subject matter of the original decree. At that time, the more important issue dealt with the pricing structure of beer.

The cost was to be preset according to measure (quart and ½ quart) and the time of year (apparently, 16th-century Bavarian beer was more expensive in the summer months when demand was greater — a concept not lost on my electric company).

The Duke realized that the well-regarded Bavarian brewing industry could be developed into a taxable powerhouse, and history proved him right.

The Reinheitsgebot has defined the basic building blocks of quality beer. It cast these guidelines in stone and has been honored and respected for some 480 years by the German brewing industry. In 1919, all German breweries reaffirmed their informal allegiance to the law — something that loyal German consumers hold dear.

As recently as spring 1986, a brewer named Helmut Keininger was arrested for putting chemicals in his beer. The infraction was considered so professionally devastating that he ended up committing suicide in his Munich jail cell.

Purist beer nuts planning a pilgrimage should know that the original copy of the Reinheitsgebot is on display at the Bavarian State Library in Munich.

The Reinheitsgebot is not applied to beer being exported from Germany. Some of the most popular German beers imported to the U.S. are not brewed according to the Reinheitsgebot; the recipes have been legally altered with adjuncts and preservatives both for U.S. tastes and for added shelf life. That may be why many U.S. travelers to Germany say that German beers never taste as good "back home" as they do in Germany.

Beer watchdogs

Several large-scale, consumer-oriented, quality-conscious organizations promote the moderate consumption of good beer. All these consumer organizations sponsor events large and small in their respective countries and are often cited in beer periodicals. Beer events may include pub crawls, beer treks, beer tastings, beer festivals, and in some cases, educational classes and seminars. See Appendix C for information about such organizations.

I'm sure that all these organizations would concur: Don't just drink up — speak up! Demand the finest possible product from brewers!

Watchdogs through the ages

Throughout history, sporadic attempts have been made to patrol the brewing industry and perform the equivalent of quality-control analysis, purity law or no purity law. We beer lovers take this stuff seriously!

✔ The first watchdog was an Egyptian fellow, in the time of the Pharaohs, who held the title of Chief Beer Inspector, or something to that effect. It was his responsibility to maintain the level of quality of the beer being produced for the Pharaoh's household. No mention is made of penalties for failure.

✔ One of the oldest public offices in England is that of the ale-conner, or taster, a post created by William the Conqueror in the 11th century in order to keep ale prices and quality in line.

Not only was the ale-conner an expert judge of beer, but he had the power to condemn a batch of beer or order its sale at a reduced price if it did not meet his high standards.

This token civil position still exists in England, paying a small annual allowance with free beer thrown in for good measure. (William Shakespeare's father, John, was an ale-conner, an appointment of considerable significance in Elizabethan England. The young bard obviously learned to appreciate

a good beer: "Blessing of your heart, you brew good ale." — *Two Gentlemen of Verona*)

Besides tasting the liquid wares, the resourceful ale-conner evaluated the new brews in a most peculiar way. Garbed in leather breeches, he would pour out a measure of ale on a wooden bench and dutifully sit in the puddle of beer for no less than a half hour.

If his breeches then stuck to the bench, the ale was deemed young and imperfect — with too much sugar — and the ale-conner could levy a penalty against the brewer. (Brewers may have felt that they were getting the short end of the stick when, in fact, they were getting the sticky end of the shorts.)

✔ In 18th-century Alsace, sworn beer assayers were called Bierkiesers. In the neighboring regions of Artois and Flanders, their equivalents were called Coueriers, Egards, or Eswerts. Their job was to taste freshly tapped beer in order to ensure that it met local standards, which closely mirrored the Reinheitsgebot. The addition of any unauthorized ingredient was a punishable offense.

"Guinness Is Good for You": Nutritional Content

In the U.S., the BATF doesn't allow the Food and Drug Administration's Nutrition Facts chart to appear on a beer bottle or can. And in the E.U., proposals to mandate the listing of ingredients have fallen by the wayside.

The governments fear suggestions of "curative and therapeutic claims" stemming from the fact that well-made craft-brewed beer can have more protein than a dry bowl of corn flakes, with half the carbohydrates and twice the potassium and without the additives or preservatives so often found in prepared foods as well as in some megabrewed beers.

In a February 1993 article in *Seattle Weekly,* Jack Killorin, a BATF spokesman, is cited as saying that listing a beer's nutrients would suggest that beer is a food. According to the article, Killorin said that beer is not a food, because alcohol is bad and the FDA does not allow bad food. (Now, I ask, does this statement refer to TV dinners and marshmallows, too?) Regardless of this statement, there are now strong indications that this attitude is changing and that nutrition labels will eventually be listed on beer products.

In fact, in the U.S., the governmental guidelines on which these kinds of things are based are reviewed every five years. The 1995 revised Dietary Guidelines for Americans, released by a joint committee of the Agriculture Department and the Department of Health and Human Services, actually *reverse* the ages-old government line. These guidelines state that accumulating evidence suggests that moderate drinking (*read:* no more than one or two beers a day for women or two beers for men) may lower the risk of heart attacks and may enhance the enjoyment of meals.

This modest statement is downright revolutionary for the U.S. government. After all, the 1990 guidelines said that drinking had *no* net health benefit.

It's not like they're inviting you to a big party, though. Moderation is key, as is a well-balanced, low-fat diet combined with exercise. The guidelines rightly go on to warn that higher levels of alcohol intake are risky in terms of raising blood pressure and incidents of stroke, heart disease, and some forms of cancer, as well as being the less direct cause of birth defects, suicide, and accidents. The guidelines continue to remind us of the dangers of drinking and driving as well as irresponsible overconsumption in general. The government warning on labels remains in effect.

Cholesterol free! Fat free!

For years, the great Irish stout, Guinness, has been advertised with the slogan "Guinness is Good for You." Americans take that kind of statement too seriously, so it wasn't used in the U.S. But it was partially correct: Beer is actually nutritious, though it should be consumed only for pleasure and thirst-quenching.

Beer is free of cholesterol and fat. More good news: 12 ounces of a typical American pale lager beer actually has fewer calories than 12 ounces of 2 percent milk or even apple juice (a bit less than wine, too)! And some lower-alcohol styles, such as dry stouts, have even fewer calories. Beer may not be diet delite, but I'll bet you're happy to know that it has good dietary qualities.

Beery nutrition facts

If the government *did* allow the listing of nutritional content on beer labels, here's what the content of a standard "Nutrition Facts" chart might be for a 12-ounce (355-milliliter) bottle of a typical megabrewed U.S. lager:

- ✔ 151 calories (two-thirds from alcohol)

- ✔ 0 grams fat

- ✔ 0 milligrams cholesterol

- ✔ 25 milligrams sodium

- ✔ 13.7 grams carbohydrate

- ✔ 1.1 grams protein

- ✔ Trace amounts of calcium, potassium, and phosphorus and many of the B vitamins

Remember: Two-thirds of the calories in beer come from the alcohol.

What's cool is that as the quality of the beer increases, so do the good numbers. For example, compare a high-quality, microbrewed beer such as Grant's Scottish Ale, produced in the state of Washington, with most nationally distributed megabrewed pale lagers. Grant's has 6 fewer calories, 1 gram fewer carbohydrates, and 1.14 *more* grams of protein, along with measurable amounts of riboflavin (B_2), niacin, folacin, and pyroxin (B_6), 195 grams of potassium, and almost twice the recommended daily allowance of vitamin B_{12}. And no additives or preservatives. (Most light beers check in at 95 calories.)

Drink beer, live longer

One of the greatest little tidbits of news that beer drinkers ever heard was the spring 1996 report that dark beer can help prevent heart disease.

This nice news came from John Folts, the director of the Coronary Thrombosis Research and Prevention Laboratory at the University of Wisconsin, the man who discovered that aspirin helps prevent heart disease. The key to dark beer's role, along with red wine and black tea, is that it contains vitaminlike compounds called *flavenoids* that inhibit platelet activity in blood, making it less likely to clog arteries. And other studies show that moderate consumption of any alcohol may increase HDL (good cholesterol) levels as well as help your longevity.

I'm not suggesting that you should go out and drink beer for medicinal reasons. On the contrary, increased consumption of tea, grape juice, or fruits and vegetables is the better way to go. But still, this information gives you a great excuse (if you need one) to drink beer.

Those Germans sure know a good thing when they see it

In mid–19th-century Munich, some nursing mothers and wet nurses went out of their way to drink up to seven (sic) pints of beer a day, thinking that amount was required to adequately breast-feed a child. In 1876, the Munich city health department tried to break this habit, stating that only two pints a day were necessary.

Things haven't changed so much, either: In 1987, a German federal petition to the European court on a related matter stated that as much as 25 percent of the average German man's daily nutrients came from beer. That's serious consumption.

Beer Advertising and Marketing

Oddly, most of the emphasis in U.S. beer promotion is on name recognition, so ads feature humor or social situations unrelated to the taste, ingredients, or general quality of the beer. In other words, while advertising should extol the virtues and the various features of a product, megabrewed beer advertising tends to ignore the beer itself (don't get me started as to why). For examples, try a Swedish bikini team, baseball in the Rockies, and animated frogs. Get the idea? Fun, though. Great creativity. Effective, too. But they say little about beer. Same with the labels.

Little white lies on labels

Some of the buzzwords peculiar to the brewing industry include *unique blends, select grains, premium hops,* and *pure spring water.* The two most overused terms (despite the fact that they say very little about the taste of the beer) are *smooth* and *mellow.* In too many cases, *insipid* and *lifeless* would be more apt.

Megabrewers aren't alone in label latitude: Many labels on craft brews tout the variety of hops or water used. Can you imagine being told which kind of corn was used in your corn flakes? That kind of detail matters to brewers, but for the rest of us, it's largely hype. What really matters is how all the ingredients are put together and how the beer turns out. It's the beer, folks. You can ignore the rest.

And all our bottles are made from the finest carbon

The following is copied verbatim from the bottle-neck label of a popular and excellent craft-brewed beer (with good ingredients) whose marketers have simply gotten carried away (and also forgotten some of their punctuation lessons):

Ajax Traditional Pale Ale {name changed to protect the guilty} *is brewed with six specially blended malts, hopped with English East Kent* Goldings and American Cascades to give this traditional ale a distinctive yet drinkable quality.

Especially impressive is the ability of the beer to retain a "drinkable quality" after all those malts and hops. What else should it be? Paintable? Wearable? Come on! *Drinkable?*

Try not to be taken in by flowery language and fancy packaging.

Beware the sheep in wolf's clothing

Recently, the lion (megabrewers) has been noticing the thorn in its paw (craft brewers), leading to some clever marketing and business strategizing. Megabrewers like the craft brewer's cachet of quality — and premium prices.

In an illustration of the maxim that imitation is the sincerest form of flattery, some of the big U.S. megabrewers have either bought or become partners with a number of successful regional craft brewers; some of the big guys have also started making their own craftlike brands disguised as microbrews through clever marketing (one wag dubbed them "stealth micros"). In the U.K., the big brewers are pushing *nitrokeg* beer (filtered and pasteurized keg beer artificially carbonated and pressurized with a nitrogen/carbon dioxide blend) disguised as the more costly and appreciated naturally carbonated, unfiltered, unpasteurized, and hand-pumped cask-conditioned ales. The brewers even supply fake hand pumps. Traditionalists are in an uproar.

Although some of the stealth brews are terrific, quality, and award-winning traditional brews, many are the plain old same old light stuff masquerading as good stuff. *Caveat emptor.*

The lowdown on contract brewing

Microbreweries (brewers who make fewer than 15,000 barrels a year) have sort of cornered the image market on gourmet beer: Most of these beers sell for more because consumers consider them superior, largely due to the freshness that comes from being made locally and in small batches. Or the cachet of being small and hand-crafted, just as with bread or furniture.

That's an assumption, of course, and assumptions are not always good.

Stealth micros?

Here's a rundown on the megabrewers who have put out craftlike brews:

✔ Miller 'fessed up to being the brewer of Red Dog, instead of crediting the phantom "Plank Road Brewery" — the original name of what is now the Miller Brewing Company — but still boasted of winning the Best Beer Advertising of the Year award for the scheme.

Miller has bought an interest in micro/regional brewers Celis Brewery, Leinenkugel Brewing Co., and Shipyard Brewery; Miller markets beers such as Celis Witbier and Blue Fin Stout through its American Speciality and Craft Beer Co. division.

✔ Coors sells its Killian's Red and Blue Moon as brewed by Unibev Corporation and Blue Moon Brewing Co., respectively. Blue Moon ales, targeted at microbrew enthusiasts, include such exotics as a Nut Brown Ale, a Honey Blond Ale, a Belgian White Ale, and a pumpkin ale. Some were originally made in the Coors Sandlot microbrewery at Coors Field in Denver, home of Major League Baseball's Colorado Rockies.

✔ Anheuser-Busch, the world's largest brewer, has recently started a line called American Originals that replicates the wonderfully tasty beers originally brewed by A-B's founder at the turn of the century, including a full-bodied lager, a porter, and a deep copper lager. A-B's Specialty Division markets Elk Mountain, Elephant Red, and Red Wolf. A-B has even brewed an Amber Bock under the venerable Michelob name.

✔ Stroh brews Augsburger and Red River beers but for now distributes them mostly in the Midwest and Pacific Northwest. Red River beers include a Select Red Lager, a Honey Brown Ale, and a Red Ale. Stroh's G. Heileman unit markets Boar's Head, Windy City, and Emerald City beers under its H. Weinhard division.

A lot of the best and best-known craft brews (gourmet beers made in a wide range of classic styles, using quality ingredients) are not microbrewed but are *contract brewed* in larger volumes than a microbrewery can handle. Contract brewers hire underutilized but well-equipped regional breweries to produce a recipe with the contract brewer's own ingredients and formulas. The giveaway label lingo, if you can find the small print along the edges, is something like "Brewed by XX Brewing Co. under special agreement, XYZ Brewing Co., ABC State." The only other way to learn what is contract brewed is to read brewspapers and beer magazines (see Appendix D for a list of these media).

Who are these contract brewers? The well-known Pete's Wicked Brewing Co., Boston Beer Company (Samuel Adams and so on), Oregon Ales, and even Brooklyn Brewery, just to name a few. You will see a definite trend, as certain brands become successful enough to build up national demand that can be met only by regional brewing, which is better than having to resort to adjuncts and preservatives.

Nothing wrong with that — the quality is the same. Still, you may find it disconcerting. Your full-of-character beer with its artsy label and catchy name reeking of homemade goodness and local freshness may not be made nearby by some wonderfully talented beer nuts slaving away on homemade equipment; it may actually be produced at an industrial site hundreds of miles away, perhaps financed by venture capital and moved by top-notch marketing muscle. For example, Chicagoans with a fondness for the "hometown" State Street beer may be surprised to find that it is produced in Evansville, Indiana.

However, if the beer tastes good, don't worry! The taste — and your satisfaction — is all that really matters.

The label as an art form

A final note: One of the nicest aspects of the American craft-brewing renaissance is the artwork on the labels. Some labels are downright inspired and splendid works of art (see the figure in this sidebar, which shows a label of the Casco Bay Brewing Co.). Appreciating them brings a whole new dimension to beer drinking. And the brand names! They're creative and humorous, making the spirit of beer live inside and outside the bottle.

KATAHDIN

GOLDEN

12 FLUID OUNCES

MADE IN MAINE

Chapter 9

Better Beer Buying

In This Chapter

▶ Knowing your enemies

▶ Understanding your defenses

▶ Picking your packaging

*B*eer is food. Sometimes you hear Europeans refer to beer as *liquid bread* (I hope they don't try to slice it). And like most foods, especially bread, beer is perishable and becomes stale over time, so the fresher the beer, the better it is.

Therefore, beer consumers on the way to enlightenment want to consume beer that is freshly made or want to be sure that it is handled properly to maintain freshness — particularly if, as do most good beers, it has no preservatives.

Beer freshness has three enemies: time, heat, and light. In this chapter, I tell you how to deal with these problems and become a more informed consumer.

Purchase or Perish

Most people aren't the least bit self-conscious about squeezing tomatoes, thumping melons, sniffing ground beef, or reading the freshness date on bread wrappers at the supermarket. And don't wine enthusiasts pay great attention to the harvest (vintage) year? Why, then, should beer drinkers be willing to dash into a store, grab any old six-pack off the shelf, and assume that the beer is fresh? Why ask why?

Cans can fool you

Don't be fooled by bottled and canned products that are called *draft* or *draught* anything. Draught means "drawn fresh from a tap" — period! Having draught beer in a can or bottle is literally impossible, despite the artfully worded labels.

Brewers in the U.K. have devised a can (labeled *Pub Draught*) containing its own miniature nitrogen canister (called a *widget*) that bursts when the can is opened, thus creating the fine-bead carbonation and creamy mouthfeel of a freshly "pulled" pint of ale. Just like the beer from hand-pumped taps of London pubs? It's good and close — but only *close* — to the real thing.

Time (is not on your side)

As I mentioned, beer gets stale over time. Three months is the average window of freshness (the shelf life) for pasteurized bottled or canned beer. Some beers have a longer shelf life than others. Those that are fully pasteurized (heated for up to one hour, as are most megabrews) are more stable than those that are flash-pasteurized (heated for only one minute, as are most craft brews). Also, hops and alcohol serve as natural preservatives, so well-hopped and stronger beers have a longer shelf life.

Conscientious brewers demand that their beer be pulled from the shelves if it doesn't sell within the appropriate time. Unfortunately, many of the small stores in the U.S. that are just beginning to carry craft and imported beers may unwittingly keep old stock on sale long after it should be returned. Don't buy old beer!

Calling it close

There's a saying, "Beer should be drunk as close to the brewery as possible."

Guinness (an Irish stout) doesn't travel well, fans say. One fan tested this out, with an amusing result. He made a pilgrimage to the famed Dublin brewery in order to have the ultimate, freshest possible, perfect pint of his favorite brew. But before his first sip, a local wag managed to put him off a bit with classic Irish wit by saying, "Oh, I don't know. It's pretty far from here to the vat. It doesn't travel well, you know."

Aging like fine wine — not!

With the following handful of styles, not only can you keep the beer for a long time, but you can actually improve its character with short-term aging of about six months to a year. These complex, strong beers tend to mellow over time, much as whiskey and wine do.

- ✔ High-gravity barleywines
- ✔ Old ales
- ✔ Triple Bocks
- ✔ Some of the higher-gravity Belgian Trappist beers (dubbels and tripels)

Although some beers, like Thomas Hardy's Ale (an old ale), are still good after a decade (developing some sherrylike tastes), even the hardiest beer is likely to wither beyond a year or two because oxidation will take its toll and the beer will go stale.

Many people collect beer bottles and cans, but no one in his or her right mind (and surely that doesn't disqualify any of you) would collect vintage beer without planning to drink it. Besides, only a few brewers (of the styles noted previously) date their beers by vintage. Wine is vintage-dated and is subject to good and bad years; certain vintages keep well for many years and are prized possessions in the cellars of those who own them. For the wine collector, owning these wines is often more important than drinking them. No such aspirations exist among beer drinkers, because no beers inspire such pretensions. Besides, I'm lucky if a good bottle of beer lasts a weekend around my house, never mind years!

Beer is really much more democratic than wine: Anyone can have a cellar full of the best beer.

Left out of the cold

Heat makes beer go stale really fast. Refrigeration is therefore the ideal way to extend the shelf life of beer. However, lack of proper refrigeration is a major problem for beer retailers and distributors. Beer retailers often have limited cooler space, and most tend to reserve refrigeration space for big-name beers. Distributors often store vast amounts of other beers in cavernous, unrefrigerated warehouses that may subject the beer to extreme temperature fluctuations.

Life's not fair: Go have a beer and ponder this.

So what beer gets the dreaded warm reception? Beer that is not supported with at least one mainstream form of advertising, beer distributed by a company with shallow pockets (*read:* no freebies for the retailer, no neon signs, no plastic clocks), or any Johnny-come-lately beer that has yet to find an audience. These beers are usually left to languish on warm store shelves or in sunny window displays that look enticing but are terrible for the beer. And these beers may be among the best-tasting ones!

Seeing the light

Any form of light is potentially harmful to beer. Light produces chemical reactions in the hop compounds. These reactions create a mild *skunky* (*catty* in the U.K.) odor. Incandescent lighting is bad enough, but fluorescent lighting — found in most stores — is even worse. (No, the light in your fridge isn't going to destroy your brew.) Beer's worst enemy is sunlight, however, as it is both light *and* heat.

A beer that smells skunky is said to be *lightstruck.* If you think you've actually seen a skunk in the refrigerator, you are said to be *dumbstruck;* no more beer for you!

One form of protection against light damage is colored glass. The more opaque the glass, the better: Green is good, but amber is best.

Bottom line: Don't expect beer to be any more resistant to heat, time, and direct sunlight than are other fresh foods. If your retailer stacks exposed six-packs in the front windows of the store where they are allowed to sunbathe for several hours a day, file a report with the beer police at once!

Remember: Time = Bad   Refrigeration = Good   Light = Bad

Checking out the scene before checking out

How can you, the customer, know when a particular beer arrived in the store? Unfortunately, you can't, but you can find clues in the beer or on the packaging that help you figure out which beers are fresh stock and which ones are on a long-term lease. Here are some general buying tips:

✔ Whether you buy beer in cans or bottles, always reach for refrigerated stock first.

✔ Check for a readable date stamp — a rare item indeed (see the sidebar "Breaking the code" later in this chapter). Look at the tops of the cans or the shoulders of the bottles; be wary of any wearing a mantle of dust.

- ✔ When buying bottled beer, consider the color of the bottle (remember that green glass allows more light to penetrate than brown glass does, and clear allows the most light).

- ✔ Hold a bottle up to the light and assess the beer's clarity. Except for beers that are purposely bottled in the unfiltered state, a fresh filtered beer should be crystal clear. Look for sediment. Unless the beer in your hand is a hefeweizen or a bottle-conditioned beer (see Chapter 1), sediment suggests that the beer has been sitting around a while.

- ✔ Give the bottle a gentle shake. Any little chunks of stuff swirling around are probably protein flakes that have settled out of the liquid — a definite sign that the beer is eligible for social security.

Making friends

Get to know your local beer retailers. If they carry a varied beer selection, make your face well known. Let them know you're a beer geek. Don't be afraid to ask questions. After a relationship is established, you may want to approach them about their storage and stock-rotation practices. You'll probably get straight answers, especially if the proprietor is a dedicated beer lover. In time, you may even suggest additions or deletions to the stock. Who knows — before you're through, they may just make you a business partner.

Another way to ensure a supply of quality beer, especially if you don't live in a major urban area, is to join a beer-of-the-month club. Several are listed in Appendix C, and most send you 12 bottles, along with a newsletter, for about $25 per month. This kind of connection serves the dual purpose of bringing you fresh beer as well as exposing you to a variety of microbrewed beers that are not normally distributed nationally.

Did You Get Burnt?

After you've plunked down your money and taken your carefully scrutinized brew home, the post-purchase evaluation begins.

Popping your top

Your evaluation of the beer starts with the removal of the bottle cap. Did the bottle give a quick, healthy hiss? Did it gush like Mt. Vesuvius or fail to release any carbonation at all? Unless the bottle was allowed to get very warm or you did the hokey-pokey with it just before opening, a gusher indicates a potential wild fermentation in the bottle — not a good thing, but not anything that'll kill you, either. If a quick sniff doesn't verify this possibility, a follow-up taste will. Vinegary tastes and aromas are usually good indications of a fermentation gone wild, but proper pasteurization makes this occurrence infrequent.

Breaking the code

All major American brewers date-stamp their product so distributors can keep track of their stock. Distributors are generally expected to remove and return an outdated product to the brewer, but occasionally a distributor and retailer agree to sell outdated beer at a drastically reduced price — without informing the consumer how old it is. Checking the date stamps before buying seems like the common-sense thing for a customer to do; however, some brewers use encrypted date stamps, so only those who know the code (and probably certain CIA operatives) can understand the information.

Some enlightened craft brewers, who live and die by freshness of product, have begun date-stamping their product with uncoded, easy-to-read freshness dates, as has one megabrewer for one type of beer. Kudos to them.

Certain megabrewers' date stamping indicates not only at which brewery the beer was brewed but also on which production line it was packaged — accurate down to the 15-minute period of production! But when written in 12-figure alphanumeric code, the information may as well be in hieroglyphics. A prize of one fresh beer to anyone who can break it.

If you didn't get the usual *fizzzzt* from the bottle, either the beer was improperly carbonated at the brewery (very unlikely) or the cap's seal had a leak that allowed the carbonation to escape. These types of problems are virtually unheard of in well-known brand-name beers and are usually limited to products from small, technologically challenged breweries.

There's rain in your beer!

The following is totally useless information.

Ever notice the cloud that appears in the neck of a beer bottle when the cap is removed? It's a real cloud, just like outside!

The airspace in the unopened bottleneck contains carbon dioxide and water vapor. Because the inside pressure is approximately twice air pressure at sea level, when the cap is removed, the gases and vapors expand rapidly. This decompression causes a precipitous drop in temperature (remember your high school science?) within the neck of the bottle — estimated to be approximately −30 degrees F (−34 degrees C) That's cold, man!

This instantaneous drop in temperature causes the water molecules to become so sluggish that they become *nucleation sites* for water droplets (condensation) — the same way clouds form in the sky.

Wow. And here you were just looking for the *meaning* of life, not the origin.

Oxidation blues

Any beer that has been lying around too long, regardless of whether it was pasteurized or not, reaches a point when it goes stale (becomes *oxidized*). The result is a beer that smells and tastes papery in the early stages and cardboardy in the advanced stages. Refrigerated beer is far less likely to become oxidized, but it can still happen over time.

Check the airspace (the *ullage*) at the top of the bottle. The proper ullage should be no more than 1 inch from the top of the liquid to the cap. A larger-than-normal ullage may promote oxidation, especially with unrefrigerated beer. Don't buy that bottle!

Cans, Kegs, Bottles, and Barrels

Beer drinkers argue endlessly over whether beer is better bottled or canned. Rather than make an authoritative pronouncement and give you my opinion (which, of course, is the right one), this section presents the facts and lets you arrive at your own conclusions.

On second thought, let me give my opinion straight away: The beer can seems to offer the most convenience, but you can't argue against the aesthetics of the old brown bottle — call me old-fashioned. Besides, where would great bottle-neck slide guitarists like Eric Clapton and Bonnie Raitt be without glass beer bottles? Have you ever heard of an aluminum-can slide guitarist?

The cancan

The bottle predates the can by, oh, about 4,000 years. Beer cans, first intro-duced in 1935, revolutionized the brewing industry. People went from drinking fresh, draught beer at a neighborhood tavern (or carrying it home in a bucket) to buying it in stores, in bulk. Canned-beer packages (six-packs) were much lighter, quicker to chill, and more convenient than bottles all around. Sadly, the beer all too often tasted like the can it came in. Eventually, a synthetic liner was invented that shielded the beer, and the can became more popular than ever. Somewhere along the line, the old tin can was replaced by the newer, lighter, linerless aluminum can, and partly due to the rise of mass marketing, the beer industry hasn't looked back since.

Bottled or canned, the beer should taste the same. However, craft brewers use bottles almost exclusively because canning equipment is more expensive than bottling equipment and also because consumers seemingly associate cans with mass-market beer.

Canning trivia

Collectors, take note!

✔ Krueger Cream Ale (Gottfried Krueger Brewing Co.), released January 24, 1935, was the first beer ever sold in a can.

✔ The Coors Brewing Company was the first brewery to package its beer in aluminum cans (back in the early 1950s).

✔ The Pittsburgh Brewing Company was the first to introduce the lift-tab aluminum can (in 1962).

Pain in the glass

In spite of the beer can's popularity, the beer bottle never really faded away. The only notable changes have been in the realm of convenience. The old, heavy returnable bottle was replaced in most markets by a lighter throwaway version and a twin with a twist-off top.

Not only do devotees of beer in glass argue in favor of bottles, but they also argue over the bottle size and shape that most enhance the beer, such as long-necks versus stubbies (I've yet to hear an argument convincing enough to convert me to any particular bottle style). Today, dozens of beer-bottle shapes are used by breweries around the world; some of the more curious (Mickey's Big Mouth, for example) are made according to individual brewer specifications.

Keg parties

You may not often need to buy a keg of beer, but at least once, you'll probably get one for a picnic, a softball tournament, a 30th birthday party (or a 40th, or 50th), or a burn-the-mortgage bash. And at least some of you belonged to the popular fraternity Tappa Kegga Bru in college. Besides, the only way to have fresh, unpasteurized draught beer is to buy a keg.

Buying a keg is easy; transporting it is the hard part. The big ones are really, really heavy — like 150 pounds. Don't lift one yourself! Have it picked up by someone big and strong or delivered straight to your party.

You need to figure out how many people will be attending the festivity and their level of "participation" in order to determine what size keg to order.

See Table 9-1 for the breakdown of keg sizes. Keep in mind that in beer parlance, a "barrel" — 31 gallons — doesn't really exist except for accounting and brewery-capacity purposes. Also, see Figure 9-1 for an example of a popular keg.

In the U.S., beer from other countries usually comes in 50-liter (13.2-gallon) and 30-liter (7.9-gallon) kegs. To further complicate matters, vendors sometimes use different names for these items, confusing brand names with sizes and nicknames. *Solution:* Always return to the volume figure (gallons or liters).

Table 9-1	U.S. Kegged-Beer Serving Table	
Size of Keg	*Number of 12-ounce Servings*	*Number of 8-ounce Servings*
Half barrel (15.5 gallons)	165	248
Quarter barrel (7.75 gallons)	82	124

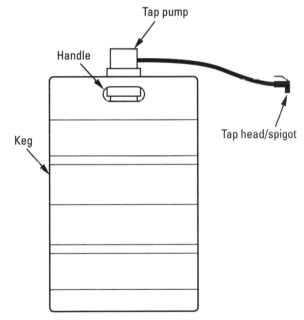

Tap pump

Handle

Tap head/spigot

Keg

Figure 9-1:
A 15.5-gallon Sankey beer keg is one of the most common and easy-to-use kegs. Don't pump too much — try serving into pitchers to keep wasted foam to a minimum.

Here are some tips for better keg parties:

🖊 Make sure that you get the right tap for your keg when you pick up the keg or accept the delivery. You're charged a refundable deposit for the tap equipment, so treat it with care.

🖊 The two most common keg systems in the market are the straight-sided, easy-to-use Sankey kegs — used by Anheuser-Busch, Miller, and other biggies — and the Hof-Stevens kegs, with their "bulging" sides and obvious *bung hole* (the corked opening where the keg is filled).

The Hof-Stevens system must be screwed carefully onto the keg (watch out for spray!). Make sure that these taps are clean and properly seated on the openings, or else the keg won't pressurize properly. If the keg doesn't pressurize, you don't drink! Such pain that would cause! Pain and, shall I say, disappointment.

🖊 Keep the beer as cold as possible. If you don't have a humongous refrigerator, place ice on top and around the base of the keg while it stands in a large bucket or plastic garbage can.

🖊 Always expect the first gallon or so to be a little foamier than usual — after all, it's probably been jostled a bit during delivery — but the beer eventually comes out normal. Letting the keg sit for a while helps, as does filling a pitcher and serving from it instead of filling individual cups. Fooling around with the air-pressure pump also leads to foamy beer; serving from a pitcher prevents that problem as well.

🖊 Some people may say that you can never have too much beer, and no good host wants to run out. That means possible leftover beer. If you don't want to return that precious nectar along with the keg after the party, plan ahead: Thoroughly clean some plastic milk jugs and empty the keg into them. Refrigerate immediately and drink within a day or two.

One for the ditch

Talk about being sure to drink your beer before it goes stale — back when England still held public hangings, the tradition was to give the condemned a free glass of ale on the way to the execution. (What a way to go!)

Part IV
Making Beer: Homebrewing

The 5th Wave   By Rich Tennant

SUCCESSFUL BEER-MAKING ESSENTIALS

Barley   Hops   Malt

Water   Yeast   Drinking Buddy

In this part . . .

Those of you who really like good beer may find that making it yourself is only a short leap from buying it. Surprisingly easy and rewarding, homebrewing is a very popular hobby. In this part, I offer some beginning and intermediate instructions, just enough to get you hooked — and keep you out of trouble.

Even if you're not into making beer yourself, these chapters are excellent for learning the details that make good beers so special. Read on to understand what those brewers and reviewers you admire are talking about. Who knows? Maybe you'll start brewing after all!

Chapter 10

Homebrewing for the Beginner

- -

In This Chapter

▶ Why brew at home?

▶ Getting the right equipment

▶ Cleaning and sanitizing

▶ Ready, set, brew!

▶ Bottling, fermenting, record keeping

- -

*O*ne of the recurring questions about homebrewing is "Why should I go through the trouble of brewing beer if I can just buy my favorite beer at the store?" After homebrewing for 11 years, teaching an occasional homebrew class, and making a video on the subject, I can offer you several good answers to that question.

First, homebrewed beer may be every bit as good as some commercial beer or even better, with more flavor and character than most. In fact, avoiding mass-marketed beer is the original inspiration for homebrewing. Second, if you can cook, you can make beer (with store-bought malt extract); third, with practice and experience, you can make any style of beer you want.

Something's brewing here

According to 1996 estimates, the U.S. has more than 1.5 million homebrewers, more than 1,500 homebrew-supply retailers, and more than 600 homebrewing clubs. The clubs are mostly small, but the national group, the American Homebrewers Association (AHA), boasts 25,000 members. Homebrew associations around the world are growing, too — on all continents. For a listing of some homebrew associations, see Appendix E.

Here are some other reasons people make stove-top beer:

- ✔ Participate in the current do-it-yourself homebrewing trend — what other hobby allows you to drink the fruits of your labor? (Okay, growing tomatoes for sauce or grapes for wine.)

- ✔ Make beers comparable to hard-to-find microbrews and expensive beers from around the world.

- ✔ Win awards in homebrewing competitions.

- ✔ Share homebrewing as an entertaining pastime with friends and family members.

However, before you go on, I suggest that you read the "Legalities of U.S. homebrewing" sidebar to determine whether or how you can proceed, legally speaking.

Legalities of U.S. homebrewing

With the repeal of the 18th Amendment in 1933, homebrewing should have been made legal right along with home winemaking. Unfortunately, the phrase "and/or beer" never made it into the Federal Register, ostensibly through a stenographer's error.

This situation remained unchanged until 1979, when a bill was signed into law by President Jimmy Carter, and after almost 40 years, homebrewing was legal again, as far as the Feds were concerned. Because the right to brew beer at home opened the door to abuses of the privilege, some safeguards were built into the law. Following are the two most important federal laws for homebrewers to abide by:

- ✔ Homebrewers are limited to 100 gallons of homebrew per year (or 200 gallons per year per household).

- ✔ Homebrew is not, *under any circumstances,* to be sold.

Despite the federal government's recognition of the right to brew at home, individual state laws may supersede the federal statute. Because only 29 states have "statutorily recognized" homebrewing, the situation is confused in the remaining 21. The American Homebrewers Association (see Appendix E) is currently lobbying to get all 50 states in step with one another.

Meanwhile, check with your state and local governments regarding the legalities of homebrewing before starting out. You can call the AHA at 303-447-0816 or visit its Web site at http://www.aob.org/aob to check whether homebrewing is legal in your state.

Getting Started

New homebrewers are no different from other hobbyists; they're champing at the bit (foaming at the mouth?) to get started with their hobby. Although this enthusiasm is good, jumping headlong into the unknown is not. I wrote this chapter for those of you who have never brewed beer and want to know about the essential tools and procedures needed to produce a simple, no-frills, malt-extract beer.

If you want to try your hand at brewing without the commitment — what, me, afraid of commitment? — you may want to visit a Brew On Premises (BOP) outfit where you can use the facility's equipment, recipes, and ingredients. See Chapter 12 for more details.

You can turn to Appendix E for information about helpful books and other homebrewing media and to Chapter 12 for software information.

Supply shopping

The first thing you should do is locate a local homebrew-supply store. Start with the Yellow Pages, under "Beer Homebrewing Equipment and Supplies." Or check out the mail-order ads in any of the magazines listed in Appendixes D and E; Appendix E lists other kinds of sources as well. Call or stop in at a store and ask for a catalog and price list if the store offers one. Look at the equipment and supplies and ask questions about the stock — especially the ingredients.

Remember: Freshness counts. Get to know the folks who run the shop — they'll be invaluable resources as you delve into homebrewing.

Pots, pans, buckets, brushes, and such

What you need to get going is not so exotic. This section lists (and Figure 10-1 shows) what you need at a minimum and recommends nonessential time- and effort-saving tools. Forget any preconceived notions about shiny copper kettles and coils taking up the entire kitchen or huge wooden vats bubbling and churning in the cellar — such are the product of a vivid imagination. This whole process is much more like baking bread.

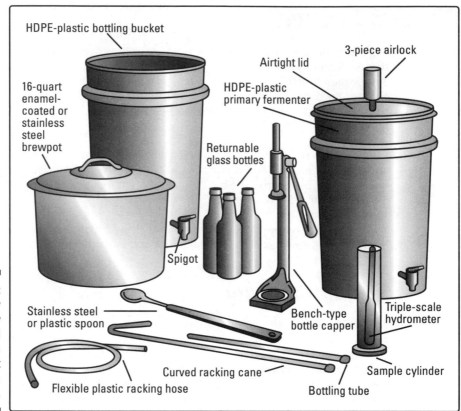

Figure 10-1:
Many
homebrew
shops sell
this basic
equipment
as a
startup kit.

Starter kits, sold by shops or mail-order houses, can range from bare-bones to top-of-the-line quality; you can find good ones for less than $100. Before buying a kit, consider your needs and what you are willing and able to spend. Following is a list of necessary items with descriptions and approximate costs.

✔ **Airlock:** Inexpensive, but a simple, efficient way to allow carbon dioxide to escape from the fermenter without letting any air in and compromising the hermetic seal of the lid. This three-piece gizmo has a cylindrical outside piece with a tubelike stem, an internal float piece that resembles an inverted cup, and a cap to fit over the cylindrical part. A similar contraption, called a *bubbler,* is a two-chamber device that works on the same principle. The difference is that an airlock can be easily cleaned and sanitized on the inside, whereas the totally enclosed bubbler cannot. *Cost:* $1.00 or less.

✔ **Bottles:** Heavy, returnable bottles, without a threaded opening (a bottle crown cannot seal properly across the threads). You need enough to hold 5 gallons of beer: 54 12-ounce bottles, or 40 16-ounce bottles, or any

Conversion equations for homebrewing

Here are some approximate metric conversions for the liquid and length measurements used in this chapter:

1 cup = 237 milliliters; ³/₄ cup = 177.75 milliliters
1 ounce = 29.6 milliliters;
12 ounces = 355 milliliters;

16 ounces (U.S. pint) = 473 milliliters;
20 ounces (imperial pint) = 592 milliliters;
22 ounces = 651 milliliters

1 gallon = 3.8 liters; 5 gallons = 19 liters
1 inch = 25 millimeters; 1 foot = 30 centimeters

combination that adds up to 640 ounces. *Pounders* (22-ounce bottles) are popular with homebrewers. *Cost:* Cost of retailer deposit, or from $6.00 to $20.00 per dozen if purchased, depending on the style.

You can buy new bottles from a homebrew supplier, but used bottles from commercial breweries are much cheaper. Find out whether a local liquor store sells any beer in returnable bottles (not the cheap, recyclable kind). If so, buy a couple of cases, drink the beer, and voilà — you have 48 bottles (not to mention a swollen bladder) right off the bat for the cost of a deposit. An (expensive) alternative is to get self-sealing swing-top bottles (also called Grolsch bottles, after the Dutch beer that popularized them).

The upside of swing-top bottles is that you don't need to buy bottle caps or cappers; the downside (besides the initial expense) is that the rubber gaskets eventually wear out. Swing-top bottles also require closer attention at cleaning time than regular bottles do, and they are not allowed in most homebrew competitions.

Local recycling bins can be a gold mine of used bottles, especially on days when bars drop off their booty.

✔ **Bottle brush:** Important piece of equipment. You need a soft-bristle brush to properly clean inside the bottles before you fill them. *Cost:* $3.00.

✔ **Bottle capper:** Affixes the fresh caps to the just-filled bottles. Cappers come in all shapes, sizes, and costs. Most work equally well, but I suggest that you choose a *bench capper* over the *two-handed* style, even though bench cappers cost more than two-handed cappers. A bench capper is free-standing and can be attached to a work surface, leaving you with one hand free to hold the bottle steady. The two-handed cappers can be tricky to use if nothing is holding the bottle steady. *Cost:* $7.00 (two-handed) to $30.00 (bench-type).

✔ **Bottle washer:** Curved copper apparatus that threads onto a faucet. Works as a spraying device for the insides of bottles — an added convenience for cleaning bottles. Not a necessity, but for the money, you may as well take advantage of it. *Cost:* $7.00 to $15.00.

If you buy a bottle washer, take note of which faucet in your home you'll be using. Utility faucets usually have larger hose threads; other types, such as bathroom and kitchen faucets, have fine threads and require an adapter. Make sure that the bottle washer and any adapters you buy have a rubber washer (gasket) in place.

✔ **Bottling bucket:** HDPE (high-density polyethylene — food-grade plastic) plastic vessel that you need on bottling day. Doesn't require a lid but is considerably more efficient if it has a removable spigot at the bottom. Also called a *priming vessel* because your fermented beer is primed with corn sugar (dextrose) just before bottling (a process discussed in detail later in this chapter). *Cost:* $10.00.

✔ **Bottling tube:** Long, hard plastic tube with a spring-loaded valve at the tip. Attaches to the plastic hose (which attaches to the spigot on the bottling bucket or the *racking cane,* or tube); the bottling tube is inserted into the bottles for filling. *Cost:* $3.00.

✔ **Brewpot:** Stainless steel or enamel-coated metal pot. Don't use pots made of aluminum and lesser grades of steel; they impart a metallic taste to the beer. Your brewpot should have a 16-quart minimum capacity because the more *wort* (unfermented beer) you boil, the better your finished beer. A big, old, inexpensive enamel lobster pot is perfect, as long as the enamel isn't chipped. *Cost:* $22.00 and up.

✔ **Brew spoon:** Stainless steel or plastic spoon with a long handle — 18 inches or longer. Never use wooden spoons for brewing: They can be difficult to clean properly. Use your brew spoon only for brewing beer. *Cost:* $2.50 (plastic).

✔ **Flexible plastic hose:** Important, multifunctional piece of equipment used to transfer beer from bucket to bucket or from bucket to bottle. Be sure to keep it clean and undamaged. Need at least 3 feet of hosing; any more than 4 feet can be a nuisance. *Cost:* $2.00, at 50¢ a foot.

✔ **Primary fermentation vessel:** Plastic bucket in which to pour cooled wort shortly after the brewing process. Must be sealed airtight for the duration of the fermentation. Must have a 7-gallon capacity to accommodate a 5-gallon batch of beer and still have room for all the vigorous bubbling action and yeast build-up *(barm)* of the fermenting beer. By the time the primary fermentation phase is over, much of this gunk will have settled to the bottom of the fermenter. *Cost:* $10.00.

I recommend plastic over glass for the fermenter because it is so much easier to clean and won't break. The plastics used in homebrewing are of the same quality and standards as the plastics used in the food industry (HDPE plastics). These plastics, unlike lesser grades of plastic, restrict — sufficiently, although not completely — gaseous transfer through the plastic.

For ease of use, you can buy specially made plastic fermenters with removable plastic spigots. If your fermenter has no spigot, you need a *racking cane* to siphon the beer out of the primary fermenter. Make sure that your plastic hosing fits the racking cane.

✔ **Rubber stopper:** Fits over the stem of the airlock or bubbler to act as a sealed wedge when the airlock is inserted into the hole in the fermenter lid. These so-called drilled stoppers are sized by number (for example, #3 stoppers). Buy a stopper that fits the opening in the fermenter lid; your equipment supplier will know what you need. *Cost:* $1.00 or less.

✔ **Triple-scale hydrometer:** Device used to determine the gravity of your brew, which, in turn, allows you to calculate the alcohol content (see Figure 10-2 later in this chapter). Easy to use and not very expensive. I suggest learning to use one if you want to progress in homebrewing. Also be sure to buy a plastic *cylinder* (sometimes called a *flask*) to hold the test sample. *Cost:* about $8.50 for both.

A *hydrometer* — be it triple scale or not — is a fragile measuring device, used solely to determine the density of liquids. When the weighted end is submerged in liquid, the calibrated stem projects out of the liquid at a height determined by the density of the liquid; that height gives you the reading. For more information on hydrometer reading, see Step 12 in the "Ready, Set, Brew!" section later in this chapter.

First draught: brew ingredients

Okay, you've got your pots, buckets, tubes, spoon, and whatnot. Moving on to buying the ingredients for your first batch of beer is easy, almost a no-brainer. You go into a homebrew-supply shop or fill out a mail-order form and buy an extract kit, a can of hopped malt extract (with a packet of yeast included), corn sugar (*dextrose* — ²/₃ cup minimum), and enough caps *(crowns)* for 50 to 60 bottles. Done. That's it!

The beer you are about to make is going to be *kit* beer — no grains, no hops, no muss, no fuss. A kit comes with its own packet of dried yeast and is sold by beer style.

Extract

When making beer from a kit, your only decision is what style of beer you want to make. Liquid malt extract (syrup) comes in a variety of colors and flavors, clearly labeled according to the style of beer that it is meant to produce.

The typical can of liquid malt extract is 3.3 pounds. For full body and taste, buy two 3.3-pound cans to make one full batch of beer (5 gallons).

The rather odd — by U.S. standards — measure of 3.3 pounds is due to the fact that the British pioneered the malt-extract–producing industry. The majority of kits on the market are from the U.K., where, translated to 1.5 kilograms, a 3.3-pound can is the standard size.

Crowns can be bought

Bottle crowns sometimes are sold by the batch (60 crowns, which is enough for 54 bottles, with a few extras) but more typically by the gross (144 crowns, which may include extras). Although bottle crowns may seem to be equipment rather than ingredients, they are consumable objects because you can use them only one time; so I call them ingredients (just not very tasty ones).

Here are some things to keep in mind when buying your kit:

- Make sure that you buy *hopped malt* (extract with hop bittering added) and not an unhopped version. Unhopped malt is for more advanced brewing as described in Chapter 11.

- For the sake of reality and authenticity, stick with an ale kit. Quality lager beers are impossible to make at the beginner level.

- Just for laughs, read the directions that are included with the kit; then burn them. These directions often call for large additions of cane sugar (much like Prohibition-era homebrew) and suggest brewing methods that do nothing to improve your beer. Follow my instructions, and you'll do fine. Trust me! (By the way, did I mention that I have a bridge to sell. . . ?)

Sugar

At bottling time, you need a type of sugar called *dextrose*, or *corn sugar*. This highly refined sugar is used to prime the beer just before it is bottled. *Priming* is the procedure in which a measured amount of corn sugar is mixed with the already fermented beer in order to create carbonation in the bottle (see "Ready, Set, Bottle!" in this chapter). Dextrose is inexpensive and can be purchased in any volume, although many homebrew suppliers sell it in prepackaged amounts. For one 5-gallon batch, you need $^3/_4$ cup of corn sugar for priming.

Water

Water is the ingredient that makes up the bulk of your homebrew, but it is too often taken for granted. I recommend bottled water over tap water. Tap water can present various problems, including the following:

- If the water that you're using for brewing is from an underground well, chances are that it's high in iron and other tastable minerals.

- If your water is softened, it's probably high in sodium.

- If your water is supplied by a public works department, it may have a high chlorine content.

Chlorine is very volatile and can easily be boiled off, but you'd have to boil all 5 gallons — a daunting task. Chlorine can also be filtered out, but even if you have a good water softener and a good chlorine filter, you're better off buying bottled water for brewing; in most cases, it costs less than a dollar per gallon. Your homebrew-supply shop can advise you on choosing the right water from the many kinds available at most supermarkets.

Department of Sanitation

Before moving on, I need to discuss one *major* factor in making good beer: If you want your beer to taste fresh and be drinkable and enjoyable, you need to protect it from the millions of hungry microbes that are waiting to ambush your brew. Germs are everywhere; they live with us and even on us. Look out! There's one now!

Bacteria and fungi, the two bad guys of the germ world that you need to worry about with beer, are opportunistic; if you give them half a chance at a free meal, they take it without reservation. (Wouldn't you, if it were your wonderful beer being offered?)

Fungi consist of mold spores and wild yeast. Beer yeast fall into the fungus category, but they're the friendly variety. Only a couple of strains of bacteria show up in beer — usually in spontaneously fermented Belgian beers.

Fungi and bacteria thrive in very warm temperatures — often up to 120 degrees F (49 degrees C). Microbial activity tends to decrease as the temperature drops, so cooling down the hot wort as quickly as possible is imperative.

"Cleanliness is next to godliness"

I don't know who first said that cleanliness is next to godliness, but I'd be willing to bet that he or she brewed beer. Scrupulously clean equipment and a pristine brewing environment are the keys to making good beer. "Clean" doesn't mean just soap-and-water clean; when it comes to beer, serious sanitation is a necessity.

You can't possibly kill *all* the bacteria in your home. The idea is to keep the germs from enjoying your beer before you have a chance to; if they get to the beer first, you may not want it.

I cannot make this point too often: Anything and everything that comes into contact with your beer *at any time* must be either sanitized or sterilized.

Bad guys

Because unfermented beer is warm and sweet, it is the perfect breeding ground for all the micro-biological bad boys. However, none of the bacteria that grow in beer are remotely as dangerous as the *e coli* or salmonella bacteria that occur in uncooked meat, fish, and eggs. The germs that breed in beer are just freeloading little buggers that make the beer taste bad. Beer germs won't kill you (although having to throw out an entire batch of brew might). You certainly don't have to attain the same level of sterility in your home brewery that you expect in an operating room.

Sterilizing refers to disinfecting items (such as the brewpot and the brew's ingredients) by boiling. *Sanitizing* refers to cleaning and disinfecting all the rest of the equipment by using chemicals (and is not to be confused with *sanity*, which you can lose during all the cleaning you'll have to do).

Soaps for suds

The chemicals that are used to clean homebrewing equipment include iodine-based products, chlorine-based products, ammonia, lye, and at least one environmentally safe cleanser that uses percarbonates. Following are the pros and cons of various chemicals:

- ✔ *Iodine* is widely used in the medical field and the restaurant industry as a disinfectant. The disinfectant properties of iodine can be applied to homebrewing, but unless the iodine solution is well diluted, it will stain plastics as well as human skin.

- ✔ *Ammonia* is best used for cleaning bottles in a dilution of 1 cup ammonia to 5 gallons of water — if you can stand the pungent odor. Ammonia requires a thorough hot-water rinse.

- ✔ *Chlorine* is in simple household bleach, which is very effective and cost-efficient for cleaning homebrewing equipment. A 2-ounces-to-5-gallons dilution ratio is sufficient, making a gallon of generic bleach an incredibly good deal. Be sure to buy an *unscented* bleach and to rinse all equipment thoroughly. Good old plain bleach is best.

   Just so you don't try to double up on your sanitizing procedures, *never* mix ammonia with chlorine. This combination releases toxic chlorine gas.

- ✔ *Lye* should be used only to remove the most stubborn stains and obstinate organic material from bottles or glass carboys. Always wear protective gear, such as goggles and rubber gloves, when you work with lye.

✔ *Percarbonates* supposedly accomplish their cleaning activity with oxygen molecules; exactly how is beyond me. Sanitizers that contain percarbonates do not require rinsing.

Several brand-name sanitizers — including Iodophor, One Step, and B-Bright — are available through homebrew suppliers. The capacity of these products to sanitize homebrewing equipment is in direct proportion to the way in which they are used, meaning if you don't follow instructions, don't blame the manufacturer for a blown batch of beer.

For my money, ordinary unscented household bleach is still the best bet.

General cleaning practices

The best place to handle sanitizing procedures is a utility basin or a large-capacity sink. (A bathtub will do in a pinch, but remember that bathrooms harbor tons of bacteria and also, on occasion, small children. Remove both prior to use.) The most effective methods of sanitizing involve soaking rather than intensive scrubbing.

Never use any abrasives or materials that can scratch your plastic equipment, because pits and scratches are excellent hiding places for those wily bacteria. A soft sponge, used only for cleaning homebrew equipment, is the way to go.

Sterilizing and sanitizing your equipment is the fifth step in the brewing process — see the next section.

Ready, Set, Brew!

Making and bottling a batch of beer, like building Rome, can't be done in a day. On the other hand, it doesn't take a heck of a lot longer than a day, either.

Because the raw, sweet wort must undergo fermentation before it officially becomes beer, bottling can't take place until fermentation is complete. Fermentation of a 5-gallon batch usually takes a minimum of seven days, depending on the yeast. So you need to set aside two days, about a week apart, for the job. Allow three hours each day to set up, brew (or bottle), and clean up. Patience is a virtue; good homebrew is its own reward.

Remember: Everything that comes in contact with the beer can potentially contaminate it. Keep your equipment clean, keep your brewery clean, keep your hands clean, and practice good hygiene; every cough or sneeze is a threat to your beer. You may even want to consider banishing Spot and Sylvester from your brewing area until clean-up time. Beer's not serious, but sanitation is.

Here are the steps for making a simple extract beer:

1. **Fill your brewpot two-thirds full of cool water and place it on the stove, with the burner set on medium-high.**

   Use the largest burner available.

   The quantity of water used in this step is not important, but you should boil as much as possible. Don't worry — you'll make up the difference to 5 gallons by adding more water to the fermenter later.

2. **Heat the thick, syrupy malt extract to make it thinner and easier to scoop out of the can.**

   You can heat the can by immersing it in hot water.

3. **Open the can, scrape all the extract into the brewpot, and use your virgin brew spoon to give the mix a vigorous stir.**

4. **Set a timer or note the time when you poured extract into the brewpot. Boil *uncovered* for 1 hour, stirring regularly and keeping the brewpot at a slow, rolling boil.**

   The universally suggested minimum boil is 1 hour — the amount of time required to mix and boil the ingredients properly.

   Be prepared to reduce or turn off the heat — or throw in a handful of ice cubes — if the foam threatens to rise over the top. Stirring regularly should keep the wort from scorching, a problem especially prevalent on electric ranges.

   Also, sticky, sweet stuff all over your stove is not a good thing — not to mention a waste of potential beer. So remember, to prevent boilovers, do *not* cover the brewpot.

5. **Sanitize the equipment that you need for fermentation.**

   Those items that you need to sanitize are

   - Fermenter and lid

   - Disassembled airlock or bubbler

   - Rubber stopper

   - Clean coffee cup or small bowl (for the yeast)

   - Hydrometer (not the cylinder)

   Place the fermenter in the utility tub (or large sink) and begin drawing cold water into the fermenter. Add cleansing/sanitizing chemicals, according to package directions, or 2 to 3 ounces of unscented household bleach. Allow water to fill the fermenter; then shut off the water. Immerse the remaining equipment in the fermenter, including the fermenter lid (you will have to force it in a bit).

Then crack open a beer; you've got time to kill. While you're at it, stir the brewpot (with the spoon, not the beer bottle!).

6. **After half an hour has elapsed, remove and rinse the various pieces of equipment.**

   If your fermenter has a spigot, drain the water through it to sanitize it, too. Rinse everything in hot water and place the items on a *clean* surface. Allow them to air-dry.

   The fermenter lid, placed upside-down on a clean surface, is a good place to put the smaller items.

7. **When 1 hour has elapsed since you poured in the extract, turn off the burner and *now* place the lid on the brewpot.**

8. **Cool the wort (after it's mixed with water, the extract is transformed into *wort*).**

   Put a stopper in the sink drain and carefully place the covered brewpot in the sink. Run cold tap water until the sink is full, making sure that you keep the water from seeping into the brewpot and the boiled wort. Heat from the brewpot will be drawn away by the cold water, which won't stay cold for long.

   Drain the water and repeat this procedure two or three times, or as often as necessary. When the water surrounding the brewpot no longer gets noticeably warm in the first couple of minutes, you can stop.

   Adding ice to the water speeds the cooling process. If you live in a cold climate, snow banks work well for cooling wort. Do *not* add ice directly into the brewpot, or you may contaminate the wort.

   You need to cool the wort as quickly as possible at this point because cooling inhibits the growth of bacteria and readies the wort for the addition of the yeast.

9. **While the wort is cooling, fill a sanitized cup or bowl with lukewarm water (90 to 100 degrees F, 33 to 38 degrees C), tear open the yeast packet, and sprinkle the yeast into the water.**

   To avoid contamination, do not stir. Allow the mixture to stand for at least 10 minutes, covered with plastic wrap to ensure against airborne contamination. This process, called *proofing,* is a gentle wake-up call for the dormant yeast and prepares it for fermentation.

10. **When the brewpot is cool to the touch, carefully pour the cooled wort into the fermentation bucket (fermenter).**

    Make sure that the spigot is in the closed position (you don't even want to *think* about the consequences of leaving it open).

11. **Top up the fermenter to the 5-gallon line with cold bottled water (or tap water, if yours is of acceptable quality).**

Yeast needs oxygen to begin the respiration phase of the fermentation cycle. Vigorously pouring and splashing cold water into the fermenter is an effective way to mix the water and the wort, as well as to aerate the wort for the yeast.

12. Take a hydrometer reading (optional).

As you immerse the sanitized hydrometer (see Figure 10-2) into the now-diluted wort, give the hydrometer a quick spin with your thumb and index finger. This action keeps tiny bubbles from clinging to the side of the hydrometer, which could cause you to get an incorrect reading.

Record the numbers on the scales. See the "Hydrometers made simple" sidebar for more information about using a hydrometer.

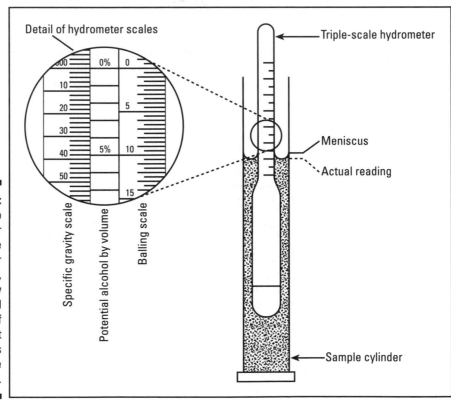

Figure 10-2:
Be sure to read your triple-scale hydrometer carefully, sighting only the actual surface of the wort, not the ridges of the meniscus.

13. **After you take the hydrometer reading (if you are working with a hydrometer), pour the yeast into the cooled wort to start the fermentation process.**

    Brewers call this step *pitching* the yeast. So as not to destroy the living yeast, the wort must be cooled to between 60 and 80 degrees F (15 and 27 degrees C); 70 degrees F (21 degrees C) is ideal. Gently pour the yeast in a wide circle to disperse it well.

14. **Close the fermenter with its lid, leaving the airlock or bubbler out, and place the fermenter in a cool, dark location, such as a basement, crawl space, or closet.**

    Do not put the fermenter in direct sunlight or someplace where the daily temperature fluctuates (such as your garage).

15. **When the fermenter is in place, attach the rubber stopper to the airlock, fill it halfway with water, and snap on the airlock cap; then position the airlock (bubbler) securely into the hole in the fermenter lid.**

    To make sure that the fermenter lid and airlock are sealed properly, gently push down on the lid. This push should cause the inner float piece to rise. If the float piece doesn't move, the seal has a breach; check the lid and the airlock.

16. **Wait seven to ten days.**

    This step is the hardest, especially for first-timers.

Hydrometers made simple

Remember, reading the triple-scale hydrometer at the beginner level is an option, not a necessity. You measure the density of your brew with a hydrometer. Knowing the beer's density enables you to calculate the volume of alcohol in your brew. More important, you can find out with certainty if your brew is done fermenting (your bottles might explode if it isn't!).

Hydrometers are like thermometers — really simple. But they can be daunting if you are unfamiliar with them. Here's how it all works: The specific gravity scale compares all liquids to ordinary water at 60 degrees F (15 degrees C), which has a specific gravity of 1.000.

✔ Taking a hydrometer reading after the wort is cooled gives you the original gravity (OG). This gives you an idea of how much fermentable sugar is in your brew before fermentation (that's the potential alcohol).

✔ Taking a second hydrometer reading after fermentation is over (just prior to bottling), you get a final gravity (FG, also called *terminal gravity*).

Subtracting the FG from the OG tells you, by way of conversion, how much of the sugar was eaten by the yeast.

(continued)

(continued)

How? When yeast eat sugar, they produce alcohol, so each decrease in gravity results in an increase in alcohol. On the triple-scale hydrometer, the alcohol-potential scale is right next to the specific-gravity scale. (If you're ready to call out for pizza, you've got company. But it's easier the second time around, believe me.)

Remember, the main reason you need a hydrometer is to avoid exploding bottles. Bottles explode when, due to fermentation problems, a lot of sugars remain in the beer when it's bottled. Average healthy yeast consume at least 65 percent of available sugars; if the final gravity reading on your fermented beer is not 35 percent or less of the original gravity, too much sugar may still be left in your beer. If the beer is bottled with priming sugar to boot, you're headed for the beer version of fireworks. Allow the beer a couple more days to ferment and check again.

Here's a sample equation: If your beer has an original gravity of 1.048, subtract 1 so that you have 0.048; then multiply 0.048 by 0.35, which results in 0.017. If the final gravity of your beer is higher than 1.017, you should delay bottling a few more days.

Note: A couple of things to remember when using a hydrometer:

✔ If your liquid's temperature at reading time is not near 60 degrees F (15 degrees C), the numbers will be skewed. Hot wort readings (OG) will be lower than they should be, and cold bottling readings (FG) will be higher than they should be.

✔ Be sure to sight your reading at the lowest point of the *meniscus* (the concave shape of the surface in the sampling cylinder).

Optional reading: Just in case you're curious, the third scale on the triple-scale hydrometer is the *Balling scale*. Its gradations are called *degrees Plato*. On this scale, water at 60 degrees F (15 degrees C) is 0 degrees Plato. You can use it in exactly the same way that you use the specific gravity scale. In fact, many megabrewers and some microbrewers use the Balling scale. The same homebrew with an OG of 1.048 will have a density of 12.5 degrees Plato. Most homebrewers and a great many microbrewers prefer to work with the specific gravity scale.

Fabulous Fermentation

Fermentation activity can start anywhere in the first 12 to 24 hours after you add the yeast to the wort. Fermentation starts slowly, gradually builds in intensity, and usually reaches a crescendo on the second or third day. When fermentation has reached its peak, the airlock may sound like an engine piston at low rev, with carbon dioxide bubbles making their hasty exit from the fermenter. A quick whiff of the escaping gas will give you your first aromatic experience of beermaking.

Leave the fermenter alone for the duration of fermentation. The exact length of fermentation depends on the health and viability of the yeast and on the temperature at which fermentation takes place. Even as the activity slows and the bubbles in the airlock start emerging slowly, one at a time, fermentation may continue for several more days. Be patient. Do *not* remove the airlock or fermenter lid to sneak a peek inside; you'll risk contaminating the beer. The general rule of thumb is to wait seven days minimum.

On the seventh day of fermentation, start paying close attention to the brew (no, it's not the day to rest). With the aid of a wristwatch or a clock that has a second hand, count the amount of time between bubbles emerging from the airlock. When a minute or more elapses between bubbles, plan to bottle the next day or very soon thereafter. If after seven days, the float piece in the airlock is not even floating, you should start bottling.

If you decide to purchase a hydrometer, fill the hydrometer cylinder with a sample of beer through the spigot of the fermenter and take a hydrometer reading to verify that fermentation is complete.

 After you take your hydrometer reading, do not pour the sample from the cylinder back in with the rest of the beer; to do so risks contaminating it. More important, don't throw the sample down the sink; it may be uncarbonated, but it's still good beer, so drink it. You'll be surprised by how good it already tastes. Ah!

Ready, Set, Bottle!

After you've made certain that the beer is fully fermented, retrieved the bottling equipment, and quarantined the family pets, you're ready to start the bottling procedures.

As always, setup starts with sanitizing all the necessary equipment, which includes the following:

- Bottles
- Bottling bucket
- Plastic hose
- Bottling tube

In addition to the items to be sanitized and a sanitizing agent, you need the following equipment:

- Bottle brush
- Bottle capper
- Bottle caps
- Bottle washer
- $^3/_4$ cup dextrose
- Two small saucepans

Here are the steps for bottling your beer:

1. **Fill your utility tub or other designated sanitizing basin about three-quarters full of cold water. Add bleach or another sanitizing agent, as directed on the package, and submerge all the bottles needed to contain the full 5-gallon batch of beer.**

   Allow the bottles to soak for at least a half hour (or according to package directions).

2. **While the bottles are soaking, put $^3/_4$ cup dextrose into one of the saucepans, dissolve the dextrose in a pint or so of water, cover, and place the pan on the stove over low heat.**

3. **Into the other saucepan, put enough bottle caps for the number of bottles you have soaking, plus a few extra. Fill the pan with enough water to cover all the caps, and place the pan on the stove over low heat.**

   Too many bottle caps sterilized and ready for bottling is better than not enough.

4. **Allow the contents of both saucepans to come to a boil. Then turn off the heat and allow both to cool.**

5. **When half an hour has passed, clean the bottles.**

   Connect the bottle washer to the faucet over the tub in which the bottles have been soaking and turn on the hot water (the bottle washer will hold back the water pressure until a bottle is lowered over the stem and pushed down). Then clean the bottles one by one with the bottle brush, drain the sanitizer, rinse the bottles with the bottle washer, and allow to air-dry. Continue until all bottles are cleaned.

   A wise idea is to visually check each bottle for cleanliness instead of just assuming that all the bottles are sanitized.

   Four dozen free-standing bottles can make for one heck of a domino effect. Always put cleaned bottles back into six-pack holders or cardboard cases to prevent an aggravating, easily avoidable accident.

6. **Drain the bottle-cleaning water out of the utility tub and place the bottling bucket in the tub. Fill the bucket with water and the sanitizing agent of your choice. Then place the bottling hose, bottling tube, and cylinder in the bottling bucket and allow them to soak.**

7. **While the bottling equipment is soaking, retrieve the still-covered fermenter from its resting place and put it on a sturdy table, countertop, or work surface about 3 or 4 feet off the ground.**

8. **Set up your bottling station, making sure that you have the priming sugar (dextrose) and bottle caps — still in their respective saucepans — as well as the bottle capper and bottles.**

   If you're taking gravity readings, have your hydrometer and cylinder sanitized and ready to use.

9. **After half an hour, drain the sanitizing solution from the bottling bucket through the spigot on the bottom. Then thoroughly rinse the remaining pieces of equipment, along with the bottles, and bring them to your bottling station.**

Whistle while you work.

10. **Place the bottling bucket on the floor directly below the fermenter and connect the plastic hose to the spigot on the fermenter, allowing the other end of the hose to hang inside the bottling bucket. Pour the dextrose-and-water mixture into the bottling bucket.**

The dissolved corn sugar is mixed with the beer as it drains from the fermenter into the bottling bucket; this procedure is called *priming*. After all the beer is bottled, this sugar becomes another source of food for the few yeast cells that remain in the liquid. As the yeast consume the sugar, they produce the beer's carbonation within the bottle. Eventually, the yeast again fall dormant and create a thin layer of sediment on the bottom of each bottle.

If by chance your beer is not fully fermented, or if you somehow added too much dextrose at bottling time, you may find out first-hand what a mess exploding bottles can make. Excess sugar — whether it is leftover maltose from an unfinished fermentation or added corn sugar — overfeeds the yeast in an enclosed bottle. With nowhere for the pressure to go, the glass will give before the bottle cap will. Kaboom! Big mess! Do not overprime! (Remember, the recommended amount of sugar to add is ³/₄ cup.)

11. **Open the spigot on the fermenter and allow all the beer to run into the bottling bucket.**

Don't try to salvage every last drop from the fermenter by tilting it as the beer drains down the spigot. The spigot is purposely positioned about ³/₄ inch above the bottom of the fermenter to allow all the spent yeast and miscellaneous fallout to remain behind.

Avoid splashing or aerating your beer while you are bottling. You'll later be able to taste any oxidation that the beer picks up now. Yuck.

12. **After the last of the beer is drained, close the spigot, remove the hose, and put all the equipment aside to be cleaned after you're done bottling.**

13. **Carefully place the bottling bucket up where the fermenter was. Connect the rinsed hose to the spigot on the bottling bucket and attach the bottling tube to the other end. Arrange all your bottles on the floor directly below the bottling bucket.**

Keeping all your bottles in cardboard carriers or cases prevents potential breakage and spillage.

14. Open the spigot on the bottling bucket and fill the bottles.

Gently push the bottling tube down to the bottom of each bottle to start the flow of beer. The bottle may take a short while to fill, but the flow always seems to accelerate as the beer nears the top. Usually, a bit of foam rushes to the top of the bottle — don't worry! As soon as you withdraw the bottling tube, the liquid level in the bottle falls. Remove the tube from each bottle when foam or liquid reaches the top of the bottle.

When you remove the bottling tube from the bottle, the level of the beer falls to about an inch or so below the opening. This airspace is called the *ullage.* Homebrewers have differing opinions as to how much airspace there should be. Some people say that the smaller the airspace, the less that oxidation will occur; others say that without proper ullage, the beer won't carbonate properly. Rather than jump into the fray, I say that if the airspace looks like the space in bottles of beer from commercial breweries, go with it.

15. After draining the bottling bucket, close the spigot, remove the hose, toss the hose inside the bottling bucket, and set everything aside to be cleaned later.

16. Place all the bottles on your table top or work surface, place a cap on each bottle (as insurance against everything that can go wrong), and cap one bottle at a time. Pull down on the capper lever slowly and evenly.

Both bench and two-handle cappers come with a small magnet in the capper head, which is designed to hold and align the cap as you start crimping. (I have learned not to trust the magnet to hold the caps in alignment; I prefer to seat them on the bottles by hand.)

Occasionally, a cap may crimp improperly. If you suspect that a cap did not seal correctly, tilt the bottle sideways and check for leakage. If you find a leaker, yank the cap and replace it (you sterilized extras, right?).

17. Store your liquid "lucre" in a cool, dark location (such as the place where you kept the fermenter) for two weeks.

Your homebrew needs to undergo a two-week conditioning phase, during which the remaining yeast cells chow down on the dextrose and carbonate your beer.

Putting your brew in the fridge is not a good idea (at least for the first two weeks) because overly cold temperatures stunt the yeast's activity.

18. Thoroughly rinse your brewing equipment in hot water and store it in a place that is relatively free of dust and mildew.

This step may be the most important one of all, not so much for your new brew but for the next one. Consider this procedure to be an insurance policy on your next batch of beer — boring but worthwhile, like most insurance policies.

After two weeks have passed, check to see whether the bottles are clarified; the yeasty cloudiness should have settled out. Chill a bottle or two for taste-testing.

Homebrew, like any commercial beer, should be decanted (poured into a glass) before you drink it. Decanting not only releases the carbonation and the beer's aromatics but also enables you to pour a clear beer; drinking it out of the bottle stirs up the sediment, creating a hazy beer.

Congratulations! As you can see, homebrewing at this level is easy. You're creating beer strictly from a kit: You just add a beer concentrate to water and then heat, ferment, and bottle it. If you can make basic breads, you can make tasty beer.

Record Keeping

The primary goal of every homebrewer is to create a drinkable, enjoyable beer. Although quality is a noble objective, *consistency* is the mark of an accomplished homebrewer.

You can achieve both quality and consistency in a shorter period of time with the help of accurate records. Pedantic though it seems, keeping track of times, temperatures, weights, and measures establishes a pattern for the homebrewer. These records tell you not only what went right but also — and more important — what may have gone wrong. You can catalog and file successes and failures for future consideration.

A few published guidebooks and workbooks for homebrewers are available, but an old-fashioned spiral-bound notebook is as good as anything. Exactly how useful a notebook is depends on how accurate and timely your entries are; they have to be good to be useful.

The data that you should track at the beginner level include brand names of malts, quantities of ingredients, length of boil, types of yeast, hydrometer readings (if you take gravity readings), and approximate fermentation times and temperatures. If you start this good habit early, record keeping at the intermediate and advanced levels — when record keeping is much more important — should come much easier and will be worth the effort.

Ten most common mistakes made by beginning homebrewers

✓ Infecting a batch of beer because of improperly sanitizing equipment

✓ Infecting a batch of beer because of improperly handling or transferring the wort or beer

✓ Causing a stove-top boilover by keeping the brewpot lid on during boiling

✓ Starting the brewing or bottling procedures without having all the necessary equipment or ingredients on hand

✓ Interrupting a fermentation (or allowing one to go on too long)

✓ Overpriming the beer at bottling time, resulting in overcarbonated beer or exploding bottles

✓ Attempting to cap twist-off bottles with threaded necks

✓ Failing to learn and understand general brewing procedures before plowing ahead

✓ Keeping poor records or none at all (to be good, you have to learn from your failures)

✓ Failing to adjust to the realities of homebrewing

What you *set out* to make doesn't matter; what you *make* is what counts. More often than not, your beer turns out to be something other than what you intended it to be. Relax and go with the flow (literally).

✓ Taking it all much too seriously

Homebrewing is supposed to be fun. It's just beer, after all.

Chapter 11

Sophomore Homebrewing

- -

In This Chapter

▶ Upgrading equipment

▶ Adding hops

▶ Using specialty grains

▶ Having fun with kettle adjuncts and miscellaneous ingredients

▶ Combining the art and science of brewing

▶ Intermediate homebrew recipes

- -

Absolutely nothing is wrong with the freshman "kit" brewing described in Chapter 10, and many homebrewers are content to brew beer in that manner. No problem there.

If, however, you have a stronger interest in homebrewing (that is, you've started to go nuts about beer), have a lot of time on your hands, or just want more control over the taste, color, and aroma of your beer, read on! You may also want to check out the various homebrewing magazines and books to round out your education (see Appendix E). In short, now you're ready to improve your beer.

For those of you who want to go beyond the two sophomore-level homebrewing recipes at the end of this chapter, please refer to the books listed in Appendix E for information.

Although brewing on the sophomore level means you use more ingredients and equipment and follow more steps, you still follow the brewing process as described in Chapter 10. In this chapter, I point out where and how you do new things. So you simply follow the steps in Chapter 10 and plug in the new directions as indicated here.

The five fundamental differences you encounter as you move from beginning- to intermediate-level homebrewing are as follows:

✔ Adding your own hops instead of using prehopped malt syrup

✔ Adding specialty grains instead of being limited to a "kit" recipe

✔ Having the options of adding flavors and increasing the alcohol

✔ Using liquid yeast rather than dry yeast

✔ Doing a secondary fermentation prior to bottling

Note: All instructions are given with 5-gallon batches in mind. Also, many of the terms used in this chapter are explained elsewhere in the book; see the index if you need help finding a term.

See Chapter 10 for some metric conversion equations that apply to homebrewing.

New Toys: Equipment Upgrades

Sophomore-level homebrewing requires some more equipment than beginning homebrewing. A more hands-on approach to anything calls for more-specialized equipment. But don't worry: You don't need to take out a second mortgage to brew at this level (on the contrary, you'll probably want to quit your day job so you can have more time to play in your brewery).

Following is a list of some necessary equipment for sophomore homebrewers who want to try all the procedures noted in this chapter (this stuff is in addition to what you need as a beginning homebrewer — see Chapter 10 for the most basic requirements). See Figure 11-1 for a look at two such items. For those of you who are not compelled to progress to *all* these levels, you can just pick and choose those items that best suit your needs.

Figure 11-1:
A glass carboy and a hand-cranked grain mill are among the more important additions that you may want to make to your home brewery.

Don't run out and buy all this stuff till you've read through this entire chapter!

✔ **Airlock (or bubbler):** You may have an airlock from your adventures in beginning homebrewing (see Chapter 10); however, you need a second one if you're going to have two brews fermenting simultaneously. *Cost:* $1 or less.

✔ **Carboy cleaning brush:** For proper cleaning of your secondary fermenter, or carboy, you need a carboy cleaning brush. This heavy-duty, soft-bristle brush is similar to a large toilet scrubber (please don't confuse the two types at home!) and is specially made to reach every curve and corner of the carboy. *Cost:* $3.50.

✔ **Curved racking tube (or cane):** Because carboys are not made with a spigot, a hard plastic, curved racking tube is needed to siphon out the beer. *Cost:* $2.50.

✔ **Drilled rubber stopper (for carboy):** You need a drilled rubber stopper to fit the carboy's neck (usually a #6 or #7 stopper) — in addition to the rubber stopper that you use for beginning homebrewing (see Chapter 10 for more details on stoppers). *Cost:* $1 or less.

✔ **Funnel (12-inch, plastic):** Because the opening of the carboy is so small, a large funnel is handy for pouring stuff into the carboy. *Cost:* $6.

✔ **Glass carboy:** Primarily used as a secondary fermenter. Can be a water jug that bottled-water companies deliver only to businesses or can be a jug purchased from homebrew-supply shops — with or without water! (*Note:* You can't use the plastic carboys delivered to private residences.) The carboy represents one of the biggest differences in equipment from the beginning stages. *Cost:* $15 for a 5-gallon glass carboy (for bottled water and deposit — less if you can buy it empty).

✔ **Grain mill:** Looks a bit like a meat grinder. Used to crack grain prior to mashing or steeping it. Grain can be bought precracked, but many homebrew stores or store personnel don't crack it properly, and precracked grain can also go stale more quickly. Cracking your own grain is a terrific advantage. *Cost:* $39 and up.

The mill-less homebrewer can find inventive ways to crack the grain, such as putting it into a large, sealable bag and rolling it with a rolling pin or baseball bat, but a mill is the way to go.

Whatever you do, don't use a coffee grinder to do your grain milling: Your grain will end up looking like sawdust (and how it looks is just the beginning of your problems; finely ground grain can lead to harsh and unpleasant tastes in your beer).

✔ **Immersion thermometer:** Because temperature control becomes more and more important in brewing at the intermediate level, you need an immersion thermometer to track the temperature of your brew. A lab-quality immersion thermometer is capable of temperature readings above the boiling point (212 degrees F, 100 degrees C, at sea level) and as low as 40 degrees F (4 degrees C). *Cost:* $6 (lab immersion thermometer).

✔ **Scale:** Once you start brewing beer according to homebrew recipes, you'll find that many ingredients (like hops and specialty grains) are called for in small quantities, often less than an ounce. A good kitchen or postal scale, because it can measure fractions of ounces, is vital to getting these quantities right. *Cost:* $20 to $30.

✔ **Sparge/hop bags:** Basically, incredibly big tea bags. Sparge bags are effective for steeping grain or keeping hops under control in the brewpot. You can buy reusable nylon bags with drawstrings or the inexpensive, throwaway cheesecloth kind. *Cost:* $4 (reusable nylon), 40¢ (throwaway).

✔ **Strainer (10-inch diameter or larger):** At the sophomore stage of homebrewing, you're adding loose grain, hops, and other ingredients to your brewpot — making a bowl-shaped strainer with a handle a necessary piece of equipment. Kitchen-grade steel mesh is better than plastic. Don't settle for one with a diameter of less than 10 inches. *Cost:* $5 to $10.

The Right Stuff: Obligatory Ingredients

Now that you've spent next month's rent on brewing equipment and your home is beginning to look like Dr. Frankenstein's lab, you need to get up to speed on all those wonderful ingredients — like malt, hops, grains, and yeast — that are going to help you win the blue ribbon at the next homebrew competition. The right stuff will make your next batch of beer irresistible. The main reason, of course, for choosing the right stuff is to brew a particular *style* of beer (see Chapter 1).

If your goal is to make beers like those you've enjoyed elsewhere, I'm happy to say that it's a very attainable goal. The quickest way to improve your beer and begin duplicating various styles is to take personal control of the ingredients. The less you depend on the malt-extract producer to make your beer, the fewer constraints you have to overcome.

Beer style is basically determined by the following four things, all of which are directly related to the choice of ingredients (of course, various brewing techniques can also affect these things):

✔ Gravity (largely influenced by the use of base grain or malt extract)

✔ Bitterness (largely influenced by the use of hops)

✔ Color (largely influenced by the use of specialized grains and techniques)

✔ Yeast (chosen from a wide array of various strains)

The gravity, bitterness, and color of any given beer are determined while the beer is still in the brewpot. The effects of the yeast take place during fermentation. All can be specified and/or quantified in a recipe.

> ## Storing your homebrew ingredients
>
> When you buy homebrewing ingredients that you aren't going to use immediately, always store them properly. Grains, hops, and yeast packets should all be refrigerated, and hops should be frozen for long-term storage. Never allow any ingredients to lie around in a warm environment or in direct sunlight. The easiest ingredient to store is canned dry malt extract, which is perfectly happy in a kitchen cupboard or closet.

Malt makes it: gravity and dry malt extract

The malt you use influences the beer's *gravity*, the figure that indicates a beer's density or thickness (you use a hydrometer to measure the density of a liquid, as discussed in Chapter 10).

For example, the original gravity for an Imperial stout is roughly twice that of a brown ale. With that in mind, common sense tells you that you need roughly twice as much malt extract to achieve the original gravity of Imperial stout as you do for the original gravity of brown ale.

Usually, homebrew recipes call for a specific number of pounds of extract needed to achieve a target original gravity. When no specific number of pounds is called for, try using this formula (it's not perfect, but it'll get you in the ballpark):

```
target gravity (drop the whole number 1) x 5 = Y;
Y ÷ 0.04 = number of pounds needed
```

That is, if your target gravity is 1.048, your formula is $0.048 \times 5 = 0.24$; $0.24 \div 0.04 = 6$ pounds.

Note: This formula is designed to work with the specific gravity scale (as opposed to the Balling scale — see Chapter 10), based on a 5-gallon batch size. For a listing of approximate gravities by beer style, see Appendix F.

Specialty grains

Another sophomore-level benefit is that you can add all kinds of colors, flavors, and textures to your beer by using specialty grains along with your malt extract. *Specialty grains* are grains that are added in order to get some special characteristic. They're not used as a substitute for malt extract (like adjunct grains are) but rather as an enhancement.

Dry extract versus syrup

Dry malt extract, also called powdered extract or DME, is just a dehydrated version of the malt syrup that figures so prominently in Chapter 10. Dry extract is made the same way as malt extract syrups but with the added process of being spray-dried completely (which, by the way, makes it more expensive). Dry extract is usually sold generically; it's not prepackaged according to any style, though you can still get it in light, amber, and dark variations.

The best thing about dry extract in comparison to syrup is its convenience. Retailers usually sell it by the pound in any quantity you want. If it comes in a resealable bag, you can use a portion of it and put the rest back in the refrigerator for later use, whereas unused portions of sticky malt syrup are difficult to store. Dry extract is also good to have around for yeast propagation and yeast cultures — see "From yeast to west (liquid yeast versus dry yeast)" later in this chapter.

Using dry malt extract in place of malt syrup extract affects your original gravities slightly in a pound-for-pound comparison. Syrups contain approximately 20 percent water content, whereas the dry extract has almost none. The difference adds up to about 1 specific gravity degree per pound, the dry extract having a greater yield than the syrup. That is, 6 pounds of syrup achieve a specific gravity of 1.048, while 6 pounds of dry extract achieve a specific gravity 6 degrees higher, or 1.054 — not a major difference, but something you should know.

Specialty grains

- ✔ Have been *kilned* (roasted) to various degrees of roastedness after they've been malted (in some cases, unmalted and still-wet malted grain are kilned as well)
- ✔ Are added to give the malt extract the following two things:
    - A variety of visual, aromatic, and taste enhancements
    - Head-retaining and body-building proteins and dextrins (the beer's body, not yours)

 In a 5-gallon batch, you don't need much grain to create a noticeable effect. Depending on the grain, quantities of as little as a quarter pound are detectable. For measurement conversions, 1 cup of *cracked* grain equals approximately ¹/₄ pound; hence, 1 pound of grain fills 4 cups.

Note: Specialty grains are not normally added directly to the brewpot. And like all other grains in the brewing business, they should never be boiled; they are meant to be steeped in hot water just long enough for them to yield their goods. Twenty minutes to a half hour should be enough.

Steeping can be done in the brewpot with the rest of the brew, but I can think of two reasons to consider not using this method:

- ✔ If you don't use a sparge bag, you'll need to strain all the grain out before you can bring the extract to a boil.
- ✔ If the grain is in the brewpot at the same time as the extract, the grain's yield will not be maximized.

Steeping in clear water captures all that the grain has to offer. Try steeping the specialty grain in a separate pot and then adding it to the extract, or steep it in the brewpot before you add the extract. After it is properly steeped, pour the now-flavored water into the brewpot through a strainer, keeping all the grain out of the brewpot.

In order to capture as much of the grain flavor as possible, sparge the grain: Pour hot water through the grain in the strainer (and into the brewpot) until the water runs clear. About a half gallon of water should do the trick.

Be sure to remove all the grain before boiling the extract.

Here are the most common specialty grains and their typical uses:

- ✔ **Black malt:** Roasted to such a high degree that all malt flavor and aroma have been burned off. Because of its charred aroma and flavor, this malt should be used sparingly; overgenerous use creates an unpleasant harshness in flavor and mouthfeel. Typically used in schwarzbier, porter, and stout.

- ✔ **Chocolate malt:** A malt that has been roasted to a dark brown color, retaining a hint of its malt character. Used in conservative amounts, actually imbues beers with a distinct chocolate aroma and taste. Used in brown ales and bock beers, among others.

- ✔ **Crystal malt:** Named for the kilning procedure that crystallizes the caramelly sugars inside the still-moist grain. Adds a caramel-like sweetness to the beer, along with some color and an improvement in head retention (it's sometimes called *caramel malt* for obvious reasons). Not the cure-all for bad extract beers that some homebrewers think it is, but a step in that direction.

- ✔ **Roasted barley:** Not called a malt, because this barley is not malted before it is kilned. The kilning procedure calls for gradual increases in temperature so that the grain is not charred like black malt. This dark brown grain gives a rich, roasted, coffeelike aroma and flavor. Used primarily in stouts.

- ✔ **Victory malt (also called biscuit malt):** A lightly kilned grain that is primarily used in pale ales and several brands of red beer. Smells and tastes a bit like toasted bread; can also give a beer a nutty quality.

Lovibonds to love and HCUs 4 U 2 C

All the various maltsters who produce the grain for the U.S. brewing industry produce it in much the same way, each following the same standards as the others.

One of the industry standards they follow is the production of kilned grains according to a color scale called the Lovibond scale (no, this is not about commitment in your relationship). Actually, the Lovibond scale can be applied to wort, malt extract, and beer as well, but these others all trace their roots to the malt house.

Because differences in color depth are easy to *see* but nearly impossible to *describe* accurately, the Lovibond scale designates a specific number to a specific color depth. Each of the specialty grains listed here is assigned its own "degree" on the Lovibond scale (though Lovibond can be abbreviated as "L," most packages and recipes just use the number without the L word). Here are those numbers, including some base malts for comparison:

✔ Pale lager: 1.6 (base malt)

✔ Pale ale: 1.8 (base malt)

✔ Vienna: 3

✔ Munich (light): 10

✔ Munich (dark): 20

✔ Crystal: 20–120

> *Note:* Crystal malt is produced and sold in a variety of degrees Lovibond, usually jumping in 20-degree increments — 20, 40, 60, and so on.

✔ Chocolate: 350

✔ Black malt: 530

✔ Roasted barley: 530

Because the color of the grain has a direct effect on the color of the beer, being able to calculate the cumulative color of all the grain called for in a recipe is important. The Homebrew Color Units scale was developed for just this reason.

Homebrew Color Units, or HCU, is a crude method of establishing beer color, based on a simple formula of adding up the pounds of each type of grain, multiplying by the degrees Lovibond for each, and dividing by the total number of gallons in the batch of beer. So: 10 pounds pale malt @ 1.8L = 18; 4 pounds Munich dark @ 20L = 80; and 1 pound crystal malt @ 60L = 60. Add them all together, and you get 158, which divided by 5 gallons equals 31.6 HCUs.

You usually don't have to mill highly roasted grains. Because they are somewhat brittle, they have a tendency to crumble during the milling procedure, and that fine, dark grain powder should be avoided because it creates a harshness in the beer.

With the ability to add color and flavor to your beer by using specialty grains, you no longer need to buy amber or dark extracts to make amber or dark beers; you can make them all with light malt extract. In fact, once you're comfortable using specialty grains, you're better off deriving these colors and flavors from grain anyway; the taste difference is appreciable. You have more control over the taste and color by using real grain any day than by using premade extract.

Let's go to the hops

Now that you're a sophomore homebrewer, you can begin exerting your beery autonomy by making strategic choices in hop varieties and adding them as you see fit. About 50 hop varieties are grown around the world, with new or experimental cultivars being introduced regularly. Each hop variety offers different nuances: bittering intensity, aromas, and flavors. The average homebrew-supply shop stocks at least a half-dozen types and has access to many more. Availability is subject to crop failures, seasonal conditions, and market demand (see Chapter 2 for more information about hops).

Hops for homebrewing can be purchased in three forms (shown in Figure 11-2):

- ✔ **Whole-leaf hops:** The hop leaves are, for the most part, still intact and look like small pine cones. Their disadvantage is that they're packaged loosely and, therefore, take up considerable space in already-cramped home freezers. That's why a true homebrew geek has a spare fridge in the garage or basement.

- ✔ **Pellets:** This form is a pulverized and compacted hop product, about the width of a No. 2 pencil. Ounce for ounce, pellets take up only a quarter of the space of whole-leaf hops, but the process that pelletizes the hops also ruptures the hop lupulin glands. To guard against oxidation, pelletized hops need to be packaged in nitrogen- or oxygen-barrier bags. One advantage to using hop pellets is that because the lupulin glands have been ruptured, the resins and acids within the glands are more easily *isomerized* (dissolved) and thus require less boiling time.

  Compression makes packing and storing hops more efficient, and the hop is rendered more stable.

- ✔ **Plugs:** The most recent form to be developed, which seems to be the best of both worlds: whole-leaf hops that have been compressed into a 1-inch-diameter, $^{1}/_{2}$-inch-thick hop "chip." Plugs combine the freshness of whole hops with the convenience of pellet hops; the difference is that plugs are typically packaged and sold in 5-ounce quantities — a big commitment if you're using only 2 or 3 ounces of hops per batch and especially if you like to experiment with different varieties. You have to be sure to store them properly — in a plastic bag, purged of oxygen, that is kept in the freezer.

  Hop plugs were developed with commercial dry hopping in mind (see the "Dry hopping" sidebar in this chapter); plugs fit neatly through the bung holes in kegs and casks. They're not good for playing checkers or milkcaps.

Figure 11-2:
Because whole-leaf hops are delicate, they're often compressed into pellets or plugs and packed in oxygen-barrier bags.

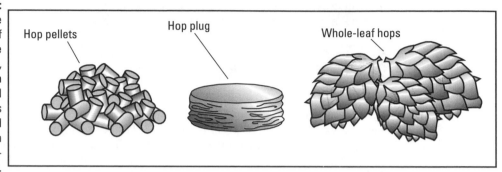

Hop pellets

Hop plug

Whole-leaf hops

Fresh hops!

The freshness of your hops is vital to the outcome of your beer. Fresh hops that are whole or in plug form usually have a light, almost lime green color; pelletized fresh hops are a darker shade of green. (A few hop varieties, such as Goldings, have a yellowish cast.) Hops that look browned and curled are probably pretty old; if the tiny lupulin glands are orange instead of yellow, the hops are oxidized (in other words, they've gone bad). Check your hops for aroma, too: A hop variety that smells like pungent cheese is also old and oxidized. These off aromas and flavors can be detected in your beer.

Bittering potential

After freshness, bittering potential is the next most important consideration in your choice of hops. At harvest time, hops are measured for their *alpha acid content* — the component that correlates to bitterness. The alpha acid content is expressed as a percentage of its weight relative to the weight of the whole hop flower. For example, Bramling Cross produced in 1996 has an alpha acid content of 5.5 percent.

Different hop varieties are known to have higher or lower acid content than others and are used accordingly. Alpha acid contents also vary slightly from one growing season to the next, depending on the elements, and from one place of origin to the next — American-grown Hallertau hops can differ considerably from those grown in Germany. In a way, hops are to beermakers what varietal grapes are to winemakers.

Don't worry! You don't need an advanced degree in plant physiology to brew beer. Depend on the gang down at your homebrew-supply store to help you out. Those folks are full of expert advice about hops and everything else under the sun (though I can't vouch for their advice on everything else). See Table 11-1 for some of the more "technical" information about hop bittering.

Dry hopping

Dry hopping is adding hops, in any form, to the beer after primary fermentation in order to give your beer an added touch of hop aroma. If you want to dry hop your beer, secondary fermentation is the stage in the fermentation process to carry it out.

You'll find two schools of thought as to whether you can dry hop without contaminating your beer. One side says that the hops are unboiled and may potentially contaminate your brew, while the other (the one with which I agree) says that the alcohol now in the fermented beer should be antiseptic enough to keep any bacteria at bay. Either way, whatever you put into the secondary fermenter needs to be strained out of the brew on bottling day.

Table 11-1	Alpha Acid Content of Prominent Hop Varieties	
Hop Variety	*Alpha Acid*	*Comments*
Bramling Cross	5% to 6%	Goldings hybrid; good flavoring hop
Brewer's Gold	8% to 9%	Good for bittering ales; pungent aroma also
Bullion	8% to 9%	Good for bittering; poor stability
Cascade	5% to 6%	Excellent for finishing U.S. ales
Centennial	7% to 8%	Cascade hybrid; excellent aroma hop
Chinook	9% to 12%	High alpha; coarse bittering
Cluster	6% to 8%	Popular bittering hop for U.S. national breweries; low aromatic potential
Comet	9% to 11%	Very rare variety; very bitter
Eroica	10% to 12%	Coarse bittering
Fuggles	4% to 6%	Excellent aroma hop; traditional ale hop
Galena	12% to 13%	Coarse bittering
Golding (Kent)	4% to 6%	Excellent aroma hop; traditional ale hop
Hallertauer	5% to 6%	Traditional German lager hop; all-purpose
Hersbrucker	5% to 6%	Traditional German lager hop; all-purpose
Mt. Hood	5% to 6%	American Hallertauer clone
Northern Brewer	7% to 9%	Universal bittering hop
Perle	7% to 9%	American Northern Brewer clone

(continued)

Table 11-1 *(continued)*

Hop Variety	Alpha Acid	Comments
Pride of Ringwood	7% to 9%	Australian bittering hop
Saaz	4% to 6%	Traditional Pilsner hop; excellent for finishing
Spalt	6% to 8%	Traditional German lager hop; all-purpose
Styrian	5% to 7%	Aromatic ale hop from former Yugoslavia
Tettnanger	4% to 6%	Traditional German lager hop; all-purpose
Willamette	5% to 6%	American Fuggles clone; excellent for finishing

Aromatic hops

Certain hop varieties are chosen strictly for their ability to lend piquant aromas to beer. Because you can't measure the aromatic "content" of hops, brewers have to make these choices based on accepted tried-and-true histories. Aroma hops, also called *finishing* hops, are recognized by names that can be rattled off by accomplished homebrewers like they were blood relatives — Fuggles, Goldings, Cascades, and Tettnanger, among others.

Brewing royalty

Noble hops are those varieties that have relatively low alpha acid contents but are prized for both their aromatic and flavoring characteristics. Among the noble varieties are Hallertauer, Hersbrucker, Spalt, and Tettnanger in Germany; Fuggles and Golding in England; Saaz from Bohemia in the Czech Republic; and Styrian from the former Yugoslavia. Noble hops have been cultivated for centuries. They are more expensive than the U.S-grown, derivative hop varieties, so many homebrew-supply stores and catalogs do not feature them — but commercial beer labels often boast of their use.

Newer U.S. hybrids are being cultivated for better stability and for resistance to disease. Most of these hybrids are high-alpha hop varieties that are more cost-effective because smaller quantities are needed to achieve higher bittering potential. That's progress. (There's actually a new hop variety called Progress — how about that?)

Note: Hop *stability* (how well the hops keep over time), though certainly an issue with the commercial brewers, is rarely one for homebrewers unless you buy in bulk quantity. Stability ratings are simply good, fair, and poor.

Using hops

Aromatic and bittering hops can be used interchangeably, but there's no point in doing that — aromatic hops usually have much lower alpha acid content, and you would need larger quantities to accomplish the job of bittering the beer. Conversely, many bittering varieties don't have as much of the essential oils needed for good aromatics.

Hops can be added to the brewpot at any time. Typical bittering hop additions are done by quarter-hour, half-hour, and one-hour increments. Recipes are written accordingly.

At what point in the boil you introduce hops depends on what you want to get out of them. Adding smaller quantities at various intervals imbues your beer with a more complex aromatic, flavoring, and bittering profile than if you add a whole bunch all at once. Regardless of whether the hops are pelletized, plugged, or loose, you have the choice of dropping them into the kettle freely or putting them into a *hop bag,* a sort of big tea bag. A hop bag allows the hops to steep in the boiling wort but eliminates the job of straining them out later.

Note: *Flavoring hops* are hops that are put into a boiling brewpot about 15 minutes before the boil is done in order to add hop flavor — 5 minutes or less if they are intended for aromatics only.

A good, rolling boil is needed to blend the hop resins and acids in the beer.

Substituting hop varieties by calculating AAUs

Many homebrew recipes call for a certain hop variety by name or require a certain number of Alpha Acid Units (AAUs). What if you want to make a particular beer and can't find the hop called for in the recipe? Substitution is the obvious answer, but how do you go about substituting one bittering hop for another? By figuring the AAUs. This equation is simple, assuming that you know, or your supplier knows, the alpha acid content of the hops to begin with.

If you know the alpha acid content, here's what you do: If the recipe calls for 3 ounces of Northern Brewer hops and you know that Northern Brewer hops have about 7.5 percent alpha acid, then the recipe is calling for 22.5 AAUs

(3 ounces × 7.5 alpha). For bittering purposes only, you should be able to use 2 ounces of Chinook hops (for example) with an alpha acid content of 11.25 percent (2 ounces × 11.25 = 22.5 AAUs).

Note: I say for bittering purposes only because Chinook hops and Northern Brewer hops do differ in taste.

AAUs are so much easier to deal with than IBUs (International Bitterness Units, or just plain Bitterness Units). The internationally used formula for determining IBUs in commercial beer is so complex, I don't even understand it enough to share it with you. Relax. Don't worry about it.

Complete *isomerization,* or solubility, doesn't take place until the brewpot has been boiling for 30 minutes or more, depending on whether you use whole hops, plugs, or pellets. Although the hop resins responsible for bittering are not easily dissolved, the hop oils that contribute hop flavor and aroma are extremely volatile and evaporate quickly.

From yeast to west (liquid yeast versus dry yeast)

Yeast is another one of the ingredients that you can change and improve at this level of homebrewing, and it is also the fourth variable in the beermaking process (after gravity, color, and bitterness).

As discussed in Chapters 1 and 2, yeast is largely responsible for how the finished beer turns out. The time, effort, and high-quality ingredients that you put into your brew are all for nothing if your yeast ruins the entire batch. You can guard against making lousy beer by replacing dry yeast with pure, healthy, liquid-culture yeast strains.

The dry yeast that is included with the beginning homebrewer's extract kit (and also sold separately) is more than adequate for making drinkable beer, but that's the same as saying that a 1971 Ford Pinto is more than adequate for getting you to work in the morning. Think about it. Why settle for "reliable transportation" when you can drive a *real* car?

On the other hand, liquid yeast cultures are produced in a sterile environment and come with limited guarantees of good results. Further, liquid yeast is cultured according to individual beer styles. The largest and best-known producer of liquid yeast cultures for homebrewing is Wyeast Laboratories in Oregon. To give you an idea of the degree of classification, Wyeast produces seven traditional cultures for ales and another seven for lagers, eight "advanced" yeast cultures for unique beer styles, and two yeast culture blends that are concentrated for larger volumes of beer.

Freeze-dried yeast

Dry yeast is freeze-dried, so it is designed to last a long time. Unfortunately, the freeze-drying processes that dehydrate these yeast are not entirely sterile; mutant yeast and bacteria mingle with the good yeast in these packets. You can only hope that the good yeast cells far outnumber the bad. Also, dry yeast is sold in relatively generic packets labeled "ale" and "lager" — no further classification is attempted. Dry yeast is also known to consume more of the available sugars in the wort, resulting in lower terminal gravities (see "Malt makes it: gravity and dry malt extract") and drier beers — almost as if they're drinking up for lost time.

Squirmy yeast

Liquid yeast is typically sold in foil pouches that contain both a small amount of pure yeast culture and a smaller sealed plastic packet with a small amount of a sterile liquid medium and malt nutrient (packaged this way, the yeast are not allowed to eat until their food is sprung from its plastic prison). While holding the foil pouch firmly on a flat surface with one hand, locate the inner packet and pop it with the heel of the other hand. The little packet is squirmy, so popping it may take a couple of tries. Once the packet has burst, the foil pouch needs to be shaken to fully mix the yeast and nutrient.

Caution: Do not burst the inner packet into a corner of the foil pouch — I've heard of homebrewers blowing out a whole corner of the pouch!

If the maturing yeast outgrow their foil pouch before you're ready to brew, you can create the perfect sterile "holding tank" by doing the following: Have one sanitized beer bottle, a small rubber stopper (to fit the bottle), and an airlock/bubbler handy. And here's where it pays off to have some dry malt extract on hand (see "Malt makes it: gravity and dry malt extract" earlier in this chapter). Boil a cup of water with a tablespoon or three of extract mixed in. After it cools, pour the cup of wort into the bottle and position the stopper and airlock (if you use a funnel, make sure it's sanitized!).

Using liquid yeast does have its negatives: Because the yeast may take several days to consume the malt nutrient and multiply to the proper "pitching" rate, brewers need to carefully plan their brewing itinerary in advance so their yeast is perfectly ready. Also, because of the yeast's carbon dioxide flatulence, the foil pouch in which liquid yeast is sold may pop if it is not watched. Always read and follow the directions. And did I mention that liquid yeast is also almost five times the cost of dry yeast?

Optional Goodies

Besides the four groups of ingredients — barley, hops, yeast, and water — found in every beer, you can add some optional goodies at various points in the brewing process. These goodies include sugars, flavorings, and, of course, herbs and spices.

Sweet kettle adjuncts

As mentioned in Chapter 3, commercial brewers sometimes add sugars to their brew kettles to supplement the natural malt sugar from the barley. This addition is done to give the beer different flavors and to boost the alcohol content of the beer by giving the yeast more to eat.

These sugars are called *adjunct sugars* for the same reason that rice and corn are called *adjunct grains:* They're not one of the primary ingredients used in beermaking. Here, they're referred to as *kettle adjuncts* because they can be thrown right into the brew kettle with the wort, as opposed to adjunct grains, which are dealt with in a cereal cooker, separate from the mash.

These other sugars can take many different forms. Some of these sugars are sweeter than others; some are more fermentable than others. Just as malt sugar is called maltose and corn sugar is called dextrose, some of these other sugars have their own *-ose* suffixes:

- ✔ **Fructose:** Found in fruits and malted grain
- ✔ **Glucose:** Derived from starch (on a molecular level, glucose and dextrose are identical)
- ✔ **Lactose:** Found in milk; unfermentable by beer yeast
- ✔ **Sucrose:** Can be found in malted grain; a compound of one molecule each of glucose and fructose

Stay away from processed white sugars in brewing (cane and beet sugar are especially high in sucrose), because if white sugars account for more than 20 to 25 percent of the brew's fermentables, the beer gets a noticeable cidery smell and taste. Also, white sugars are so highly fermentable that you'll have a measurable increase in alcohol and a measurable decrease in body and mouthfeel. Dextrose (corn sugar), also a refined sugar, should be reserved for priming the beer at bottling time (see Chapter 10).

Here are some ideas for kettle adjuncts in which natural sugars can be found:

- ✔ **Honey:** Very fermentable; adds a delicate sweetness or perfuminess.
- ✔ **Rice or corn syrup:** Use brewer's grade only.
- ✔ **Maple syrup:** The more natural, the better.
- ✔ **Brown sugar:** The darker, the more flavor.
- ✔ **Molasses/treacle:** Usually comes in three colors — light, dark, and blackstrap.
- ✔ **Fruit extracts:** Much easier to use than real fruit; widely available and never out of season.

Keep in mind that these are sugars to be added sparingly to your brew and should not constitute a large percentage of the total fermentables.

Unforgettable unfermentables: almost 31 flavors!

Beyond adding adjunct sugars to your brew, you can add several unfermentable flavorings. The key when using these is to complement the underlying beer flavor, not to create a whole new one. Remember that all these ingredients should be introduced to your beer in the brewpot so that they're disinfected by boiling.

- **Chocolate:** Don't expect chocoholics to beat a path to your door. Beer with chocolate is an esoteric brew that doesn't seem to inspire many brewers (or drinkers). Use only unsweetened baker's chocolate, not milk chocolate or sweetened chocolate. One or two 1-ounce squares should be used for a 5-gallon batch.

- **Fruit flavorings:** Some fruit flavorings come without the added sugar. You use them the same way you use fruit juices or extracts, but they don't require extra fermentation time. Doses vary depending on the fruit, brand, your personal taste, and so on.

- **Ginger:** Gingerroot in beer is very reminiscent of ginger ale (soda). Ginger was a common ingredient in beer made in the U.S. during colonial times. Use freshly grated gingerroot, not ginger powder, and use it sparingly (gingerly?) — 1 ounce for 5 gallons should do it.

- **Licorice:** Even when it's not added to a beer, licorice flavor is often experienced in dark beers. Brewers who like this flavor can add all they like to their own beer; unsweetened brewer's licorice is sold by most homebrew suppliers. Never overuse licorice, as 1 or 2 inches is sufficient in 5 gallons. Restrict its use to porters, schwarzbiers, and stouts.

- **Smoke:** Another esoteric brew. Fans of German rauchbier can emulate their favorite style by using liquid smoke extract. You can find this extract at well-stocked grocery stores, but be careful not to buy cheaper brands that contain vinegar or preservatives. Use only pure extracts; a tablespoon or two in 5 gallons goes a long way.

- **Spruce:** A tip of the cap to colonial beers, spruce beer was an early American favorite. Using the new spring growth (the needles) of the spruce tree was the old-fashioned method. Today, you can buy spruce essence through homebrew suppliers. Five teaspoons or less should give your beer a refreshing spruce taste.

- **Vanilla:** Although you can use pure vanilla extract or vanilla beans in beermaking, its use is not widely acclaimed. Most brewers reserve this flavor for once-a-year spiced ale or Christmas beer.

- **Old galoshes:** Just wanted to see whether you were paying attention!

Another thing you can add to modify your brew's flavor is a liqueur. Liqueurs are a great alternative source of flavors for the following reasons:

- They come in a variety of fruit flavors.
- Syrups used in liqueurs are usually of high quality.
- Because they contain alcohol contents of up to 40 percent, liqueurs are already antiseptic; you don't need to boil them.
- Liqueurs also contain a fair amount of sugar. One 750-milliliter bottle contains just about enough to prime a 5-gallon batch of beer (you may want a couple more ounces of corn sugar, to be sure).

All you need to do is add a 750-milliliter bottle of liqueur to your bottling bucket; in doing so, your beer gets flavored and primed at the same time. As far as the added alcohol is concerned, the total content is not likely to rise more than 1 or 2 percent per 5 gallons, maximum. Good shortcut.

Never use cream liqueurs — only translucent ones.

Herbs and spice and everything nice

At some point in your blossoming brewing career, you're likely to grow the same wild hair that every other homebrewer has grown. One day you'll be contemplating your next brew over an odoriferous plate of Italian food when out of nowhere it hits you — "Hmmm, I wonder what garlic beer would taste like?" You may laugh, but garlic beer has been done (unfortunately for those who tasted it). In fact, in the world of homebrew, very little *hasn't* been done. If it can be put in beer, it's probably been tried.

Herb and spice beer is the category that really pushes the envelope, although what seemed alien a half dozen years ago is now reaching the mainstream. Coriander seems to be the *herb du jour* (or is it a spice — I'm not even sure). Allspice is on the rise, and ginger is making a comeback, while cinnamon and cloves are now considered passé. Of course, all these ingredients have been used at one time or another over the past few thousand years.

Mushroom beer

A highly respected homebrewer with a penchant for making "weird" beers topped himself a few years ago. To this day, he is the only person I know who's made a beer with chanterelle mushrooms! I hear that the beer improved greatly after I tried it. . . .

Before adding herbs or spices to your beer, you should probably reflect a bit. Try to imagine the taste of the beer you have in mind (you might even try brewing a little herb or spice tea and adding it to a commercial beer). Is it something you want to drink two cases of? If so, make your move cautiously, remembering that using too little of the ingredient is better than using too much. If the taste in your first batch is too subtle, you can always revise your recipe and try again.

You can introduce herbs and spices at two stages in the beermaking cycle:

- ✔ Add them directly to the brewpot.
- ✔ Put them in the secondary fermenter (see "Secondary Fermentation").

If you go the brewpot route, wait until the last 10 or 15 minutes of the boil. Allowing certain herbs or spices to boil in the wort for a long time can sometimes cause an astringency or harshness similar to boiling grain.

If you hold out until the secondary fermenter stage, the ingredients need to be sanitized. Hold the bleach — this is a job for distilled alcohol. Whatever consumable spirits (whiskey, vodka, gin) you have in your house should get the job done. Pour a half cup of whatever you have on hand and allow the herb/spice to soak for about a week prior to putting it in the secondary fermenter (what you do with the leftover cup of spiced booze is your business). Seal the mixture with foil or food wrap and store it in the fridge.

To make this ingredient-soaking process easier, try fashioning a small filter/pouch out of a coffee filter or a fresh tea bag that's been emptied of its contents; use a twist-tie to close it.

Secondary Fermentation

Your first step toward becoming a sophomore brewer has to do with adding more and better ingredients. The second is about conditioning your brew differently, and fittingly for a second step, it's called *secondary fermentation*.

Secondary, or two-stage, fermentation is all about conditioning your beer. At the beginner's level, you put the fresh wort in the primary fermenter, let the yeast do its thing, and then bottle the beer (see Chapter 10). The beer has about two weeks to condition in the bottle before you start sucking it down. That's the right thing to do when your equipment and expertise are limited, but you can do better.

Taking the freshly fermented beer out of the primary fermenter is necessary in the beginning process not just because the initial fermentation is over but also because all those little yeasties, fresh from a gluttonous feast, are about to start consuming themselves. That's right: Given the opportunity, sugar-crazed yeast will cannibalize. This horrific event is called *yeast autolysis.* Autolysis can impart a sulfury, rubbery stench and flavor to your beer. Leaving your fresh, young beer sitting on that bulging layer of self-destructing yeast dregs is akin to letting your child wallow with pigs in the mud — and you wouldn't want to smell either one of them when they were done.

So, you say, if bottling the beer after one week works at the beginner's level, why not do the same thing at the sophomore level? You can, but now that you are introducing more ingredients to the brewpot, more flavors and textures in the beer need to blend, and for this melding process, time has no substitute. By allowing the beer to undergo a secondary fermentation — by expanding the fermentation's time — you are promoting a mellowing process, one that will make a noticeable improvement in your beer.

Because most of the consumable sugars in the wort have already been eaten, secondary fermentation yields very little yeast activity and rarely produces a measurable amount of additional alcohol. This stage is just an opportunity for all the beer's ingredients to acclimate and establish a tasty relationship.

Secondary fermentation isn't worth the effort unless you allow the beer to mellow in the carboy for at least one week; two to three weeks is the norm, and a month or more may be needed for barleywines, Imperial stouts, and other complex and high-gravity beers. Thus, bottling will be delayed considerably, giving you more time to sanitize all that glass and contemplate your capacity for patience.

One final vote in support of secondary fermentation: Using this procedure, not only do you have nothing to fear regarding unfinished primary fermentations (and exploding bottles), but you can actually cut the primary fermentation time by a day or two and rack the beer over to the secondary fermenter at your convenience. Racking is possible *only* after the peak fermentation activity subsides.

Remember: No phase of homebrewing is exempt from cleaning and sanitizing. Adding another fermentation phase means disinfecting all the equipment that goes along with it. Might as well get used to it and stop complaining.

The Art of Siphoning

The use of a carboy in homebrewing requires the brewer to practice siphoning techniques because carboys don't come equipped with spigots. A curved racking tube — or cane, as it is sometimes called — is needed along with your plastic hosing.

Homebrewing = rocket science — not!

What is the driving force behind the principle of siphoning? This force is gravitational acceleration × mass (F = mg). The beer (or any liquid) is pulled by gravity and pushed by the weight of its own mass. As its own mass decreases, so does the pushing pressure; gravitational pull remains constant. (The next lesson concerns the other well-known homebrewing formula, $E = mc^2$.)

The opening of the siphon hose must be lower than the bottom of the vessel from which the beer is being siphoned to be effective (the lower the better). Keeping large air bubbles out of the siphon hose increases siphoning efficiency; air bubbles can slow or stop liquid flow and can also oxidize the beer.

You can start a siphon in a handful of ways, but not all of them are acceptable for homebrewing. For speed and simplicity, sucking on one end of the siphon hose will surely get a flow going, but this opens the door to all kinds of contamination possibilities. Some brewers feel that a good gargle and rinse with whiskey or vodka is a good way to prevent this problem. (Just limit yourself to rinsing so you don't mess up the rest of the job.)

Another, more widely accepted practice is to fill the plastic hosing with water just prior to fitting the hosing onto the racking tube. After the tube and hose are connected (with the cane resting in the carboy), just dropping the open end into the bottling bucket automatically starts the flow of beer. This method may take a few tries before you get the system down.

Sophomore Homebrew Recipes

Here are two easy homebrew recipes that incorporate the addition of bittering and finishing hops, specialty grains, and secondary fermentation. As you can see in this section, intermediate-level homebrew recipes are not much more than a list of ingredients, because the brewing steps at this level are basically the same for each style.

The steps you follow to brew the two recipes in this chapter are in addition to the 16 brewing steps in Chapter 10. You simply incorporate the new steps into the former ones, so, for example, Steps 1a and 1b follow Chapter 10's Step 1. The new steps are required for you to use specialty grains, add hops and kettle adjuncts, use liquid yeast, and do a secondary fermentation.

So to begin, you simply start with Step 1 in Chapter 10 and incorporate the extra sophomore-brewing steps into the individual steps as needed.

Remember: The numbers in these steps correspond to the brewing steps in Chapter 10.

Here are the two additional steps you follow when using specialty grains:

1a. While you heat the water in the brewpot, steep your specialty grains. Place the grain (either loose or in a sparge bag) in a saucepan, fill with enough water to cover the grain, and heat for 20 to 30 minutes as hot as possible but without boiling. *(Do not boil!)*

1b. Pour this water into the brewpot through a strainer (to catch the grain) and then sparge the grain: Continue to pour water over the grain in the strainer until it runs clear (this process should take a half gallon or so). Dispose of spent grain (which is great for composting, for all you gardeners out there).

Here is the extra step for adding hops to the brew kettle. *Remember:* In sophomore brewing, you use *unhopped* malt extract, which means you have to add hops.

4a. Add bittering hops to the brew kettle anywhere from 30 minutes to 1 hour before the boil is done (the more bitter you want the beer to be, the longer you boil the hops). You don't add finishing hops until a couple of steps later.

Note: Whether hops are added to the brew kettle loosely or in hop bags, the hops need to be strained out of the wort before it is poured into the fermenter.

Here are the extra steps for adding kettle adjuncts — sugars or miscellaneous flavorings:

4b. Introduce additional sugars and miscellaneous flavorings (honey, molasses, licorice, spruce essence) to the brewpot early to benefit from a full boil.

4c. Add herbs and spices to the brewpot in the last 15 minutes of the boil (they're better off being treated similar to flavoring hops).

Now, to add hops (again!):

4d. Add finishing hops in the last 5 minutes — just long enough to kill bacteria, but not long enough to boil off the volatile aromatic oils.

Adding hops a little bit sooner, in the last 15 minutes of the boil, imbues the beer with additional hop flavor without extracting the hops' bitterness.

Here is the step for using liquid yeast:

13. **Just add liquid yeast from the foil pouch directly into the fermenter.**

    Note: This step *replaces* the original Step 13 of Chapter 10. You do the liquid yeast procedures in place of the dry yeast procedures, not in addition to them.

When you use liquid yeast, you have to start the yeast-activating procedures a couple of days before you actually brew the beer. Be sure to follow package directions closely.

Here are the steps for secondary fermentation. *Note:* Because secondary fermentation is not discussed at all in Chapter 10, this is an additional procedure that just uses old techniques. And remember, all sanitizing procedures still apply!

16a. **After you determine that your beer's primary fermentation is complete, simply drain the beer from the primary fermenter into your glass carboy, using the spigot and plastic hosing (if necessary, top off the carboy with boiled and cooled water, leaving an inch or two of airspace).**

16b. **Seal the carboy with a rubber stopper and airlock or bubbler and allow the beer to mellow another two weeks (*you* can mellow out, too).**

    A hydrometer reading at this time is optional but recommended.

After two weeks, start bottling according to the bottling procedures outlined in Chapter 10. The only difference this time is that because (unlike a plastic fermenter) a carboy lacks a spigot, you must siphon the beer from the carboy into the bottling bucket by using a racking cane and plastic hosing. Hints and tips for doing just that are found in this chapter (see "The Art of Siphoning").

So now you can get brewing!

The original and terminal gravities and the ingredients and their quantities are not hard-and-fast rules, just general parameters for the style. Ingredient substitutions based on availability or preference (such as with hops, or powdered versus syrup extract) are a homebrewing fact of life, so don't worry — go ahead with confidence.

Beer Style: British Pale Ale

Here are the ingredients for a widely popular style, commonly known and sure to please a range of friends. It's a good stepping-stone recipe on your way to more-complex brews, too.

Original gravity: 1.046; terminal gravity: 1.012

Malt extract: 6 pounds (light)

Specialty grains: 1 pound 20L crystal, 1/2 pound toasted malt

Bittering hops: 2 ounces Brewer's Gold (substitute: Northern Brewer)

Finishing hops: 1 ounce Goldings (substitute: Fuggles)

Yeast: Liquid ale yeast (Wyeast #1028 or #1098)

Boil at least 1 ounce of the bittering hops for a full hour. Put the second ounce of bittering hops into the brewpot for no less than 30 minutes (the longer the second ounce is in the brewpot, the more bittering you get; conversely, the less time the second ounce is in the brewpot, the more hop flavoring you get).

Beer Style: London-Style Sweet Stout

A bit different from the pale ale, this relatively sweet beer is a good place to start for stout lovers (that is, beer drinkers who love stout, not stout beer drinkers who are in love, though that is certainly possible).

Original gravity: 1.048; terminal gravity: 1.014

Malt extract: 6 pounds (light or amber)

Specialty grains: 1/2 pound chocolate malt, 1/4 pound roasted barley, 1/4 pound black malt

Kettle adjunct: 8 ounces lactose powder (milk sugar)

Bittering hops: 2 ounces Brewer's Gold (substitute: Bullion or Northern Brewer)

Finishing hops: 1 ounce Fuggles or Goldings

Yeast: Liquid ale yeast (Wyeast #1028)

Because of the added sweetness of the lactose, both ounces of the bittering hops should be boiled for a full hour. Besides, hop flavoring is not part of this stout style's flavor profile.

Chapter 12

Homebrew Geekdom

· ·

In This Chapter

▶ Brewing like the pros

▶ Getting more homebrew gadgets

▶ Making your own equipment

▶ Competing with other homebrewers

▶ Homebrewing on premises (BOPs)

· ·

*W*hen you are confident in your ability to brew good and consistent extract-based homebrew, you may want to take up the challenge to brew beer from scratch — just like the professional brewers do — and exercise even more control over your ingredients.

For more details on the equipment and processes than this chapter can provide, you need to buy or borrow some in-depth homebrew resources, such as books, magazines, videos, and computer software. You have plenty to choose from — see Appendix F. (and also the software section of this chapter) for information.

If you haven't already, now is definitely the time to contact the folks at the American Homebrewers Association (P.O. Box 1679, Boulder, CO 80306-1679; phone 303-447-0816, fax 303-447-2825). They can pinpoint nearly every homebrew-supply store and homebrewing club in the U.S. for you, as well as many clubs around the world. As a member, you receive five issues per year of their magazine, *Zymurgy.* The magazine contains plenty of advertisements for homebrew equipment and ingredient suppliers. (Your local homebrew-supply shop is also a good source for more information.)

To locate a local club on your own, check out the nearest brewpub or beer bar — beer geeks are regulars at these places, so that's where you're likely to find members of any local beer appreciation or homebrew club. For more information on clubs, check out Appendix E.

From Syrup to Grain: Equipment and Ingredients for Advanced Homebrewing

Fundamentally, advanced homebrewing means *all-grain* brewing, and all-grain brewing means *mashing* grain to make your wort rather than buying malt extract as the base for your beer. This is the definitive step in the mastery of brewing beer at home, where science begins to overcome art (as in "the art and science of brewing"). You have to master different methods of mashing (three kinds!), more-complex fermentation techniques, and more-complex recipes — all beyond the scope of this book. The culinary equivalent is chefs growing their own food, finding specialized sources of exotic ingredients, and making their own stocks and pastries. Everything is made from scratch for control, pleasure, and better brews. And this level takes a lot more attention and effort than I can even hint at here. You've been warned!

Getting more equipment (or making it yourself)

As you progress up the homebrewing evolutionary ladder, you need to beg, borrow, or steal (just kidding) the proper equipment for your brewery. Some of this stuff is absolutely necessary, and some can be considered extravagant — it all depends on your perspective (at this point, your brewery may start to look a lot like the Jet Propulsion Laboratory).

For the serious advanced homebrewer, equipment costs begin to add up quickly, but you have alternatives to signing over your paycheck to the homebrew-supply house. Some expensive pieces of equipment can be made on the cheap, fairly easily if you're not all thumbs. Most homebrew books describe how to make these contraptions.

The advanced homebrewer needs much of the same equipment as the intermediate homebrewer — lab immersion thermometer, grain mill, kitchen or postal scale, and so on (see Chapter 11). The following list describes some of the additional pieces of equipment you need for "from-scratch" brewing and gives you some basic directions for those items that you may be able to make yourself. (See Chapters 3 and 10 for more information on how some of this equipment fits in the brewing process. Chapter 10 contains some metric-conversion equations.)

- ✔ **Large-volume brewpot:** Instead of buying a huge and expensive stock pot from a restaurant-supply store, do what many savvy homebrewers do: Fashion one out of a used beer keg.

- ✔ **Lauter tun:** Essential to mashing grain, as it allows you to capture the wort while holding back the grain. This important piece of equipment can be made very inexpensively with little more than a couple of 5-gallon food-grade plastic buckets.

- ✔ **Immersion wort chiller:** Highly effective piece of equipment that isn't too expensive, either. A long coil of copper tubing, two short pieces of garden hose, and a couple of hose clamps get you where you want to go. See Figure 12-1.

- ✔ **pH papers:** Used to measure the pH (the alkalinity or acidity) of your brewing water — a necessity for mashing.

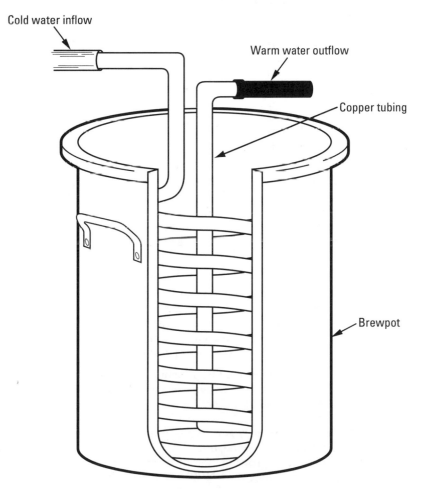

Cold water inflow

Warm water outflow

Copper tubing

Brewpot

Figure 12-1:
An immersion wort chiller, shown in a homebrewing brewpot, is easy to make. Cold water enters at one end and exits at the other as warm water, like a radiator in reverse.

✔ **Gypsum and calcium carbonate:** These minerals are used to "correct" the pH of your brewing water.

✔ **"Cellar" (second fridge):** In order to brew authentic lager beers, you need the ability to "lager" your beer in a cool lagering "cellar" for relatively long periods of time. Not many homebrewers have the Alpine caves in which the process was originally developed; get a second fridge and modify it with a beer-friendly thermostat.

Growing, roasting, and smoking your ingredients

No, the smoking doesn't refer to something done with cigarette papers. In addition to buying equipment upgrades and building your own equipment, you probably want to take a more active role in the production of your brewing ingredients. Here's a peek at some things that can confirm your position in the world of beer geekery (geekiness?).

✔ **Yeast:** Logical first choice for advanced involvement in the control over your beer's ingredients. If you have success with the yeast-handling techniques outlined in Chapters 10 and 11, you should have no problem "banking," "ranching," or "farming" your own yeast.

✔ **Grain:** Few homebrewers venture into grain husbandry, probably wisely so because grain-growing and malting procedures require vast amounts of land, equipment, capital, and expertise — and are best left to the farmers and maltsters who can provide you with a product more efficiently and cheaply than you can produce for yourself. You can, however, do a couple of things to assert more control over your grains (especially recommended for Type A personalities):

   • **Roast grains:** Roasted grains give your beer complexity by imbuing it with a variety of toasty, roasty, and nutty flavors. When you roast your own grains, you can control the duration and intensity of the roast. Of course, you can just buy similarly roasted grains at your local homebrew supplier, but how much fun is that?

   • **Smoke grains:** Besides roasting your grains, you can also opt to smoke them on a grill or in a smoker, especially if you have acquired the rare taste for rauchbier or other smoked beers.

✔ **Hops:** Not many homebrewers — even serious advanced ones — get involved in hop growing, but it does have its proponents. Much as cooks get a kick out of growing their own vegetables, homebrewers can get some kicks out of farming the one beer ingredient that they possibly can (unless you count well water as an agricultural product).

Back to your roots

Not only do homebrewers benefit from the bounty of the commercial hop-processing trade, but they're also now able to take advantage of the much smaller but equally satisfying glut of hop rhizomes.

A *rhizome* is a root cutting — the easiest way to start a new hop plant. Hop rhizomes can be purchased through many homebrew suppliers, though they are usually available only very early in the growing season (February to April).

Hops can be successfully grown just about anywhere between the 40th and 50th Parallels, north and south of the equator. Some micro-climates are better than others for hop cultivation, obviously, but as long as the hops have ample sunlight and receive plenty of moisture, they can thrive.

Investing in optional gadgets and gizmos

In the ever-expanding world of homebrewing, armies of people are trying to build a better mousetrap, metaphorically speaking. Someone is always coming up with a new and better way of making beer at home. Tremendous changes have taken place in the past decade, and the "science" of homebrewing will continue to evolve as more helpful and time-saving innovations continue to appear.

The following items can make your brewing easier and more convenient. Most can be found at a well-stocked homebrew-supply store or in a complete catalog. They are not absolutely necessary for making good beer, and a few can put a real dent in your pocketbook. But for the serious homebrewer, these items are a good way to spend your disposable income.

- **Amazing Wheel of Beer:** Handy little slide-rule–type calculator (see Figure 12-2). Use it to calculate gravity when you are mashing. By using it, you can quickly calculate the gravity you'll get from 20 different malts, grains, and extracts in both OG and Balling scales.

- **Beer filter:** Boxy set of pads or cartridges in a canister. You need a carbon dioxide system to force the beer through and to carbonate the beer after the yeast has been filtered out.

- **Carbonator (brand name):** Convenient little gizmo that allows those of you who normally keg your beer to bottle a little for tasting away from home. A one-way pressure valve, it fits on 1- or 2-liter plastic soda bottles. Requires a carbon dioxide system.

Figure 12-2:
The Amazing Wheel of Beer is a laminated set of plastic discs. To calculate the gravity from the different ingredients, match up the gallons and the pounds of each ingredient that you are using.

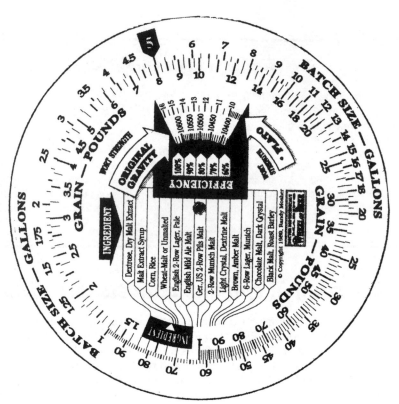

Dr. Bob Technical's Amazing Wheel of Beer copyright © Randy Mosher. Reprinted courtesy of Randy Mosher.

✔ **Counter-pressure bottle filler:** Allows those of you who keg your beer to transfer the beer to glass bottles without losing carbonation. This process is important if you want to send bottles of your beer to competitions. Requires a carbon dioxide system.

✔ **Digital pH meter:** If you are mashing, electronic, digital equipment just makes the job a little easier and a lot more accurate than when using papers.

✔ **Digital thermometer:** Again, the electronic, digital version of this basic tool is simply easier to use.

✔ **External thermometer:** If your carboy or keg is sitting in an environment that is not thermostatically controlled, such as a basement, you may want to use a stick-on thermometer. This instrument is great for keeping track of fermentation temperatures.

✔ **Five-gallon soda kegs, with carbon dioxide tank, regulators, hoses, and fittings:** Don't bother with the commercial kegs — they're too big. If you want to keg your own beer, get a Cornelius kegging system.

Shopping at homebrew stores

More than 1,500 homebrew-supply stores operate in the U.S. Some are old home winemaking shops that made the transition to accommodate wine's sister beverage; many are long-established businesses that cater to the dyed-in-the-wool homebrew fanatics. But most are mom-and-pop stores that decided to diversify and rope the newest cash cow.

Because many of these homebrew-supply stores do mail-order business, you no longer need to look for one in your hometown (though having one nearby is more convenient). Check out your local homebrew or beer appreciation club (see Appendix C or see the sources in Appendix E), whose members are more than happy to guide a novice to a good place.

✔ **Hop-Go-Round:** Another easy-to-use, circular little slide-rule–type calculator. This one is for calculating hop bitterness units.

✔ **Siphon starter:** Diaphragm device that works by shaking. Prevents possible contamination of your beer.

✔ **Wort aeration system:** Combination of air pump and sterile filter with a "beer stone" that diffuses oxygen into the beer, not unlike aerators used in fish tanks. Very effective. Creates a better environment for yeast.

Another item that you may want to invest in is a keg system. One thing homebrewers seem to universally agree on is that bottling is the worst part of homebrewing — the cleaning, storing, sanitizing, and capping of so many bottles is tedious and time-consuming. Well, kegging the brew is a viable option for anyone with a little cash to burn and a good beer appetite.

The system to get is a 5-gallon soda keg system, such as the very common Cornelius brand. The reason for using these kegs is that they are easier to clean, fill, handle, and obtain than commercial beer kegs. Commercial beer kegs require special tools and equipment and are almost impossible to clean properly (not to mention that they don't come in 5-gallon sizes).

Brewing by the Byte

Nineteenth-century brewing and 20th-century technology are on a collision course. The result? Computer software for homebrewers: point, click, brew. You could easily subtitle this section "Where Beer Geek Meets Computer Geek" because this subject truly is the epitome of geekiness. I don't claim to be a die-hard member of either camp (the old-fashioned way versus the high-tech way), so this section is a lean look at some of the existing software, presented without major judgment.

This list is short because the market for this software is somewhat limited. Few programs that you may find listed or even advertised in magazines are actually available — the producers either have gone out of business or just aren't professional enough to respond to inquiries.

Homebrewing software

Some of the following software is located online. If you're not familiar with the Internet and the World Wide Web, check out *The Internet For Dummies,* 3rd Edition, by John R. Levine, Carol Baroudi, and Margaret Levine Young, or *The Web After Work For Dummies,* by Jill and Matthew V. Ellsworth (IDG Books Worldwide, Inc. — who else?).

✔ ***The Interactive Complete Joy of Home Brewing with Charlie Papazian:*** MediaRight Technology. $49.95 (CD-ROM, Windows only). Available at homebrew shops, software stores, or direct (phone 212-966-7383).

The biggest-selling and best-known of all homebrewing programs (see Figure 12-3). Offers brewing instructions, recipes, a batch journal, a hop calculator, and an updated list of homebrewing resources. The presentation is great, too — plenty of video clips, online help, music, tables, and snazzy graphics. One drawback: The program requires a full 15MB of free disk space to run!

✔ ***BrewMeister Version 1.0:*** Freeware (Macintosh only). Available for downloading at the `http://hyperarchive.lcs.mit.edu/HyperArchive/Archive/art/brew-meister-10.hqx` World Wide Web site.

One of the rare homebrewing programs dedicated to the Macintosh platform. Offers IBU, color, original/final gravity calculators, batch logging, and a recipe generator. Beware of the preprogrammed recipes, though — one listed rather ambiguously as a pale ale calls for 1 pound of honey. Whoa, there!

Mingling jargon

A beer geek asks a computer geek: "What do you do when your mash gets stuck?" The computer geek responds: "Grab your hard drive and RAM it through!"

Figure 12-3:
Here's a
screen from
the popular
homebrewing
program
called *The
Interactive
Complete
Joy of Home
Brewing
with Charlie
Papazian.*
This
CD-ROM
has plenty
of material
to search,
including
book text
and brewing
recipes and
videos.

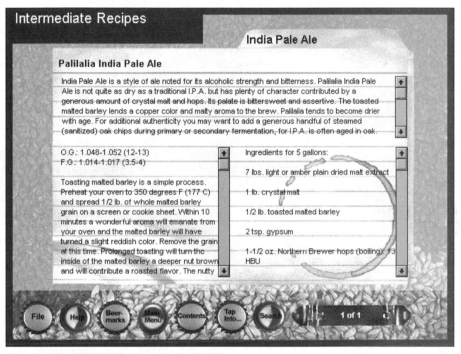

Reprinted courtesy of MediaRight Technology, Inc., New York, N.Y.

✔ *Brew Chief:* Chicago Beer Company. $29.95 (Windows only). Available direct (P.O. Box 642893, Chicago, IL 60664; phone 312-248-0474).

A versatile program with a load of features for the homebrewer. Recipe logs, converters, calculators, online help, and bottle/keg label templates should handle most of your brewing needs. 1996 AHA style descriptions and guidelines are also included — a nice touch.

✔ *Beer Recipe Formulator Version 2.0:* Shareware (MS-DOS only). Available for downloading at the `ftp.stanford.edu./pub/clubs/homebrew/beer` Internet address.

This formulator is simple and easy to use and is geared toward novice homebrewers. It can formulate recipes of any size, but measures are limited to gallons, pounds, and ounces, and no conversion program is included. Dust off your slide rule!

You can find more programs by checking out the various Internet and Web sites listed in Appendixes D and E.

Shareware — caveat emptor

Shareware is software that is usually distributed through the Internet, from Bulletin Board Systems (BBSs) or by regular old floppy disk. Authors of shareware software rely on the honor system to get paid — if you like and use a shareware program, you are supposed to send the creator a nominal fee for its use (*freeware,* on the other hand, carries no such obligation). This fee may entitle you to benefits not available to the "shareware sneak," such as free or cheap upgrades to new versions and limited product support.

Although shareware can be of good quality (some titles have evolved into programs that are sold by big-name software companies), remember that ultimately, you get what you pay for. Don't expect million-dollar graphics, instruction manuals, or 24-hour, 800-number technical support. However, shareware *can* be an inexpensive way to find out whether computerized homebrewing is right for you.

BOPs Are Now S.O.P.

BOPs (Brew On Premises) are another phenomenon born of the North American brewing renaissance. A BOP is, for all practical purposes, a homebrewery (actually several small ones) for rent, sort of like a Laundromat — only the suds are a lot more interesting.

BOPs offer on-site brewing equipment that allows many "home" brewers to brew individual batches of beer simultaneously. Most BOPs feature at least six brewkettles, so six brews can be boiling at once. Bring your pals for help!

Oh Canada!

The original Brew On Premises was conceived in Canada, not so much in the name of good beer as in the name of affordable beer: Canada levies painfully high taxes on beer and other alcoholic beverages. The average case of beer (and I do mean average) costs about $28 Canadian (roughly $20 U.S.), thanks to taxes. That's a lot.

In the U.S., BOPs didn't catch on until about 1993, and in fact, they still haven't, compared to Canada. At last count, fewer than three dozen were spread around the country, but the number is likely to increase as the general public becomes aware of the existence and convenience of BOPs. And now a few can be found in Europe.

BOPs for you and me

Here's a partial list of BOPs in the U.S. To find more, ask around at various brewpubs, beer bars, or homebrew-supply shops.

- ✔ **California:** Hamilton Gregg Brewworks (Hermosa Beach); phone 310-376-0406

- ✔ **California:** Brew City (San Francisco); phone 415-929-2255

- ✔ **California:** The Brew Factory (San Luis Obispo); phone 805-594-1669

- ✔ **Colorado:** The Beer Store (Boulder); phone 303-494-7000

- ✔ **Idaho:** Brewworks (Boise); phone 208-853-4677

- ✔ **Illinois:** Chicago BOP (Chicago); phone 312-404-1000

- ✔ **Massachusetts:** Modern Brewer (Somerville); phone 617-629-0400

- ✔ **New York:** Lager Heads, Inc. (Orchard Park); phone 716-667-2335

- ✔ **Oregon:** Glisan St. Brewhouse (Portland); phone 503-223-9566

- ✔ **Pennsylvania:** America U-Brew (Philadelphia); phone 215-627-2337

- ✔ **Washington:** U Brew Seattle (Seattle); phone 206-782-2537

The BOP supplies the malt extract, the grain, the hops, the yeast, and various other brewing ingredients for one all-inclusive price. Single-batch prices are set according to the particular style of beer you want to brew. The cost of one brew not only covers your ingredients and the rental of the brewing equipment but also usually includes instructional help and the storage of your beer during fermentation and aging. When the brew is ready to be bottled, you're given full reign of the in-house bottling equipment.

Homebrew Competitions

Just like chili cook-offs and pie bake-offs, homebrew competitions provide a competitive platform for amateurs who like to make good beer. In 1985, only about a dozen such competitions were held across the U.S., with a couple hundred entries total; now hundreds of events take place annually, attracting thousands of entries. They're hosted at local, regional, and national levels, in the U.S. and around the world, and offer a variety of rewards to the winners.

I feel sanctified

Because today's homebrew competitions have so much at stake, the American Homebrewers Association (AHA) established the Beer Judge Certification Program (BJCP) to standardize judging and scoring procedures at all

AHA-sanctioned events. Any competition that does not request and receive AHA-sanctioned status is considered a maverick event. Neither judges nor contestants are quick to participate in nonconformist events — judges because they won't earn BJCP judging points and contestants because they aren't guaranteed a high level of competency from the judges.

The typical sanctioned event may have as many as 30 major classifications and another 50 subcategories open to entries. It includes categories for beer styles as well as those fermented but non-beer cousins, cider and mead (mead is fermented from honey).

After all the beer categories are judged and score sheets are tabulated, the best beer from each category goes on to the Best of Show round. The most senior and experienced judges (those who don't have their own competing brew eligible for the Best of Show, that is) are hand-picked to judge the beers at that level. At this point, no score sheets are used; the judges arrive at the two or three beers that best represent their respective categories by process of elimination. When the final two or three beers are left standing, first-, second-, and third-place honors are bestowed.

The prizes awarded at homebrewing competitions nowadays are nothing to sneeze at — mostly, they're something to drink to. Generally speaking, the larger the competition, the more that's doled out to the winners. The national competitions run by the AHA are exceptionally generous to grand-prize winners (especially the annual National Homebrew Competition, or NHC). These competitions offer top winners all-expenses-paid trips and the like, thanks to donations from large breweries and allied businesses worldwide. Runners-up console themselves with merchandise and nifty ribbons. See Chapter 14 for more details about competitions.

Acceptance of BOP brew as homebrew is left to the discretion of the individual competition director. Check with the ruling body of the competition before sending your entry.

A choice award

One of the most incredible awards is getting your homebrew replicated and sold by a nationally distributed brand — kind of like if your mom's chocolate-chip cookies were made by Sara Lee. Three brands do this: Pete's Wicked Brewing Co. (for a seasonal brew), Boston Beer Company (for winners of a worldwide contest marketed as "Longshot"), and Goose Island Brewing Co. (in conjunction with Beer Across America). These homebrews are among the best and most distinctive brews you can find and a real tribute to the skill and creativity of homebrewers. A tribute that pays royalties, no less! Cool.

Even losers are winners

Entering your homebrewed beer in a sanctioned competition can be a very gratifying aspect of homebrewing. Beyond winning ribbons and prizes, competitions offer clear and objective evaluations of your beer by competent and knowledgeable beer judges.

For each brew you send to a sanctioned competition, you are guaranteed to receive all the judges' score sheets. These score sheets go beyond assigning a simple numerical score to your brew; BJCP judges are trained to offer intelligent and coherent feedback.

Though some of the judging still may be guesswork, the judges' comments may point out important negative attributes in your beer and your brewing technique that can help you improve your beer and eventually your enjoyment of homebrewing. Your friends will always tell you that your homebrew tastes wonderful — or just plain awful — so you need a source of professional objective analysis. This information alone is worth the entry fee.

Becoming a barrister of beer

So you think you'd like to be a beer judge? You say it sounds like an easy gig? You think you'd get to drink a lot of free beer? Actually, it is great fun, but becoming a certified beer judge is no cake walk (pub crawl?). It takes time, practice, experience, perseverance, and a genuine desire to be good at judging beer.

Your enthusiasm is undiminished? Your resolve unflagging? Good! There may be a place for you in the BJCP. For more information, contact Beer Judge Certification Program, P.O. Box 375, Hayward, CA 94543.

To many judges, what's more important than actually judging beer competitions are the knowledge and satisfaction that they gain and the expertise and appreciation of beer that few others ever achieve: the very tasty pinnacle of beer geekdom!

Beer judge rankings

The BJCP was established in 1985 to educate already-knowledgeable people in proper procedural judging techniques and to standardize scoring methods. After judge candidates have proven their knowledge and ability by passing a three-hour essay and tasting entrance exam, they progress through the program by earning experience points for judging, stewarding, and organizing competitions. How many points they receive depends on the position they held and how large the competition was (measured by the number of entries). As they accumulate experience points, they can advance to the next level. Here are the levels, the required minimum test score, and the required experience points.

- **Recognized Judge:** 60 percent; no judging experience points needed to start at this level

- **Certified Judge:** 70 percent; at least 5 experience points required

- **National Judge:** 80 percent; at least 20 experience points required

- **Master Judge:** 90 percent; at least 40 experience points required

- **Honorary Master Judge:** A temporary designation bestowed by the BJCP upon certain persons widely known for their judging skills and mastery of the craft, for whom an exam would be superfluous — for example, Michael Jackson. (I mean, of course, *the* Michael Jackson, who's acclaimed as the world's foremost authority on beer and brewing — *not* the singer.)

Or maybe you someday — why not?

Part V
Going Nuts over Beer: Travel and Collecting

The 5th Wave   By Rich Tennant

"Douglas, it's time we talked about this beer paraphernalia hobby of yours!"

In this part . . .

For some people, drinking the darn stuff just isn't enough. I'm talking about those of you (okay, me, too) who are interested in further exploring the *subject* of beer. Well, there's a solution: beer travel and breweriana collecting. Yes, you can find plenty of beery things to see and do around the world —and plenty of things to bring home (some beautiful, some pretty weird). Whether with memories, experiences, or objects, you can take beer to new levels of enjoyment.

Chapter 13

European Beer Touring: Brewspots and Shrines

*O*kay, beer fans: If you've got the beer bug bad, you're going to want to experience firsthand the thrill of drinking fresh beer where it has always been loved most, made best, and served just right. That means Europe (the U.S. isn't exactly dry, either — see Chapter 14). Although beer wasn't born in Europe, it grew up there and became the world's most popular beverage because of European brewers. Commercial brewing has been serious business there since the 12th century.

So do some serious beer touring. You've got to be able to say someday, "Ah, yes — been there, done that!"

Outside Europe — with the possible exception of Australia — probably only the U.S. and Canada have created a beer culture you can actually visit. No other countries offer a beer enthusiast much to explore, beerwise. The major breweries established outside Europe and North America have generally been created by German or British brewers (the home of Tsingtao beer, in China, looks like a Bavarian village) and are not distinctly local; the recipes and the styles are European (mostly light lagers, although stouts are brewed in Ghana, Nigeria, South Africa, Sri Lanka, Barbados, Jamaica, and Singapore, among other places). So let's face it: World beer travel — just like world beer styles — is European beer travel.

You can drink well or revel in beer stuff in almost all European countries, but the crown jewels of beerdom for beer tourists are, hands down, Germany (especially Munich and Bavaria as a whole), the U.K., Ireland, Belgium, and the

Czech Republic. Certified beer nuts, your pilgrimage awaits, complete with beer shrines (biggest, oldest, original, and so on). For the more sane among you, a little bit of beer trekking can provide a really great accent to a more normal trip, say a business trip or a family vacation.

Beer Trekking Tips

The pub culture in most of the major brewing nations is mostly intact, and a visit to practically any local bar is likely to yield a good beer discovery. In Germany, you can become overwhelmed by the sheer number of breweries that exist (Bavaria alone has more than 800), while beer trekkers in Belgium may get thoroughly bewildered by the variety of unusual beer styles served at any given bar.

The best way to get over being confused and overwhelmed is to get a little serious. Start tasting the beers deliberately and without apprehension. As you would at a beer tasting or festival, take good notes — preferably on paper, but coasters and bar napkins will do in a pinch (see Chapter 14 for beer festival tips). Anywhere you land in these countries, be a beer explorer: Ask for something local, something full of flavor. Something different, made with care. Keep a record, and your experience is transformed into a keepsake (and also might make more sense). A record also helps when you get back home and want to buy bottled versions of what you had on your trek.

Some of the best beer parties anywhere in the world are European festivals. Quite often rooted in religious or obscure historical contexts, they now usually serve only as modern-day justifications for fun. Joyous celebration is the purpose of these festivities; beer is an integral means to that end. And it's easy to join the party!

Some excellent guidebooks are must-reads for beer nuts prior to making their yeasty pilgrimages. They are listed in Appendix D.

Packaged goods were never so fine

For those who like company and knowledgeable guides, a new business has begun: beer tours. Beer lovers can pick such prepackaged, self-proclaimed "mildly educational" tours as Beer and Brewing Tour of England and Belgium (including the Great British Beer Festival), Historical Pub Tour, and The Great British Pub Tour (British Network Ltd, phone 800-274-8583 or 201-744-8814); Oktoberfest and other German festivals (any number of travel agents); or Brewing Traditions of England and Scotland, The Best of Bohemia and Bavaria, and Artisan Breweries of Holland & Belgium (MIR Corporation, phone 800-424-7289 or 206-624-7289) — just to name a few. The national airlines of most brewing countries can also be of help.

Germany

Germany is for beer lovers.

You have, no doubt, heard that Germans like beer? That they kind of wrote the book on brewing? *Ja?* Nowhere is the beer culture more established and ingrained than in Germany. As many as 1,300 breweries are located in unified Germany, more than in any other country in the world. And most are in the southeastern province of Bavaria, centered on Munich.

Munich alone is home to 13 brewers of various sizes, some of whose bottles are easily found in the U.S.: Spaten, Augustiner, Hacker-Pschorr, Lowenbräu, Paulaner, and Hofbräu. Each of these six breweries also operates beer halls in Munich; all are outstanding places to sample the local fare (Muncheners consume more than just about any other group of people). During the hot summer months, entire families flock to the many refreshing beer gardens; at some, you bring your own food. Even better are the local, small breweries scattered mostly throughout Bavaria. The whole thing is all much better than you could ever find back home (wherever that is), just in case you need another excuse to go.

Many of Germany's other large cities, such as Berlin, Dortmund, and Köln (Cologne), can each boast of having several large breweries. Even more impressive, each of these cities (including Munich) has its own beer style, almost like a wine appellation (see Chapter 1 and Appendix B for more on styles). Some smaller villages also boast several breweries. Germany is saturated with beer and has been for hundreds of years.

The seven-minute pour

In Germany, you are likely to encounter something completely unknown in the U.S., or anywhere else for that matter: the "seven-minute pour." This is a way of serving a beer with a firm, rocky head that can rise up and over the rim of the glass without spilling.

This method requires that the bartender draw beer into the same glass three or four times, each time allowing several minutes for the head to properly condense and strengthen. So that customers are not made to wait a full seven minutes for their beer, a good bartender has several glasses waiting at various stages of readiness.

One Chicago-area brewer of a high-quality Pilsner beer (Baderbrau) once asked all his draught outlets to serve his beer this way but was scoffed at: They all said no American would ever wait that long for a beer.

German shrines

Here are the shrines to visit in Germany. Note that you can't taste all of Munich's beers at one place: Each place either has its few favorites or is a *tied house,* which is owned by one of the breweries and features only that brewer's brand. Good guides list the beers served at each location.

The Hofbräuhaus (Court brew house), Munich: The oldest and most famous beer hall in all of Germany (and thus, probably, the world — see Figure 13-1). Because of its enormity (it can seat over 4,000 people on three levels), its antiquity (it was commissioned in 1589 by Duke Wilhelm V), and political history (both Adolf Hitler and Vladimir Lenin plotted here), the beer may seem secondary — but it's not! Standards plus seasonals such as Delicator in March, Maibock in May, and Märzen from September to October are all wonderful.

Zum Uerige, Düsseldorf: A brewpub of local renown, said to brew the finest altbier in all of Germany.

Köln: Any one of the dozens of small local brewhouses that serve the local delicacy, Kölsch beer (P. J. Fruh's is a tourist favorite).

Villages: Some small villages boast their own breweries, each with a distinctive recipe. Try the local stuff: The perfect liter may await you (and modern ways make these small-fries somewhat endangered).

Figure 13-1: After strolling the Marienplatz and watching the daily tolling of the famous Neues Rathaus Glockenspiel, tourists flock to the Hofbräuhaus by the thousands to soak in the beer and sway to the music.

Photo reprinted courtesy of the German Information Center, New York, N.Y.

German festivals

Germany has no shortage of festivals. To attend one is to experience what Germans call *gemütlichkeit,* a distinctly German easy-going, genial good time. At the top of the heap is the revered and sometimes reviled Oktoberfest. Many others occur throughout the year and throughout Bavaria.

Oktoberfest (Munich), September–October: Ironically, this most famous fest *ends* on the first Sunday in October, having begun the second-to-last Saturday in September. All Oktoberfests began as harvest-time country fairs, but Munich's Oktoberfest bears little resemblance to a country fair today. Over six million people attend the event every year, the majority of whom do not live in Munich — or Germany, for that matter! Reservations are essential (full meals are served, and you can drink only when sitting down). Many travel agents sponsor all-inclusive tours; check with yours. Some "country fair": It even has its own World Wide Web site (http://www. munich-tourist.de)!

Canstatter Volksfest (Stuttgart), October: This autumn festival harkens back to the days of the simple country fairs and is considerably smaller than Oktoberfest. Noticeably missing are the tourists, but the beer is every bit as good and plentiful. Bavarian locals are more likely to do their celebrating here. The Volksfest begins just about the time Munich's debauch comes to a close.

Fasching (Bavaria), February: The German equivalent of Mardi Gras, a raucous pre-lenten celebration, Fasching ("fasting") is celebrated primarily throughout Bavaria, which has Germany's greatest concentration of Catholics.

Fruhjahrsbierfest (Munich), March: Begins on March 19 of each year (St. Joseph's Day).

Starkbierfest (Munich), March: Referred to as Munich's secret beer festival, the Starkbierfest is said to be every bit as big and rowdy as the Oktoberfest, but it is devoid of stark commercialism and drunken tourists (but not necessarily drunken Muncheners). The Starkbierfest ("strong beer fest") is held when the city is still shaking off the winter chill. For good reason: The Starkbierfest is a celebration of the annual release of the doppelbocks (doppelbock, locally called a "spring beer cure," usually sets the alcohol meter off at 7.5 percent alcohol by volume).

Schützenfeste (Hanover), July: Held throughout Germany, but the most notable is held each July in Hanover. Originally a sharpshooter's competition, this gathering of civil vigilante groups has been diluted over the centuries to become just another good excuse to have a beer party.

The biker's mug

In June 1922, when Franz Kugler, an enterprising young Munich tavern owner, blazed a bicycle path through the woods that skirted his Gasthaus property, over 13,000 cyclists tried it out. Realizing an impending shortage of blond beer, Herr Kugler quickly decided to mix the more plentiful dark beer with bottles of clear lemon soda that he happened to have in abundance. Not one to miss a promotional opportunity, Kugler told the cyclists that this concoction was something he invented especially for them so they would not get too tired or inebriated for their return ride home. The *Radlermass* ("bicyclist's mug"), as he named it, became a hit, and mixed beer drinks were born.

Beers to look for in Germany:

Andechs	Bitburger Pils	Maisel's	Weihenstephan
Augustiner	Hannen Alt	Paulaner	
Ayinger	Küpper's Kölsch	Spaten	

German museums

Brauerei Museum (Dortmund): Part of the Kronen Beer Works.

Brauereimuseum (Luneburg): Located in a building that served as a brewery for over 500 years. A large stein collection is the centerpiece.

Schwaebisches Brauereimuseum (Stuttgart): Museum of brewing history as well as current brewing techniques.

U.K. (England, Scotland, and Wales)

The U.K. may lack the number of brewers that Germany has, but it makes up for it in the variety of beers offered (hundreds) and the sheer number of pubs — about 80,000. Hard work, this beer-trekking stuff, if you want to visit even a small percentage of them.

The U.K. is the ale stronghold of the world. Similar to the U.S. brewing industry, a handful of large, national breweries dominate the market, but over 200 brewpubs, micros, and regional brewers produce the more interesting and more flavorful interpretations of traditional styles for impassioned consumers, especially cask-conditioned ale (unpasteurized, unfiltered, naturally carbonated, hand-pumped beer; also called Real Ale). These delicate brews are treated

German mixed beer drinks

Altbier-bowle: Altbier poured over a goblet or small bowl of fresh fruit. Popular in the region near Düsseldorf, long associated with altbier.

Altschuss ("alt shot"): Equal parts altbier and cola.

Alsterwasser ("Alster water"): Equal parts light lager (the Munchener Helles type, not lite beer) and lemonade or lemon soda.

Bierbowle: Like the altbier-bowle, but for a half dozen people. Six 12-ounce bottles of light lager, 8 ounces strained sour cherries, the ground pulp of 1 whole lemon, 2 ½ tablespoons sugar, and 12 ounces whiskey, served cold.

Biergrog: A heated mixture of dark beer (12 ounces), 3 tablespoons sugar, and grated lemon peel to taste.

Bismarck: Dark beer mixed with champagne. A favorite of Prussian Chancellor Otto von Bismarck.

Heller Moritz: Equal parts wheat beer and champagne or sparkling wine.

Honigbier ("honey beer"): A heated mixture of light lager, 1 ½ tablespoons honey, ¼ cup oatmeal — shot of whiskey optional.

Luttje Lage: More of an exercise in manual dexterity than a drink. In northern Germany, the "tricky devil" is performed by hoisting two small glasses that are held between the digits of the same hand. One glass, held above the other, contains whiskey or schnapps that pours into the lower glass (filled with beer) as it is poured into the mouth. You only practice this so much.

Radlermass: Dark beer and lemon soda (see the "The biker's mug" sidebar).

Russ: Similar to the Radlermass; substitute wheat beer for the dark beer.

Schaumbier ("foam beer"): A heated mixture of light lager, with 2 eggs, ½ cup sugar, and grated lemon peel beaten together.

locally like estate-bottled wines are in France, and with reason: They don't travel — further justification to go there yourself. Ironically, even the beer made by the British national brewers (such as Bass) is considered premium stuff in the U.S. In short, one drinks well in Great Britain.

Almost any pub offers the British standard, *bitter,* but bitter is not so bitter — it is fairly light-bodied, lightly carbonated, and light in alcohol (the "bitter" is an ancient tag dating from when hops were first used). Not all pubs offer a wide array of styles, but many do feature big, bold, and brawny beers, such as Scotch ales, old ales, and barleywines (see Chapter 1 and Appendix B), that are so strong that they may well put you under the table quicker than you can say, "Llanfairpwllgwyngyllgogerychwyrndrobwllllantysiliogogogoch" (which happens to be the town in Wales with the longest name in the world).

Many of the pubs in the U.K. are tied houses — they are at least partly owned by a brewery and therefore can serve only the beers of that particular brewery. You can usually spot a tied house by the mention of the brewery, or the beer served within, on the pub sign. If you want to try a variety of lesser-known beers, avoid the tied houses.

Pub games

Regardless of a pub's ownership or the beers served, pub games are popular throughout the U.K. Pub games are considered by some beer nuts to be central to British culture, if not the embodiment of it. They aren't, but they are fun. Darts, of course, are commonplace, but other lesser-known games — such as cribbage, dominoes, and the British pub favorite skittles, a table-top version of nine-pin bowling that uses finger-sized *skittles,* or pins — can often be seen in play.

The Campaign For Real Ale (CAMRA) is *the* source for information on good beer in the U.K. and on the continent. In addition to reeducating their countrymen about traditional, cask-conditioned Real Ale, the folks at CAMRA publish the best, most incredibly detailed guides for the beer-oriented tourist (notes include "real fire in fireplace," "family room," and "traditional pub games played"): *The Good Beer Guide* lists over 5,000 pubs in Great Britain (England, Wales, Scotland, Northern Ireland, and the Channel Islands, all listed by county) that serve good cask-conditioned ale; nothing but the real thing makes it into this passionate beer guide — a must-have. Another CAMRA book, *Good Pub Food,* helps out with notes on a lesser-form of nourishment (CAMRA also has similar guides to Bavaria and to Belgium and Holland).

Beer drinkers new to the U.K. might be taken aback by the odd, humorous, and sometimes vulgar names given to British beers by their brewers: Baz's Bonce Blower, Bishop's Tipple, Blackout, Croaker, Double Dagger, Enoch's Hammer, Head Cracker, Once a Knight, Roger & Out, Tanglefoot, Topsy-Turvy, Willie Warmer, and Wobbly Bob can all be ordered without putting your tongue in your cheek; others might put a little blush in them.

Great Britain's great pub grub

The old standbys include ploughman's lunch (cheese and bread plate), steak and kidney pie, shepherd's pie (beef, potatoes, and veggies), bangers and mash (sausage and mashed potatoes), pasties (a northern variation on shepherd's pie), and the ever-present fish and chips (the British version of a burger and fries). Other gustatory treats may include upside-down pie (stilton cheese and bacon), jacket spud (baked potato), curries, vegetable hot-pot, and Yorkshire pudding. In Scotland, you can investigate gammon steak (ham), neeps and tatties (turnips and potatoes), and haggis (you don't want to know).

Warm is the norm

You may have heard that the British drink their beer warm. Warm, in this case, is a relative term. Compared to the palate-numbing temperatures at which U.S. lagers are served, British ales are served warm, but try taking a "warm" bath in water that's 55 degrees F (13 degrees C). This is considered cellar temperature and the proper serving temperature for most English ales. For good reason: Products that are warm-fermented do not fully express their qualities when served too cold.

Brewpubs, or *homebrew pubs,* as they are sometimes called in the U.K., are becoming increasingly popular. One well-known chain is the "& Firkin" chain: Fox & Firkin, Falcon & Firkin, Ferret & Firkin, Frog & Firkin, and so on. (A *firkin* is a 40.9-liter barrel.)

U.K. shrines

U.K. breweries and brewpubs: The U.K. has too many good breweries to put on the A list — you'll never see them all. Your best bet is to check out the local pubs in each town (some tours make a point of this). Most pubs offer good food and even better beer, not to mention an excellent opportunity to mix with the locals and hear interesting stories about past customers. Plenty of guidebooks and tours in the bigger cities exist for this purpose. (If you're a Charles Dickens fan, you'll feel quite at home at the Saracen's Head, in Bath, where Dickens wrote *The Pickwick Papers.*)

The Traquair House, Innerleithen, Scotland: A four-story manor house (now a museum) with not only a small working brewery but an abundance of history dating back to the 1500s (Bonnie Prince Charlie, leader of the Jacobite rebellion against the English Monarchy, supped here). You won't want to miss the Traquair House Ale.

Edinburgh, Scotland: A great town for walking, and its numerous pubs make it perfect for a pub crawl — Rose Street in the New Town section has Britain's highest density of pubs per square foot. Many serve cask-conditioned ale. Ales are usually labeled by strength, as in Light, Heavy, Export, and Wee Heavy (so strong it must be served in wee servings). Alternative units are expressed as 60 to 90 shillings.

Southeastern England: In addition to visiting the breweries and pubs, if you're here in the late summer or early autumn, check out the famous hop farms that dot the countryside in Kent County, "the garden of England" and home of the famed East Kent Golding variety. The high trellises are amazing to see.

U.K. festivals

CAMRA's *Good Beer Guide* lists over 100 festivals by date and location, complete with local phone numbers. Its local branches also organize regional beer festivals throughout the country and throughout the year. Consult CAMRA's monthly newsletter, *What's Brewing*.

Here's one festival to visit:

> **The Great British Beer Festival (London), August:** Held yearly in the Grand Hall at Olympia, London. The Campaign For Real Ale (CAMRA) is responsible for putting together this largest beer festival on British soil, said to rival the Great American Beer Festival in Denver, Colorado (see Chapter 14). In addition to hundreds of varieties of beer and cider, the festival offers pub games, collectibles, publications, and contact with various beer-related organizations.

Beers to look for:

Adnams	Fuller	Samuel Smith
Belhaven	Gibbs Mew	Shepherd Neame
Eldridge Pope	Marston	Young

U.K. museums

> **Bass Museum (Burton-upon-Trent, Staffs):** The big one, including the entire history of beer in general and Bass in particular, along with a small brewhouse (you can help brew!), bar, restaurant, and stables. Free entry.

> **Heritage Brewery Museum (Burton-upon-Trent, Staffs):** Working brewery; beer included in entrance fee.

> **Whitbread Hop Farm (Beltring, Kent):** Family park with Shire horses, other animals, and lots of non–beer-related entertainment.

English mixed beer drinks

Black Velvet: Stout and champagne. According to pub lore, the stout represents the common folk, and the champagne represents nobility (what a tired old stereotype). Great with oysters.

Brown Betty: Ale and brandy served warm. In Old England, this drink was served with spiced toast intended for dipping.

Brown Velvet: Stout and port wine.

Ireland

Ironically, though well known for both its wonderful pub culture (the tales! the music!) and internationally successful brewers Guinness, Murphy, and Beamish, Ireland doesn't have many breweries, museums, or festivals. Just plenty of pubs, wonderful pubs. Dry stout is the national brew, and the major brands display a range of dryness.

Guinness Brewery, Dublin: Established in 1759, the Guinness St. James Gate Brewery produces the world's finest dry stout. Check out the Guinness Museum: the history of brewing in Ireland, beer advertising, brewing equipment, cooper's tools, and free samples of Guinness Stout.

Dublin pub crawls: Done with great flair here. A traditional Irish music crawl can be improvised with advice from the locals; the Literary Pub Crawl is led by actors performing O'Casey, Beckett, Yeats, Joyce, Behand, and other Irish luminaries, with a little bit of local lore thrown in for good measure.

Belgium

Belgium is heaven for beer explorers.

Beer is Belgium's claim to fame, in beer lovers' eyes, much as wine is to France. With over 100 breweries (and almost ten times that, a few generations ago) in a country of ten million, you can see why. And the brewers produce over 50 definitive styles, in more than ten times as many brands, including more famous specialty beers than any other nation.

Belgian gastronomy, unlike its history or sociology, is legendary among European countries, perhaps ranking a close second behind French *haute cuisine*. Featuring dishes made with beer or matched to beers, *cuisine à la bière* is a Belgian specialty not to be missed. Definitely seek it out.

Belgian brewers continue to produce beer styles that were developed over centuries — some still using yeast strains that are direct descendants of the originals. Many of these beer styles are indigenous to Belgium and made nowhere else in the world; others are emulated elsewhere, often with disappointing results. Either way, that necessitates a trip to sample the local beer, freshly made and freshly drawn. The beer is often served in proprietary glassware, an interesting and amusing attraction in itself.

Shooting hops

Perhaps the most beer-appropriate dish, served only in the early spring, is a plate of delicate hop shoots, prepared and served like asparagus. This traditional peasant dish is served with a light sauce and topped with poached eggs and croutons.

Like the beers they produce, many Belgian breweries are antiquated. Sadly, they are slowly going out of business in this modern age of marketing and mergers. The century-old brewhouses are like working museums. Some brewers even refuse to brush away the cobwebs, claiming that they don't want to disturb the spiders and the very essence of the brewery. In the same vein, Belgium's specialty-beer cafés often feature collections of nostalgic beer memorabilia as their decor. Again, a location call is the only way to appreciate this. Go!

Belgian shrines

Abbey Road: Trappist ale fans should prearrange a visit to some of the five beer-producing Trappist abbeys in Belgium (there's a sixth one across the border in Holland that should be included, too): Rochefort, Scourmont (Chimay), Orval in the south and southeast, Westmalle in the north, and Westvleteren (St. Sixtus) in the west. Not only do these abbeys produce beer for secular consumption, but some of them, such as Chimay and Orval, produce abundant amounts of cheese and bread as well.

Lambic lane: Lovers of lambic beer will want to take a spin on the Bruegel route, south and west of Brussels. Named for the famed Flemish painter, the route will take you through the villages that inspired his landscapes. In many of these villages, the unique lambic beer is either brewed or blended (blended lambic beer is called *gueuze*).

Cafés: All the larger cities (and many of the quainter towns) have at least one outstanding beer bar or café (cafés in Belgium are as widespread as pubs in England). Some cafés are known to stock as many as 500 different Belgian beers. Outside of Brussels, the medieval town of Bruges has more cafés than any other town of its size.

Belgian festivals

Poperinge Hopfesten (Poperinge), every third September: Poperinge is located in the middle of Belgium's small hop-growing region. This festival features a folkloric procession of townspeople, a hop-picking contest, and a lot of beer drinking. Unfortunately, the Hopfesten is held only every three years — 1996, 1999, 2002, and so on. At other times, drive the 36-mile hop route around the 85 hop farms.

Carnaval de Binche (Binche), February: Dating back to the 14th century, this annual celebration takes place during Shrovetide (the three days preceding Ash Wednesday) and features barrel-tapping and dancing in the streets.

Leuven Bierfest (Louvain), May: Another annual beer festival, this one during Whitsuntide (usually mid-May).

Adriaan Brouwer Bierfesten (Oudenaarde), June: An annual commemorative beer festival held yearly in honor of the famous painter born here in 1605.

Beers to look for:

Boon	DeKluis	Rodenbach	Various Trappist beers
Brasserie à Vapeur	Duvel	Silly	
De Koninck	Maes	Sterkens	

Those looking for a break from Belgian specialty beers should look for the best-selling Belgian Pilsner beer, Stella Artois.

Belgian museums

Brewer's Guildhouse and Confederation of Belgian Brewers Museum (Brussels): Though it's not a brewery, this palatial museum (headquarters of the Knights of the Mashing Fork) is one of the biggest beer shrines in all of Europe, appropriately located on Brouwers straat ("brewer's street"), on the Grand'Place. In one of the city's greatest ironies, the famous fountain known as the Mannekin Pis (a cherubic child unburdening his bladder) is located right there, too.

Oud Beersel 1882 Museum (Beersel): Located at the Vendervelden Brewery, brewing artifacts in the small museum form an extension of the brewery tour. Great name for a brewing town!

Bruges Brouwerij Mouterij Museum (Bruges): Located in an old malt house, this site shows the history of brewing in the city of Bruges.

Musée Bruxelloise de la Gueuze (Brussels): A living museum-brewery of the Cantillon brewery, with displays of brewing history (tours include free beer sample). Public brewing sessions are held in March and September.

Musée Européen de Brasserie (Romedenne): Brewing equipment and memorabilia are on display in the old Bouty Brewery.

Musée des Bières Belges (Lustin): Special beers are served along with the admission fee. A remarkable collection of breweriana, including bottles and more for sale. Open weekends except by appointment and July and August; annual breweriana fair with trading and sale each May.

Czech Republic

The Czechs drink about as much beer as any population does, per capita. Locally produced beers can be found in almost every Czech town.

Pivovarske Museum (Plzen): This brewery museum is set up in a Gothic malthouse in the historically significant town of Plzen (birthplace of Pilsner beer).

Urquell Brewery (Plzen): The Urquell Brewery introduced the world to the golden, clear Pilsner beer, granddaddy of all commercial lagers. This area was the medieval kingdom of the good King Wenceslas. Devotees say the beer doesn't travel well. Try it on site — need I say more?

U Fleku Pubhause (Prague): Second largest brewpub in the world (the largest, Wynkoop, is in Denver, Colorado). Also the oldest, started in 1499. Only one beer is served here — oddly enough, a dark lager.

Budweis: Any beer from this town, once the location of the royal brewery, is called Budweiser (note the relationship to kings). It is a local brew on which Anheuser-Busch modeled its flagship brew long ago (the lawyers are still working out the details). Michelob is also based on a nearby town name. In the 1500s, there were 44 breweries, but now there are only two. Do some comparison shopping!

Other Worldly Highlights

A serious beer trekker need not stop with the major brewing countries: Other countries hold plenty of discoveries, although because of locals' loyalties to their favorite brews, finding unusual beers may be harder. As always, ask about any beer-lovers' groups as a lead to specialty bars or beer festivals.

Austria

An entire beer style — Vienna lager — is attributed to old Vienna, which still has some wonderful brewpubs but only one brewery. Throughout the country, breweries are known to operate very good restaurants, too.

Denmark

Carlsberg Brewery (Copenhagen): Site of much study and development of the lager beer style.

Carlsberg Museum (Copenhagen): A century of Danish brewing is on display at the country's largest brewing company.

The Netherlands

Amsterdam: Heineken is the world's second biggest brewer — Budweiser being the biggest — and a tour of its brewery in Amsterdam is great fun (the main facility, outside of Amsterdam, is the largest brewery in Europe).

Biermuseum de Boom (Alkmar): Displays of brewing, malting and cooperage set up in an old brewhouse.

Brouwerijmuseum Raaf (Heumen): A brewery tour is included in a visit to the museum, which features old brewing equipment.

Maastrict: Small city with 365 pubs (one for each day of the year?). Pubkeepers all over the Netherlands are famous for their passion for and knowledge of beer.

Berkel-Enschot: The only Trappist beer produced outside of Belgium, Schaapskooi beer is made at the Koningshoeven Abbey (*Abdij* in Dutch) and sold under the name La Trappe.

Bokbier Festival (Amsterdam), November: The Dutch group PINT celebrates bock beers on the first or second weekend of November. It is one of the oldest consumer organization festivals in the world.

Norway

The Aass Bryggeri (pronounced ōhss) brewery in Drammen, Norway. Outstanding quality beers in a variety of styles.

Australia

Australia gets honorable mention, especially because it's not in Europe. The Australians are notorious for their high per-capita consumption, which is on par with the Germans and the Czechs. This should come as no surprise for a hot, arid country with a wild frontier past. I understand that the Aussies prefer their beer ice cold (they probably don't get many complaints from visiting Yanks). This is one of the reasons why Australian bars serve beer in small glasses: It can be drunk more quickly, without suffering any loss of coldness.

Despite the deep Anglo influence on the Australian brewing industry and an occasional well-made ale, this is a lager beer country-continent. Some of the standout ales include Cooper's Real Ale and Stout, Tooth's Sheaf Stout, and national favorite Castlemaine XXXX (known affectionately as "four-ex").

In addition to being a thirsty lot, Australians are also said to be perennially ready for a beer party. Two people and a couple of bottles of beer qualify. Sounds like fun to me!

Locations of note include some brewpubs: The Pumphouse Brewery in Sydney, the Loaded Dog Pub in Melbourne, The Sail & Anchor Pub, and Good On Yer in Fremantle (a brewpub since 1952). While you're Down Under, take note that there seem to be plenty of brewpubs in New Zealand.

The Australian National Festival of Beers is held every July in Kangaroo Point, featuring over 50 Aussie brews on draught.

Japan

Throughout Asia, the German influence on brewing is unmistakable, and light lagers predominate. The internationally famous Japanese megabrewers have some beer gardens (Sapporo has the most famous one, in Sapporo) and theme pubs, and more and more bars are opening with large international beer selections, featuring Belgian and American microbrewed beers. Homebrewing is beginning to catch on, as are microbreweries and brewpubs. And don't forget that the Japanese have been brewing a long time: Sake is actually beer, made entirely from rice. Now sake brewers are making craft-brewed beers, thanks to recent changes on laws.

Thailand

Not only does Thailand have some well-established megabrewers, but a celebrated German brewer, Paulaner, has just opened a beer hall in Bangkok.

A beer is a bier is a pivo

Here's how to ask for a beer in various countries:

Country	"Beer"	Country	"Beer"
China	*mai chiu*	Italy	*birra*
Czechoslovakia	*pivo*	Japan	*biru*
Denmark	*ol*	Latvia	*alus*
Finland	*olut*	Netherlands	*bier*
France/Belgium	*bière*	Poland	*piwo*
Germany	*Bier*	Spain/Mexico	*cerveza*

Chapter 14

North American Beer Tours and Festivals

• •

In This Chapter

▶ Bustling through breweries

▶ Frequenting festivals

▶ Making much of museums

• •

*Y*ankee beer enthusiasts can no longer complain: Good beer is almost everywhere!

Despite beer's decidedly European roots, American beer explorers needn't travel too far to sate their curiosity. People can find lots to celebrate and explore in North American breweries, beer festivals, and even brewery museums (such as their mere existence in the country that actually tried to outlaw alcohol). And because microbrewed or brewpub beer is not distributed nationally, beer exploration in the U.S. and Canada provides great rewards at every turn. Talk about instant gratification!

With over 1,000 craft brewers or brewpubs now plying their trade in the U.S. and Canada, you can find good beer just about everywhere, though it's concentrated in the big urban areas. While beer generally isn't regional, at least one region merits special mention: the Pacific Northwest — beer nirvana, the Promised Land for American beer explorers. Great pubs, great publicans, great microbreweries, innovative brewers. Some 30 percent of the world's hops are grown here, along with 30,000 tons of barley each year.

Here are some U.S. beer highlights:

> ✔ Oregon has the most microbreweries per capita of any state (54 in 1995, or 1 for every 50,000 good citizens) and is probably the only state with a brewpub video and its own brewers' guild. Portland, where you're never more than 10 or 15 minutes from a brewpub or microbrewery, is referred to as Munich on the Willamette (ironically, Portland, Maine, is a close rival — Munich on the Atlantic?). For more information, contact the Oregon Brewers' Guild.

> ✔ Boston has instituted a very tame and short pub crawl, with the help of a beer trolley (Olde Towne). At least one tour operator offers a "Boston Pub Tour" and a week-long Maine Coast brewery tour, too.
>
> ✔ Washington, D.C., is home to several enormous brewpub beer gardens, some with outdoor seating for hundreds.
>
> ✔ Denver is home to the largest brewpub in the world (Wynkoop).

In the U.S., beer destinations have arrived. And with the 50 to 100 percent growth predicted for the industry in the next few years, new beer destinations will continue to arrive on the scene. You beer explorers will have to keep going and going and going to sample them all.

Craft beer lovers are a particularly enthusiastic lot. They've inspired or created a market for a number of guidebooks and periodicals to support their thirst for beer knowledge. Several good books list brewpubs and small breweries; others either feature or merely include beer bars. Among the noteworthy are my own book (ahem) *Beer Across America: A Regional Guide to Brewpubs and Microbreweries,* as well as *On Tap* (regional series) and *Beer Traveler's Guide.* Keep your eyes out for regional and local guides, such as the Craft Brewers Guild's *Good Beer Guide to New York City.* Two periodicals devoted entirely to traveling in search of new brewpubs and microbreweries are *Brew* magazine and *Beer Travelers* newsletter. And one enterprising artist has even created a road map for all breweries (Coop's).

For a detailed listing of these and other publications, see Appendix D.

Brewery Tours

Brewery tours are one of the few ways people can taste beer for free (or almost free) and get a brief education in brewing processes all in the same afternoon. What's more, brewery tours are nothing new — major breweries have been hosting them for years as part of their ongoing public-relations programs (Anheuser-Busch even possesses a national landmark, the Clydesdale stables), and the passion of microbrewery and brewpub owner/brewers is such that a tour is usually a sure bet for a fun thing.

Each of the big, nationally known brewhouses has regularly scheduled, multi-media tours that eventually lead to a spacious and comfortable tasting room, sure to include a gift shop in the hopes that you will feel compelled to buy something in return for the hospitality. Some regional brewers also have tours of various types, while others can't be bothered (or can't for insurance reasons).

Mexican beer

If a microbrewing movement is taking place in Mexico, it's an underground one. Mexico's current economy and peasant traditions are not likely to support any widespread effort to glamorize beer. Beer fiestas? Well, maybe someday. Presently, for the most part, beer is considered just another beverage. Surprisingly, a decade ago, the government mounted a campaign to call beer "una bebida de moderacion" — a beverage of moderation — in order to stem the rising incidence of public intoxication.

The half dozen or so major brands are mostly pale lagers, with two notable exceptions. The brewer of Corona (a minor brand in Mexico) is also responsible for producing one of the country's few dark beers: Negra Modelo. The relatively malty Dos Equis is a small wonder: a descendant of the Vienna lagers brewed there during the mid–19th-century Austrian occupation by Emperor Maximilian.

Tip: The Mexican *beísbol* (baseball) Hall of Fame is housed on the grounds of the huge Cuauhtemoc Brewing Company in Monterrey. Visitors can sample beer for free in its breezy beer garden.

Things are more casual on the microbrewery level. An advance phone call is usually enough to get you in the door. Brewpubs require only a gift for gab on the brewer's and customer's parts (and a moment when the brewer is not super-busy). In some cases, all you have to do to see the brewing operation is to turn a bit on your bar stool (my kind of exercise).

At these smaller places, given the nature of the industry, you'll be able to meet the brewmaster, the maintenance crew, the owner, and the president all with the shake of one hand. You won't find a better opportunity to learn the intimate side of brewing, and the enthusiasm for the craft at this level can be infectious. Watch out, though — you might find yourself helping to clean up!

Beer Festivals

Beer lovers love to celebrate. Craft-beer fests seem to be popping up wherever a small conglomeration of brewpubs or microbreweries exists. Could it be that beer is a good social lubricant? Something to ponder.

Americans are quickly learning that the true meaning of "beer festival" goes far beyond the ubiquitous Oktoberfests that take place in practically every two-horse town in the country. You need a little more than grilled bratwurst and oom-pah music to please the beer crowd nowadays. In beer festival parlance, *quantity* means *variety,* as in number of brewers and styles — not a high rate of consumption. And you need good beer. Craft-brewed beer.

Beer festivals are becoming somewhat standardized, with the hosts having learned from early mistakes.

- ✔ Attendees can expect to pay a healthy entrance fee, but this is easily justified in order to cover high insurance premiums, rental of the hall or festival grounds, a mess of Port-a-Potties, advertising, and festival glassware (the glasses may become collector's items, especially if they're dated).

- ✔ If the cost of the beer itself is not included in the entrance fee, then serving tickets or tokens may be purchased for a little more than pocket change. Some festivals serve as little as 1 ounce per beer (usually the festivals with all-inclusive entrance fees, of course), while others allow as much as 10- or 12-ounce servings.

Beer festivals aren't just places to taste-test beer nowadays. Many of these extravaganzas now feature homebrew demonstrations, cooking-with-beer seminars, book signings, and sponsored booths peddling all kinds of beer-related goods and paraphernalia.

At the smaller festivals, one of the treats is to chat with the brewer and get the sense of passion and artistry that is so much a part of craft brewing. As festivals tend to grow (and grow in popularity), this is unfortunately becoming rare. Staff or volunteers do the pouring and talking now.

If you're really into beer and fun, you can volunteer to be a server or guide at a festival — a good idea whose time has come and whose rewards are simple (guess what).

Beer festival do's and don'ts

As a slightly jaded veteran of many local, regional, and national beer festivals, I've come up with a list of do's and don'ts to maximize your enjoyment and learning at beer festivals — it's a rough job, but hey, somebody's gotta do it.

Do's:

- ✔ Bring a designated nondrinking driver or scout out public transportation.

- ✔ Get there early to avoid a huge crowd. Crowds can hinder any conversation you may try to have with a brewer. And parking is usually less of a problem for early birds.

- ✔ Take, use, and keep your festival program. The large and well-established festivals hand out detailed programs loaded with fun and educational information that may be useful for months beyond the festival date. Plus you need to keep on top of the schedule for demonstrations and classes.

✔ Wear comfortable shoes; expect to walk and stand around a lot. Beer festivals are not known for lounge-chair seating accommodations.

✔ Dress appropriately. Protect yourself from the sun if the festival is outdoors.

✔ Bring along a small backpack or large fanny pack (read on).

✔ Bring a portable container of drinking water. Too often, the glass-rinsing stations are out of water, and drinking fountains are either hard to find or draw long lines. Heat, humidity, and beer drinking are not the best of partners. Dehydration is a problem worth avoiding.

✔ Bring bread, pretzels, crackers, or some kind of munchies (avoid greasy or spicy items if you are taking your tasting seriously).

✔ Bring a pen or pencil and a small pad of paper and take (legible) notes of the beers you taste. You'd be surprised how valuable good notes can be the next time you visit your favorite beer store or festival. You'd also be surprised at how much you can forget after four hours of beer tasting!

✔ Bring a plastic cup to use at the festival (if you should happen to find the kind with an attached string to hang around your neck, so much the better). Commemorative festival glasses, which are almost always not replaccable, have a way of breaking.

✔ Accept anything that is handed out free. You may not want all the buttons, pins, coasters, posters, and matchbooks, but someone you know might — and they're FREE!

Don'ts:

✔ Don't let lousy weather keep you from going to an outdoor beer festival unless the weather is *seriously* bad. Most festivals are shielded from the elements under large tents. A little rain in your beer is not a problem.

✔ Don't go to a beer festival on an empty stomach unless you are sure that food is being served there. Most beer festivals offer food, but quality and variety can vary greatly. Festival concessions can also be ridiculously expensive.

✔ Don't bring children. For the safety of your kid as well as for your own enjoyment, find an alternative to dragging Junior along with you.

✔ Don't buy a book or any other heavy item until you're ready to leave, or else you'll have to lug it around with you.

✔ Don't stand around the pouring table after receiving your beer. Nothing is more irritating than having to fight through a crowd to get to the beer. Get outta da way, already!

✔ Don't hang out all day or night at the table that serves your favorite beer. Be bold, be daring — try those beers that you can't get at the local Liquor Barn. Beer festivals are the best places to learn about a wide variety of unusual beers and beer styles. Don't make one place your corner tavern.

✔ Don't make tasting every single beer at the festival your goal. In some cases it can't be done; and in most cases, it shouldn't be.

✔ Don't drive after drinking beer.

Beer festivals in the U.S. and Canada

Here are a few of the better-known festivals. New ones are being organized faster than you can say, "Oktoberfest." To find out about more, keep up your contacts at brewpubs and homebrew-supply shops and check out the brewspapers and beer magazines as well as the various Web sites mentioned in Appendix D. They all seem to feature calendars. Beer enthusiasts certainly like to celebrate and explore — nice combination.

✔ **Northwest Microbrew Expo (Eugene, Oreg.), second week of February:** Held at the Lane County Convention Center. An estimated 60 brews from 30 breweries. Focus is on Pacific Northwest beers, but others are welcome. Features include live entertainment, a food court, and 15-minute brewers' "Beer Tours" that explain the brewing processes. Phone 800-284-6529 or 541-485-3907.

The Canadian beer scene

Brewing is nothing new up north. The John Molson Brewery in Montreal is the oldest operating brewery in North America, having been established in 1786.

The west coast city of Vancouver has been on the cutting edge of the microbrewing movement since the movement began, but the densest concentration of Canadian microbreweries, brewpubs, and beer bars is in Ontario. The Quebecois are not far behind. You'll find good places to visit in the cities of Toronto, Hamilton, Kitchener, London, Guelph, and Montreal.

Virtually unknown to Americans fed a steady and very limited diet of Canadian golden lagers and pale ales, the popular Maple Leaf megabrewers such as Labatt's and Molson produce a fairly wide variety of brand names and beer styles for Canadians. A wonderful selection of bock beers, IPAs, stouts, porters, and malt liquors are common at the local government-run beer store. But they are painfully expensive: Blame it on the beer tax! And go brew your own at one of the many brew-on-premises (BOP) shops (see Chapter 12), where you can get good beer cheaper.

- ✔ **Midwest International Beer Exposition (Chicago, Ill.), spring:** A pay-as-you-go beer exposition and international celebration of beer held inside a major hotel. Runs from Friday to Sunday. Marquee names from the world of beer and brewing participate in many seminars, tastings, and events held throughout the weekend. Phone 708-678-0071.

- ✔ **Boston Brewers Festival (Boston, Mass.), second week of May:** More than 10,000 attendees annually. Provides a wide range of Canadian and American micro and specialty brews. Rollouts of new and hard-to-find brews are commonplace. Held at Boston's World Trade Center. Phone 617-547-2233.

- ✔ **Le Mondial de la Bière (Montreal, Canada), second week of June:** Competitions and over 200 beers from 25 countries are featured in this festival, held in the Old Port/Old Montreal area. Phone 514-722-9640.

- ✔ **International Brewmasters' Festival (Vancouver, Canada), second week of June:** 150 brewers from around the world compete for prizes at this popular festival, which may emphasize one style of beer each year. Phone 604-688-9609.

- ✔ **Colorado Brewers Festival (Ft. Collins, Colo.), June:** Over 10,000 thirsty people pack Ft. Collins' Pioneer Square every summer in anticipation of sampling something from each of Colorado's breweries. One product only from each of the home state's brewers — including Coors, of course — is showcased at this event. Brewers, food booths, local musicians, and assorted merchants all vie for your attention. Phone 970-484-6500.

- ✔ **Great Eastern Invitational Microbrewers Festival (Adamstown, Pa.), June, July, September:** Held at Stoudt Brewery–Black Angus Hall. Series of three weekend festivals showcasing beers produced in the eastern U.S. More than 50 specialty beers. Tasting sessions are held two a day in order to accommodate a greater number of participants. Great food to be had at the adjacent Black Angus Restaurant. Tickets sell out fast. Phone 717-484-4386.

- ✔ **KQED Beer & Food Fest (San Francisco, Calif.), July:** The Rolls-Royce of American Beer Festivals. Multinational in flavor. Showcases more than 200 beers from over 30 countries. Part beer tasting, part fund-raiser for public radio broadcasting, raising over $100,000 annually. Eclectic collection of live entertainment supplements beer and food. Well attended; advance ticket purchase is strongly recommended. Phone 415-553-2200.

- ✔ **Oregon Brewers' Festival (Portland, Oreg.), last weekend of July:** America's premier beer city is host to the biggest U.S. regional festival, featuring hundreds of beers from the numerous local breweries as well as from breweries around the world. The scenic Riverside Park in downtown Portland provides the perfect setting. A hophead's nirvana. Phone 503-778-5917; Web site http://www.jhw.com/~jhw/brewfest.

- ✔ **Great Taste of the Midwest (Madison, Wis.), third week of August:** The oldest and best one-day event in the Midwest — always a sellout. Hosted by the Madison Homebrewers & Tasters Guild. More than 40 breweries participated in 1995. Phone 608-256-1100.

- ✔ **Northwest Ale Festival (Seattle, Wash.), around Labor Day (first Monday in September):** More than just a beer festival, this is the country's biggest pub crawl — it lasts one week! With 25 to 30 Seattle-area ale houses featuring or spotlighting the beers of specific breweries. No entrance fee; just pay as you go. Sponsored by the Pint Post–Microbrew Appreciation Society. Phone 206-634-1433.

- ✔ **New York Beerfest — International Beer & Food Tasting (New York, N.Y.), September:** Two large outdoor tents erected on the Brooklyn waterfront underneath the famous eponymous bridge. Over 50 specialty beers from around the world are available for tasting. Typically New York — crowded, hectic, and incredibly festive. Phone 718-855-7882, extension 21.

- ✔ **Great Northwest Microbrewery Invitational (Seattle, Wash.), third week of September:** Held at the Seattle Center Exhibition Hall. Dedicated to microbreweries and brewpubs in the Pacific Northwest. Phone 206-232-2982.

- ✔ **Great American Beer Festival (Denver, Colo.), late September or early October:** The granddaddy of American beer festivals. Celebrated its 15th year in 1996 (see Figure 14-1). The single largest conglomeration of beers and brewers in America, with more than 1,200 beers from over 260 breweries across the nation. Join the more than 25,000 people who know where the real action is; meet the brewers, taste the medal winners, learn how to brew beer, or buy a beer book (another copy of this one?) and have it autographed by the author. The biggest and the best. Phone 303-447-0816; Web site http://www.aob.org/aob.

Kentucky Beer Camp

The Oldenberg Brewing Company in Ft. Mitchell, Kentucky, complete with a hotel and country music entertainment complex, hosts a beer festival that is altogether different.

Beer Camp is a semiannual, three-day extravaganza dedicated to learning about beer. Camp activities include discussions, seminars, and beer tastings — as many as 200 different varieties (as well as a camp oath and song, of course). Highlights of the weekend include brewing demonstrations, speakers and presentations from around the country, an old-fashioned cookout, a tour of the Oldenberg brewery, a Cincinnati pub crawl (nearby), and an opportunity to meet and speak with experts in the industry.

Beer Camp has been increasing in popularity every year, easily filling the 300 or so spots on the camp roster. Camp spirit tends to be strong — no homesick campers here! Call 800-323-4917 or 606-341-7223 for more information.

Other camplike events are becoming more and more common, such as one sponsored by the Ale Street News (see Appendix D) that combines beer tasting, expert-led classes, and dinners with a resort location. Brewpubs in resort areas have begun hosting "brewers' weekends," complete with hands-on brewing. Check with your travel agent for local versions.

Wonder what songs they sing around the campfires? "100 Bottles of Beer on the Wall"? (More like "20 Styles of Beer on Tap.") And what is the proper beer to serve with S'mores? Serious beer nuts want to know.

Logo reprinted courtesy of the Great American Beer Festival®.

Figure 14-1:
The Great American Beer Festival is well known for the coveted medals it doles out to brewers every year.

U.S. Beer Museums

Beer enthusiasts often cannot stop at the direct experience. Craving ever-more sudsy stimulation, they veer off the beaten track to the more contemplative scene of brewing museums (places that emphasize collecting rather than brewing are noted in Chapter 15). The few U.S. museums are not known for their completeness or scholarliness (some are also called — shudder! — entertainment complexes), but they come in enough variations to warrant exploration. Here are a few you may want to check out.

- ✔ **August Schell Brewing Company (New Ulm, Minn.):** An operating brewery since 1860. Tours include the brewery, the Schell family mansion, a deer park, and an on-site museum. Phone 507-354-5528.

- ✔ **City Brewery Museum (Galena, Ill.):** History of the host brewery, which closed in 1881. Phone 815-777-0354.

- ✔ **F. X. Matt Brewery, formerly the West End Brewery (Utica, N.Y.):** A veritable repository of antique brewery advertising; memorabilia is showcased on every wall of the brewery hospitality center. Phone 315-732-3181.

Old breweries

Like the F. X. Matt Brewery, most of the oldest and largest breweries in this country display a wealth of brewery antiques and advertising memorabilia. Check out the D. G. Yuengling brewery in Pottsville, Pennsylvania; the Jacob Leinenkugel Brewery in Chippewa Falls, Wisconsin; and the Dubuque Brewing Co. in Dubuque, Iowa.

✔ **One Hundred Center (Mishawaka, Ind.):** A shopping, dining, and entertaining experience. Occupies the buildings that once housed the Kamm & Schellinger Brewing Company in 1853. Plenty of relics left from the old brewery. Listed on the National Register of Historic Places. Phone 219-259-7861.

✔ **The Pabst Mansion (Milwaukee, Wis.):** Built in 1893 by Captain Frederick Pabst, founder of the Pabst Brewery. Phone 414-931-0808.

✔ **Seattle Microbrewery Museum (Seattle, Wash.):** Part of Beer Central in the Pike Place Historical District. A collection about the history of brewing in the northwest U.S. Phone 206-622-1880.

✔ **Wolf Brewery Caves (Stillwater, Minn.):** Part of a museum of an 1870 brewery. Phone 612-439-3588.

Where does a 2,000-pound horse sleep?

The Budweiser Clydesdales weigh up to 2,300 pounds and stand nearly 6 feet tall at the shoulder. Each horse may consume as much as 30 quarts of feed, 50 pounds of hay, and 30 gallons of water every day (no figures are available for beer consumption).

The ornate Clydesdale stables at the Anheuser-Busch brewing facility in St. Louis have been designated a National Historic Landmark and are a top tourist attraction.

Chapter 15

Collecting Beer Stuff

● ●

In This Chapter

▶ Collecting for fun and profit

▶ Answering the big question: what stuff to collect

▶ Joining breweriana clubs

● ●

*F*or some beer nuts, savoring a brew just isn't enough. They need something to hold on to, something to *keep*. Preferably something cheap, or free. Good beer is not cheap. So why not make up for that with beer tchotchkes?

These beer nuts become *breweriana* collectors. Anything and everything that was either used at a brewery or bar or bears the name of a brewery or a brand name is of value to these enthusiasts. Coasters, openers, labels, signs — anything goes. Or more correctly, anything stays. Not every collector is a complete maniac; casual collecting is just as much fun as compulsive collecting.

Many beer magazines have regular articles on the subject. The range of collectible items, both antique and new, is astounding. See Figure 15-1 for a couple of such items, as shown in a 1995 issue of the *American Breweriana Journal*. My collection has grown to probably over 5,000 items in little more than a dozen years. I don't specialize in anything in particular (I'll grab anything that's inexpensive), so my collection includes beer cans, bottles, coasters, bottle openers, bottle caps, bottle labels, mugs, steins, miscellaneous glassware, clocks, tap handles, beer trays, beer signs of all sizes and materials (including neon), posters, matchbooks, hats, and a couple of other items that I can't recall because they're stored in the garage attic. A curator I'm not.

Serious collectors get into more obscure promotional items, such as foam skimmers, ashtrays, brewing company letterheads, and "shelf talkers" (small, three-dimensional signs that are placed on store shelves to call customers' attention to a product). One avid brewerianist I know has old brewery hospitality-room chairs — complete with engraved brewery insignia — in his kitchen. These types of folks spend a lot of time and especially money tracking down those prized items that will make their collections "complete," although they'll never be completely satisfied. For them, breweriana collecting is somewhere between a hobby and a lifestyle. Maybe a mania.

Figure 15-1:
Brewery
promotional
items like
these are
fun to
collect.
Some are
poignant:
Schlitz
made this
decanter for
its 125th
anniversary;
seven years
later, the
business
closed.

Photos reprinted courtesy of Dick Cramer (Schlitz globe), Lynn Geyer (chalk dog), and the American Breweriana Journal.

What drives this urge? Nostalgia — lots of regional breweries are gone, but their names evoke places and times of our recent past — and the sheer fun of collecting. It's also a great link to other beer enthusiasts. Like drinking beer, collecting beer-related things acts as a great social lubricant. Collectors love to meet, organize, and swap.

Do I or Don't I?

If you think you may want to be a breweriana collector, here are some hints and suggestions to ponder before taking the plunge:

- ✔ Profit should be low on your list of reasons to start collecting. You've got to be *very* involved in the business to make any money.

- ✔ The value of breweriana is in direct relation to how rare a piece is. Obviously, older rare pieces can be very valuable. New stuff that is produced by the thousands has little to no value today, but that doesn't mean it won't have value someday.

- ✔ Educate yourself; join local and national breweriana clubs (most brewerianists' publications are a premium of membership in these organizations — see Appendix C).

- ✔ Peruse all the antique shops you want, but resist buying anything unless you know it's a good deal: Antique shops are notorious for inflating the prices on breweriana.

✔ Check out thrift shops and flea markets; some are hidden gold mines.

✔ Cruise the local garage sales in town; you never know where the good stuff can be found, and it's usually dirt-cheap! (Although I haven't been particularly lucky, a fellow collector I know has purchased items worth hundreds of dollars for only a couple of bucks.)

✔ Always gladly accept any piece of breweriana that is given to you or offered for a minimal price (that's how I got half my collection). Even if it doesn't appeal to you, you can always use it as trade bait.

✔ Specialize in one or a couple of different kinds of items; concentrate on those items specifically.

✔ Make sure that you have the space to store or display all this stuff once you bring it home.

Focusing Your Collection

Okay, now you're an active collector, and you want to specialize — what do you focus on? Remember, though, that not enough $1,000 beer glasses exist for every collector to have one (see the sidebar "The thousand-dollar pint"), so here's a list of various, more practical items and their pros and cons:

✔ **Bottles:** Two good reasons to stay away from beer bottles are (1) regular beer bottles are of little or no value (except for old, embossed bottles — those with raised lettering in the glass) and (2) bottles are heavy, breakable, and difficult to store. If you want to collect bottles, be prepared for a lot of headaches (so why do I have over a thousand of them?).

✔ **Cans:** Not as popular as they were in the 1970s, which is why you can pick up whole collections for a song, but can be of value if in good shape. "Cone tops" and cans with irregularities are still prized possessions. Cans are easy to damage if not stored right. All cans are prone to denting, and older tin cans will rust in humid conditions.

Do not store full cans — they will eventually leak!

Beer has been packaged in at least 13 different sizes of cans, from 7 ounces to 128 ounces. Nobody knows for sure how many different cans exist, but one conservative estimate suggests more than 20,000 cans of different sizes and brands.

✔ **Coasters:** Called *beermats* in the U.K. Of little value unless they're very old and in good condition (some have been auctioned for $200). Pristine coasters (no beer stains) are good for display purposes. Coasters are also easy to store.

✔ **Bar towels:** Very attractive, practically indestructible small towels used as place mats or coasters. Most good examples of brewery bar towels are found in the U.K., as they have never been widely produced in the U.S.

✔ **Bottle caps:** Of little or no value unless they're old (check for cork gasket) and in mint condition, but nice for display purposes.

The best way to avoid crimping a non–twist-off cap is to place a large coin over the cap before prying it off the bottle.

✔ **Bottle labels:** Very valuable if old, never used, and still in good shape. Require attentive storing because they are easily destroyed. Great for mounting and displaying. You may want to check out the interesting labels shown in figures in Chapters 1 and 8.

To start your label collection, write to as many breweries as you can and request fresh labels. Most will send them to you free (they think it's good public relations), although others may charge a couple of bucks for them. Include a self-addressed, stamped envelope with your request. Many labels are absolutely gorgeous; some are very funny.

✔ **Bottle openers:** Perhaps the best item to collect for a variety of reasons — bottle openers are small, easy to store, virtually indestructible under normal conditions, great for display purposes, and still functional. The downside is that very few of them have much value.

✔ **Glassware:** Glasses with brewery logos or brand names can be of great value, depending on the brewery and brand name. Also great for display purposes. I highly recommend against actually *using* the glasses in a collection, because they're so breakable. Either way, storage requires extra care.

If you're attracted to brewery glassware, consider collecting mugs instead of glasses. Mugs are generally heavier and more durable.

✔ **Matchbooks:** Very easy to store and can also be used for display purposes. Old matchbooks are fairly difficult to find, making your search a serious challenge and potentially getting you a high price for the ones that you do find.

✔ **Posters:** All paper breweriana have similar pros and cons: lightweight and easy to store but very easily damaged if not stored correctly. Paper items are good for display purposes.

✔ **Signs:** Neon signs are pretty expensive from the start and are very fragile. Unless you have money to burn and good storage or display facilities, I recommend another choice. Most of the old brewery signs were made of more durable materials, such as wood and tin. Today, many items are made of plastic and even cardboard. Consider your ability to store or display these items before purchasing.

The thousand-dollar pint

Recently, an auction record was set for a plain tumbler: A bidder paid $1,020 for the 19th-century glass that has a white porcelain surface decorated with a colored enamel logo (for the Anaconda Brewing Co. of Anaconda, Montana). Wonder what the coaster went for.

Photo reprinted courtesy of Pete Kroll, Glasses, Mugs & Steins.

✔ **Tap handles:** Great for display if you have a bar or similar setup. Made of wood, plastic, metal, or acrylic and come in all shapes and sizes. Quite a few different ones exist, but they're not cheap. If you plan to specialize in these, you'll have to break the piggy bank.

✔ **T-shirts:** This has got to be a new one. Breweries tend to try to outdo one another with their creativity and irreverence when it comes to this uniquely American apparel. Amazingly, even a T-shirt-of-the-month club exists (with the great motto "For those reluctant to change"): Brew Tees, 800-585-TEES.

✔ **Tokens and medals:** Breweries have commissioned coinlike tokens or wooden nickels for special events and promotions throughout the years. Mardi Gras seems to be a perennial favorite. Some are or were exchangeable for a beer.

✔ **Trays:** Pretty durable and fairly easy to store, offering good collecting potential. Old trays in good shape can command a respectable price. Trays also have good display value. Smaller "tip" trays are just as interesting but rarer.

Keep in mind that not all breweriana has to be old or antique. The thousands of breweries around the world currently making beer also produce an abundance of brewery items. Most of these can be bought only at the brewery. American brewpubs and microbreweries offer a wide variety of "beer wear" (hats, shorts, T-shirts, sweatshirts), along with beer glassware and the occasional traditional breweriana collectible.

The world of American breweriana collecting has progressed through basically four eras: pre-Prohibition, Prohibition, post-Prohibition, and renaissance (microbrewing). Technically, the present is both the post-Prohibition and renaissance eras. The difference is that some people stick to collecting items from microbreweries only, as opposed to those who continue to collect stuff from all other breweries. Recently defunct regional brewers seem to be more loaded with nostalgia than much older ones.

If you keep your eyes peeled, you can spot breweriana at a variety of non-brewery locations. The Smithsonian Institute in Washington, D.C., has some classic pieces of brewery antiques — signs and whatnot. Historical societies across the nation also use old brewery equipment and advertising to help tell the story of a region's development. But the best place to find breweriana is on the walls of brewpubs and bars and in some of the brewing museums noted in Chapters 13 and 14.

The little museum that can

The Museum of Beverage Containers, just outside Nashville, Tennessee (Goodlettsville, specifically; phone 615-859-5236), is dedicated to beverage containers and advertising and boasts over 300,000 beer and soda cans.

If that's not enough to can your can craving, check out the John Milovisch house in Houston, Texas, covered with over 50,000 cans, many of which were cut and rolled out. Since John's death, his son not only has continued to make small additions to "The Beer Can House" but has designed earrings made from beer-can pull tabs. It's wonderful what one family's passion can do for the world of art. (On the other hand, John's wife thought he had lost his mind when he started decorating the house with this rather unusual version of aluminum siding.)

The million-dollar, million-item collection

In 1951, Herb Haydock, a young cryptographer serving in Munich with the U.S. Air Force, bought eight locally made beer glasses, sparking a life-long interest that eventually led him to amass over 1 million beer and brewing memorabilia items from around the world.

With retirement looming on the horizon (and his house and garage bursting at the seams), Herb and his wife, Helen, were happy to find a buyer: Oldenberg Brewery and Entertainment Complex in Ft. Mitchell, Kentucky, which opened a new, dedicated home for the collection in 1987. The price was reported to be over $1 million, and

everything was meant to be on display, including frying pans, toothpicks, sewing kits, golf clubs, and button hooks.

Unfortunately, no more than 50 percent of the collection could be shown at any one time (it also overshadowed the brewing and music operations at Oldenberg), and in 1996, the collection was sold again, to the Miller Brewing Company, whose plans for the collection are not yet known.

Oldenberg has started a second breweriana collection of "only" 150,000 pieces, mostly from microbreweries.

Breweriana Clubs

Breweriana collectors are a gregarious lot. They like to share leads and swap stories as well as swap items.

You can find a number of good breweriana clubs around the country, some active, some not so. Most schedule swap meets (trading sessions) in addition to regular meetings; the national groups also hold lively annual meetings complete with tastings and brewery tours. They even have specialist groups, such as for coasters or glassware. One has a "home museum" certification program. These are dedicated folks!

A few of the larger and more dynamic associations also publish magazines or newsletters. Among the best is the bimonthly magazine of the American Breweriana Association, for which dues start at $25 per year. See Appendix C for more.

Beyond coasters and tap handles —
how about beer stocks?

So you say you love beer. You drink it. You brew it. You collect it. You bathe in it. Why not invest in it?

From providing major startup capital for a fledgling brewpub to buying shares in one of the established brewing conglomerates, you have nearly as many ways to invest as you have styles of beer to choose from. Surprisingly, fewer than a dozen brewers are listed on U.S. national stock exchanges. Many more are so small that they are registered only in their home states. One of these, the Portland Brewing Company, offers its shareholders a particularly enticing dividend: a free pint *daily* to those who own 100 shares or more.

Note: Some craft-brewing–company initial public stock offerings (IPOs) were dynamite, jumping 65 percent on the first day of trading, but they dropped 30 percent within a few weeks. As with any other investment, consider the pros and cons. Investing with any new or small business involves risks, and no stock is guaranteed to continually rise in value. Furthermore, the liquidity (how easily a security can be bought or sold) of the smaller microbrewery stocks can be very poor.

Some people are still attracted to these stocks. Could that have something to do with the ability to enjoy your favorite brew as a way to improve your bottom line?

Part VI
The Part of Tens

The 5th Wave   By Rich Tennant

"Cooking with beer? I've been doing it for years. Add it to the food? I'll have to try that sometime."

In this part . . .

Here's where you can apply your newfound knowledge and love of beer — in the kitchen, in travels, or in arguments with fellow beer nuts and neophytes. All kinds of fun and intriguing information are the chapters in this part.

I especially invite you to enjoy the wonderful recipes of Candy Schermerhorn in Chapter 16.

Chapter 16

Ten Great Food Recipes Featuring Beer

● ●

*T*he following recipes should be relatively easy to try. They should also inspire you to experiment with beer as an ingredient in other recipes.

These recipes were created especially for this book by Candy Schermerhorn, author of *The Great American Beer Cookbook* and owner/manager of Globe Brewery & Barbecue Co., a new brewpub located in the historic mining town of Globe, Arizona. In addition, Ms. Schermerhorn is a veteran culinary instructor (the featured culinary personality at the Great American Beer Festival for many years), writer, and consultant and does a weekly television cooking appearance.

Here are some common U.S. measures and approximate metric conversions:

Liquid Conversions	*Temperature Equivalents*	*Mass Conversions*
1 teaspoon = 5 milliliters	110° F = 43° C	1 ounce = 28 grams
1 tablespoon = 15 milliliters	275° F = 135° C	1 pound = 0.45 kilogram
1 ounce = 29.6 milliliters	350° F = 177° C	
1 cup = 237 milliliters	365° F = 185° C	
	375° F = 191° C	
	450° F = 232° C	

Roasted Garlic and Onion Soup

This delectable, fragrant soup will bring smiles of satisfaction to onion soup, garlic, and beer aficionados everywhere. The slightly nutty, sweet flavor of the brown ale gives the soup a whole new dimension!

Tools: *Small baking dish, two large saucepans*

Preparation time: *About 25 minutes*

Cooking time: *About 90 minutes*

3 large heads garlic	*1 teaspoon salt*
1¹/₂ teaspoons olive oil	*1¹/₂ teaspoons thyme or your favorite herb*
4 tablespoons butter	*2 tablespoons flour*
4 large yellow onions, thinly sliced	*5 cups beef or vegetable broth, hot*
2 large shallots, thinly sliced (optional)	*1 bottle brown ale*
1 tablespoon sugar	*croutons and fresh grated cheese (fontanel, kaseri, or Parmesan)*

1 Cut the tip end off each head of garlic to expose cloves. Drizzle each cut end with ¹/₂ teaspoon olive oil. Place on a baking dish and bake in a 275° oven for 45 minutes or until very soft. Cool and then pop cloves out of their papery skins.

2 In a large saucepan, heat butter over medium heat. Add sliced onions and shallots, cooking until translucent. Add sugar and salt, continuing to cook until mixture is caramel-gold. Heat broth in a separate saucepan.

3 Sprinkle herbs and flour over onions, stirring well. Cook 3 minutes. Stirring constantly, pour the hot broth over the onion mixture.

4 Mash roasted garlic with a fork. Add garlic and ale to soup and simmer for 30 minutes.

5 Serve in heat-proof bowls. Ladle in soup and top with croutons and a generous sprinkling of cheese.

Yield: 4 to 6 servings

You can roast additional heads of garlic for future use: Simply freeze the unpeeled heads in a well-sealed container.

Beer Batter Extraordinaire

This delicate batter is thin, flavorful, and crisp, with just a hint of smoky seasoning and the light crunch of cornmeal. It works best on firm foods: shrimp, onion rings, mushrooms, firm fish, and thin slices of firm veggies, such as sweet potato, eggplant, and zucchini. The batter is best used immediately after being prepared, so be sure to have all the rest of the ingredients (the food being battered) fully assembled beforehand.

Tools: *Large mixing bowl, medium mixing bowl, whisk, deep frying pan, candy thermometer*

Preparation time: *About 10 minutes*

Cooking time: *Depends on ingredients being fried*

³/₄ *cup flour*	*1 large egg, beaten*
¹/₄ *cup cornmeal*	¹/₄ *teaspoon liquid smoke*
2 teaspoons baking powder	*1 cup Kölsch or American wheat beer, ice cold*
1 teaspoon salt	
¹/₄ *teaspoon finely ground black pepper*	*oil for frying (preferably corn oil)*

1 In a large bowl, stir together flour, cornmeal, baking powder, salt, and pepper.

2 In a separate, smaller bowl, stir together egg, liquid smoke, and beer. Stir into the flour mixture and whisk briefly, but do not overmix. In the frying pan, begin heating oil to 365°.

3 Pat dry the ingredients to be fried and dust them lightly with flour immediately before dipping into the batter and frying.

Here are some hints for good frying results:

✔ Always heat oil from 350° to 375° F.

✔ Always use fresh oil.

✔ Use enough oil to cover the food by at least 1 inch (2.5 centimeters).

✔ Use a *long*-handled slotted spoon or *long* tongs.

✔ After removing food from the frying pan, place the food on paper towels.

Beer-Glazed Foccacia

This is the chewiest, fullest-flavored foccacia around, made just for beer lovers. Use the following dough recipe, or you can buy frozen bread dough, thaw, pat into a $1/2$-inch-thick circle and just follow Steps 4, 5, and 6.

Tools: *Candy thermometer, large mixing bowl, whisk, medium bowl, heavy skillet, pizza stone or baking sheet*

Preparation time: *About 2 hours (includes 90 minutes for rising)*

Cooking time: *About 20 minutes*

Dough:

$2/3$ cup water

$3^1/2$ to 4 cups bread flour, separated

1 tablespoon yeast

1 tablespoon sugar

$2/3$ cup hefeweizen (room temperature)

$1/2$ tablespoon dried basil

$1/2$ tablespoon kosher salt

$1/4$ cup grated Romano or Parmesan

2 tablespoons olive oil

$1/2$ teaspoon fresh ground black pepper

$1/2$ cup cornmeal

Glaze:

$1^1/2$ tablespoons olive oil

2 large yellow onions, sliced thin

$1/4$ teaspoon **each** salt and black ground pepper

$1/2$ tablespoon **each** dried basil and marjoram

$1/3$ cup Scottish ale

Suggested toppings: *strips of roasted red peppers, minced Canadian bacon, crumbled feta cheese, and strips of smoked provolone*

(continued)

1 Heat the water to 110°. In a large mixing bowl, combine $1/2$ cup bread flour with the yeast and sugar. Pour in water and whisk thoroughly. Let set for at least 15 minutes.

2 Stir in the hefeweizen, basil, salt, cheese, oil, black pepper, and cornmeal; beat thoroughly. Stir in more flour 1 cup at a time until the dough is too stiff to stir. Turn dough onto counter and knead, adding just enough flour to keep dough from sticking to the counter and your hands.

3 After 8 to 10 minutes of kneading, the dough will be smooth and elastic. Place in a lightly oiled bowl and cover with plastic wrap. Let rise until doubled — approximately 1 hour.

4 While dough is rising, heat $1^1/2$ tablespoons olive oil in a heavy skillet. Add onions and cook, stirring frequently until translucent. Add salt, black pepper, basil, and marjoram and cook until mixture is golden. Add Scottish ale and raise the heat. Continue to stir and cook until liquid is evaporated.

5 Punch dough down and let rest, covered, for 15 minutes. Using fingertips and a lightly oiled surface, stretch and pat dough into a $1/2$-inch-thick circle. Place on a pizza stone or baking sheet.

6 Rub dough with olive oil and spread with glazed onions. Top with peppers, bacon, feta, and provolone. Bake at 450° on lower shelf of oven until top is bubbly and bottom is golden — check after 15 minutes.

Yield: One 14- to 16-inch foccacia

Chile con Carne For Dummies

All cooks, whether novices or accomplished chefs, have their own recipes for a fast-to-assemble pot of chili. Unlike its tomato-based cousins, this recipe gives beer, chili, and beans the spotlight.

Tools: *Large skillet, large Dutch oven*

Preparation time: *About 20 minutes*

Cooking time: *About 1 hour*

$2^{1}/_{2}$ to 3 pounds super-lean ground pork, beef, or combination

2 tablespoons olive oil

2 large onions, chopped

6 large cloves garlic, minced

2 teaspoons ground cumin

$1^{1}/_{2}$ teaspoons ground coriander

2 teaspoons dried oregano, crushed

$^{1}/_{3}$ to $^{1}/_{2}$ cup mild, red chili powder

1 to 2 teaspoons cayenne (optional)

2 cups Vienna/Märzen/Oktoberfest style beer mixed with $^{1}/_{3}$ cup masa harina (or fine-ground cornmeal)

3 cups canned broth (chicken, vegetable, or beef) or water

1 16-ounce can kidney beans, drained

1 16-ounce can black beans, drained

2 16-ounce cans pinto beans, drained

salt and pepper to taste

1 In a large skillet, cook the meat over medium heat just until all traces of pink are gone (do not cook until browned). Remove from heat and set aside.

2 Heat oil in a large Dutch oven over medium heat. Add onions and cook until translucent. Lower heat and add garlic, cumin, coriander, and oregano. Continue cooking for 4 minutes.

3 Sprinkle in chili powder and cayenne (if using) and continue cooking for 1 minute.

4 Add beer, broth, cooked meat, and beans. Simmer slowly, stirring frequently, for 40 minutes. Salt and pepper to taste.

5 Serve garnished with sharp cheddar, a mixture of freshly minced scallions and cilantro, and a dollop of sour cream.

Yield: 6 to 8 servings

 For a marvelous Southwestern twist, stir in 1 large can of drained hominy during the last 10 minutes of cooking. For a heartier chili, cook $^{1}/_{2}$ pound chopped bacon and add it along with the meat and beans.

Brewers Pulled Beef

This simple-to-prepare barbecue of succulent shredded beef steeped in a deep, beer-enhanced barbecue sauce should be piled high on big sourdough buns and served with your best coleslaw.

Tools: *Large saucepan, electric cooking pot (optional)*

Preparation time: *About 35 minutes*

Cooking time (mostly unsupervised): *About 3 to 8 hours*

Meat:

1 bottle cream ale

3 cups water mixed with 1 tablespoon kosher salt

2 tablespoons dried oregano leaves

5 large cloves garlic, peeled and mashed

1 teaspoon crushed black pepper (red chili flakes optional)

4 pounds boneless beef chuck (or lean pork)

Sauce:

1 small onion, chopped

1 tablespoon cooking oil

3 large cloves garlic, peeled and mashed

1 to 2 teaspoons ground cayenne (or to taste)

1 teaspoon **each** salt and pepper (or to taste)

1 bottle Dortmunder Dark

$^1/_3$ cup **each** tomato paste, cider vinegar, brown sugar, and commercial steak sauce

2 teaspoons liquid smoke

1 In a large saucepan, heat cream ale, salted water, oregano, garlic, pepper, and chili flakes (if using) to a rolling boil. Add meat and sear it in boiling liquid, turning if necessary. (The meat will turn gray.)

2 Lower heat, cover, and simmer over very low heat 2 to 3 hours or until meat pulls apart easily **or** place in an electric cooking pot and cook on low 6 to 7 hours. Cool and pull into shreds.

3 In a heavy pan over medium heat, sauté the onion in a tablespoon of oil until golden. Add the garlic, cayenne, salt, and pepper and cook 2 minutes.

4 Pour in the Dortmunder and stir in the tomato paste, vinegar, brown sugar, steak sauce, and liquid smoke and gently simmer 10 minutes.

5 Add the pulled meat and simmer an additional 10 minutes so that meat can absorb the flavor of the sauce.

Yield: 8 to 10 servings

Arizona Quiche

Next time you need a fast but striking breakfast, brunch, or supper item, try this one. A blender, a frozen pie crust, and a few extra ingredients are tossed together for an unforgettable quiche.

Tools: *Blender or food processor*

Preparation time: *About 15 minutes*

Cooking/cooling time: *About 1 hour*

<table>
<tr>
<td>

¹/₂ cup sour cream

4 extra large eggs

¹/₃ cup chili beer (or American pale lager plus — optional — ¹/₂ seeded, chopped jalapeño)

²/₃ cup half-and-half

¹/₂ teaspoon fresh ground black pepper
</td>
<td>

1 small onion, sliced thin, sautéed until golden in 1 tablespoon butter or bacon drippings

*¹/₃ cup **each** diced green chilis (optional), diced red bell pepper, grated jack cheese*

4 ounces bacon, cooked until crisp and crumbled

1 10-inch prepared pie crust
</td>
</tr>
</table>

1 Preheat oven to 375°. In a blender or food processor, process the sour cream, eggs, beer, half and half, and pepper just until smooth.

2 Spread sautéed onions over the bottom of the pie crust. Sprinkle diced chilis, red pepper, grated cheese, and bacon over the top.

3 Slowly pour egg mixture into the onion mixture. Do not stir. Place on the lower shelf of oven. Bake approximately 40 minutes or until a knife inserted into the center comes out clean. Cool 20 minutes before serving.

Yield: 6 servings

If the jalapeño and green chilis aren't for you, go ahead and drop them.

For a lighter version, use ²/₃ cup lite sour cream, 1¹/₄ cups egg substitute, ¹/₂ cup skim milk, and pepper along with the beer. Sauté onion in nonstick pan with butter-flavored spray, use lite cheese, and replace the bacon with low-fat chopped ham. For a beer-imbued rendition of the classic French quiche, substitute Swiss cheese and ham for the jack cheese and bacon.

Publicans Hot-n-Spicy Chicken with E-Z Garlic Sauce

Rich with Dunkel and fragrant spices, this zesty marinade gives chicken an exotic, spicy flavor and a rich red color. Serve with the spicy garlic sauce for a real treat.

Tools: *Heavy skillet (optional), mortar and pestle, small bowl, large covered dish, grill*

Preparation time: *About 15 minutes*

Marinating/cooking time: *About 6 to 18 hours*

1 teaspoon **each** whole black pepper-corns, coriander seed, and cumin seed

²/₃ cup Dunkel or bock beer

2 tablespoons olive oil

2 teaspoons fresh grated ginger

4 large cloves garlic, mashed in a garlic press

1 serrano chili pepper or jalapeño, seeded and finely minced (optional, for chili-heads)

2 tablespoons sharp (or half sharp) paprika

2 tablespoons honey

1¹/₂ teaspoons salt (or to taste)

3 to 4 pounds chicken, cut in pieces and washed (or boneless chicken breasts)

1 Heat a heavy skillet over medium heat until very hot. Remove from heat and toss in peppercorns and coriander seed, stirring for 1 minute. Add the cumin and continue stirring for an additional 30 seconds or until very fragrant. **(Skip this step if you're in a rush.)** Cool.

2 Crush the spices. In a small bowl, combine the beer and the olive oil with the crushed spices and the ginger, garlic, chili, paprika, honey, and salt. Let set 10 minutes.

3 While marinade is resting, slash the chicken pieces diagonally with ¹/₄-inch-deep cuts, about 4 per piece. Rub chicken thoroughly with the marinade.

4 Marinate, covered, in the refrigerator 6 to 18 hours. Grill over medium heat until no sign of pink appears when meat is pierced with a sharp knife. Serve with E-Z Garlic Sauce (next recipe).

Yield: 4 to 5 servings

E-Z Garlic Sauce

The lemon essence of lemon-enhanced beer gives this sauce just the tang it needs! Serve with Publicans Hot-n-Spicy Chicken (preceding recipe).

Tools: *Medium bowl, blender or food processor*

Preparation time: *About 10 minutes*

Cooking time: *See "Publicans Hot-n-Spicy Chicken with E-Z Garlic Sauce"*

2 cups fresh water

5 cups torn French or Italian bread, crusts removed

7 to 8 large cloves garlic, peeled

$^1/_4$ cup lemon-enhanced summer beer (or lightly hopped pale ale with dash of lemon juice)

*$^1/_4$ cup **each** buttermilk (or sour cream) and olive oil*

$^1/_2$ to 1 teaspoon salt (or to taste)

1 Pour water over bread and let soak 1 minute. Gently squeeze water out of bread with your hands.

2 Place bread and remaining ingredients in a blender or food processor and process until silky smooth.

3 Either drape the white sauce over the red grilled chicken for a dramatic effect or serve the sauce on the side for dipping.

Bayou Shrimp

The roasty, coffee flavor of stout deepens the spicy characteristic of this Cajun-style shrimp dish. Serve with lots of chilled brew (a malty beer, like Oktoberfest or a brown ale) and crusty French bread.

Tools: *Heavy skillet*

Preparation time: *About 45 minutes*

Cooking time: *About 45 minutes*

4 tablespoons olive or canola oil

4 tablespoons flour

*1 cup **each** chopped onions, scallions, and celery*

1 cup fresh Italian parsley (flat-leaf)

3 cloves garlic, mashed

1 cup hot chicken broth

1 cup stout or roasty-tasting porter

8 whole canned tomatoes, chopped

¹/₂ tablespoon shrimp/crab boil (a commercial spice mixture for shellfish), finely ground

1 tablespoon sharp or half sharp paprika

¹/₂ teaspoon crushed black pepper

¹/₂ teaspoon salt or ¹/₄ teaspoon cayenne

2¹/₂ pounds raw, peeled, deveined large shrimp

1 Heat oil in a large, heavy skillet. Sprinkle in flour and cook over medium-low heat until browned, stirring constantly. Add onions, scallions, and celery, cooking an additional 5 minutes.

2 Add parsley and garlic, cooking an additional 2 minutes. Slowly stir in hot broth and then beer and tomatoes, stirring constantly. Add shrimp boil, paprika, and pepper.

3 Cover and simmer slowly for 30 minutes. Add salt or cayenne to taste. Toss in shrimp and cook just until shrimp turn pink (about 2 minutes). Remove from heat and serve immediately over rice.

Yield: 6 servings

 Of course, fresh crawfish are also wonderful served in this sauce. If you enjoy mussels, nestle scrubbed mussels into the sauce 15 minutes into the simmer time. Cover and continue cooking an additional 20 minutes or until mussels have opened and are fully cooked.

Chocolate Stout Silk Pie

This scrumptious pie is truly more than the sum of its ingredients. Rich, dense, silky, and irresistible, you truly must try it to believe it. If you can operate a blender, you can make this pie!

Tools: *Blender, two small saucepans*

Preparation time: *About 10 minutes*

Cooking/chilling time: *About 4 to 6 hours*

12 ounces semi-sweet chocolate chips (or chopped bitter chocolate)

24 large marshmallows

pinch of salt

$^2/_3$ cup stout (or porter)

$^1/_3$ cup heavy cream or evaporated or condensed skim milk

1 teaspoon vanilla

1 tablespoon quality bourbon or crème de cacao (optional)

1 ready-made butter-cookie-crumb or graham-cracker pie crust

Whipped cream and shaved chocolate and/or toasted crushed nuts for garnish

1 Place chocolate chips, marshmallows, and salt in a blender.

2 In two separate saucepans, heat stout and heavy cream until very hot but not boiling. (Don't heat them together in one container, or the cream will curdle.)

3 Pour the stout and cream into the blender and blend on medium for 1 minute. Add the vanilla and bourbon, continuing to blend until very smooth.

4 Pour the mixture into the crust and refrigerate 4 to 6 hours or until firm. Garnish with whipped cream and shaved chocolate or toasted nuts.

Yield: 6 to 8 servings

Chapter 17

Facts, Figures, and Misconceptions

● ●

*H*ere's an interesting phenomenon: More craft-brewed beer is being made, sold, and consumed in North America than ever before. Not only has the beer renaissance been a boon to beer drinkers, but it has also created a thriving industry where none existed two short decades ago. Craft brewing's vital signs are very vital, indeed!

Who Are the Rising North American Craft Brewers?

Beers that are craft brewed tend to come from the following types of breweries (for more information about breweries, see Chapter 3): *contract*, a brewery that hires another brewery to make its beer; *regional specialty*, a brewery that produces between 15,000 and 500,000 barrels per year; *microbrewery*, a brewery that produces less than 15,000 barrels annually; and *brewpub*, a brewery that produces anywhere from a couple hundred to 5,000 barrels annually (the finished product is sold on-premises, in a restaurant or pub). Table 17-1 provides a breakdown of the types of craft brewers in North America and their production (1 barrel = 31 gallons = 117.8 liters).

Table 17-1	North American Craft-Brewing Output for 1995
Type of Brewery	*Output (In Barrels)*
Contract	1,588,995
Regional specialty	1,806,913
Microbrewery	722,084
Brewpub	408,834
Total output	*4,526,826*

Impressive, yes — and an increase in production of more than 50 percent from 1994. To put this in perspective, though, consider that in 1995 the four U.S. megabrewers alone (Anheuser-Busch, Miller, Coors, and Stroh/G. Heileman) combined to brew an almost inconceivable 172 *million* barrels of beer! That's just about 9.5 *billion* six-packs!

The craft-brewing revolution, not surprisingly, has been led by the little guys. Although the world's largest brewpub (Wynkoop, in Denver, Colorado) brews and serves a mere 5,000 barrels a year — small even by microbrew standards — microbrewers and brewpubs far outnumber any other type of brewer. For example, only about two dozen megabrewers exist worldwide. What does that mean to you, the beer nut? Better quality, freshness, and variety — a few of my favorite things!

See Table 17-2 for a breakdown, according to number, of the craft brewers in North America.

Table 17-2	Number of North American Craft Brewers, by Type		
Brewery Type	*U.S.*	*Canada*	*Total*
Regional specialty	25	11	36
Microbrewery	349	38	387
Brewpub	553	58	611
Total craft brewers	*927*	*107*	*1,034*

Growth industry

If you think that craft brewing is just a fad, think again! In 1995, 308 new breweries opened in North America (202 brewpubs and 106 microbreweries), and only 32 closed (26 brewpubs and 6 microbreweries). While the U.S. may never reclaim the glory of the pre-Prohibition years — when, for example, the Brooklyn, New York, neighborhood of Williamsburgh alone could claim more than 40 breweries — the beer renaissance has brought craft brewing back to cities and towns from which it seemed to have vanished forever. Neat, huh?

International megabrewers

For your reference, the ten largest international megabrewers are, in descending order, as follows:

Anheuser-Busch (U.S.); Heineken (The Netherlands); Miller (U.S.); Kirin (Japan); Fosters Group, including Molson (Australia and Canada); Companhia Cervejaria Brahma (Brazil); Groupe BSN (France); Coors (U.S.); Santo Domingo Group (Columbia); Guinness (Ireland)

Collectively, craft brewers are generating sales too big for the megabrewers to ignore. See Table 17-3 for the sales volume of craft breweries in the U.S.

Table 17-3	Sales Volumes of U.S. Craft Breweries, 1995
Type of Brewery	*Revenue*
Microbreweries	$1,752,000,000
Brewpubs	$ 276,000,000
Total	*$2,028,000,000*

Generally speaking, people in the U.S. are drinking less beer, but better beer. The market share of craft-brewed beer in the U.S. in 1995 was 2.1 percent, up from 1.3 percent in 1994. On the whole, people are drinking only 21.1 gallons of beer per person annually, down from 22.7 gallons in 1985.

The U.S. is far and away the world's largest brewing nation, though per capita, Germany consumes the most beer. Table 17-4 shows just how much beer was "made in the U.S.A." in 1995 (1 barrel = 31 gallons = 117.8 liters).

Table 17-4	U.S. Beer Production and Sales
Market	*Amount Sold*
Domestic	176,930,000 barrels
Export	8,361,000 barrels
Total	*185,291,000 barrels*

Over 11 million barrels of imported beer were sold in the U.S. in 1995 as well.

Foamy factoids

- As of December 1995, 100 contract breweries were operating in North America.
- Forty-eight states and Washington, D.C., have either partially or entirely legalized brewpubs.
- Current failure rates for the industry are as follows:

> U.S. brewpubs — 1 in 7
>
> U.S. microbreweries — 1 in 6
>
> Canadian brewpubs — 1 in 3
>
> Canadian microbreweries — 1 in 2

Source: *Institute for Brewing Studies, Craft-Brewing Industry Fact Sheet, June 1996*

Malty Misconceptions

Here are some common misconceptions about beer, along with the real facts:

- ✔ *Bock beer is what is left at the bottom of the barrel.* No, only its detractors say that. Bock beers are made fresh from scratch every time.

- ✔ *Dark beer is always stronger than lighter beer.* Stronger-tasting, yes; more potent, no!

- ✔ *Ales are always stronger than lagers.* No, strength is not an ale characteristic — a wide range of strength exists among ales (and lagers, too).

- ✔ *European and other imported beer is stronger than beer made in the U.S.* Wrong again — strength varies with style, no matter where the beer is made.

- ✔ *Beer causes beer bellies.* No, bellies are just as often caused by sloth and inactivity as regular beer consumption (that stuff about genetic predisposition is just wishful thinking, sorry).

- ✔ *Beer is fattening because it is made from grain.* Actually, alcohol accounts for more calories in beer than all other ingredients combined.

Chapter 18

Just the FAQs, Ma'am: Ten Frequently Asked Questions

● ●

*B*eer is one of the more social drinks in the world, and where you find people, you find questions. More specifically, where you find beer enthusiasts or bartenders, you find beer questions. Some bartenders note that the two most common questions heard come from two extremes: the uninitiated and the homebrewer/technogeek. Examples include: What do you have that's like *(insert mass-market brand name here)* Light? And from the other end of the brewspective, "Is this made with 6-row barley?" From the bartender, the most frequently asked question should be "What can I offer you?" Here are some other questions that you may hear.

What Is the Best Beer in the World?

There is no *best* beer in the same way there is no best food, best car, or best book. That's really a matter of personal taste because of the wide variety of beer styles. About as close as you can come to a "best" is to find a beer that best represents its style, which means you'll find at least 70 "best beers" in the world (see Appendix B).

How Is Alcohol Created in Beer?

Alcohol is produced during the fermentation process. Yeast, which is added to the beer after it is brewed, consumes the natural sugars in the beer. In return for their meal, the yeast cells produce alcohol and carbon dioxide (just as they do when you bake bread). Stronger brews have more fermentable sugar in them (from the grain) to begin with.

What Is the Alcohol Content of the Average Beer?

The alcohol content of the average beer is between 4 and 5 percent alcohol by volume (3.2 and 4 percent by weight). Low-alcohol beers may contain as little as 0.5 percent alcohol. The strongest beer in the world checks in at about 17 percent, but an alcohol content this high is very rare for beer. See Appendix F for strength by style.

What's the Difference between a Lager and an Ale?

They're made differently, but both lagers and ales are beer. Ales are fermented with top-fermenting yeast strains that perform best in warm temperatures, while lagers are fermented with bottom-fermenting yeast strains that perform better in cold temperatures. Ales tend to be a bit more robust and have more complex tastes than lagers. Because lager beers are aged for longer periods of time, their flavor profile is said to be *narrower* than that of ale, and the maturing process causes a smooth mellowing of the beers' flavors. Prior to just over a hundred years ago, all beer was ale — lagering procedures were not fully developed until the mid 1800s.

Does Beer Age Well like Wine?

Absolutely not. Beer is a fragile, perishable product, meant to be consumed while it is as fresh as possible (only a few rare types of beer are meant to be aged). As with any food that comes in a jar, can, or box, only additives and preservatives or refrigeration can extend the shelf life of beer. Three months is considered the window of freshness in beer.

Does Beer Have to Be Refrigerated?

No hard-and-fast rule says beer must be refrigerated, but as with any perishable food, cold storage delays deterioration and preserves flavor. Exactly how much deterioration is delayed and how much flavor is preserved depend greatly on how the beer was pasteurized, whether it was made with additives and preservatives, and the overall quality of the beer to begin with.

What Is the Proper Serving Temperature for Beer?

Most mass-market, famous-brand beers are meant to be consumed at palate-numbing temperatures, but a well-made, craft-brewed beer is best served at slightly warmer temperatures so you can enjoy its full-flavored taste. Lagers are generally served between 42 and 48 degrees F (6 to 9 degrees C), and ales are generally served between 44 and 52 degrees F (7 to 11 degrees C); the darker they are, the warmer they should be served. Big-bodied, dark-colored, high-alcohol beers should be served at around 55 degrees F (13 degrees C), which is considered British cellar temperature.

What Is the Proper Glassware for Serving Beer?

Clean ones. Nothing is as important as the cleanliness of the vessel; dust, oily fingerprints, lipstick, and soap residue ruin the presentation. Though many different styles of beer glassware exist for the many different styles of beer, no hard-and-fast rule exists as to which one is best. However, if small portions of beer are being served, stemmed, tulip-shaped wine glasses work well. If 12-ounce (355-milliliter) portions are being served, the glasses provided should be large enough to hold the entire contents of the bottle, including ample space for the head.

What Is the Difference between Barley and Malt?

Barley and *malt* are often used interchangeably, though not correctly so. The principal ingredient in beer (after water, that is) is barley. Barley must undergo a wetting and drying process called *malting* before the brewer can use it. Only after this process is complete can the barley can then be called *malt* or *barleymalt*.

Why Is Yeast Found in Some Beer Bottles?

Some beer styles are meant to contain a small amount of yeast sediment in the bottle. Traditional German weizenbiers and certain Belgian and British beer styles undergo an additional fermentation inside the bottle called *bottle conditioning* with yeast that eventually settles down. At some small microbreweries, the filtering equipment is only capable of capturing yeast and sediments larger than 250 microns, and the smaller stuff dusts the bottom of the bottle.

What Is the German Beer Purity Law?

The German purity law, also known as the *Reinheitsgebot,* was the first consumer protection law, written by Duke Wilhelm IV of Bavaria in 1516. This law stipulates that Bavarian brewers can use only four ingredients to make their beer: barley, hops, yeast, and water, with no additives and no preservatives (the law was amended to include wheat, in order to make weizenbier). Most American microbrewers voluntarily abide by this law, which is generally seen as a symbol of quality.

Are Brown or Green Bottles Better to Use for Beer?

Light is a beer-destroying energy. Whether the light is fluorescent, incandescent, or natural, beer is harmed by its effects. Whatever can be done to shield beer from light is worth the effort. Brown glass protects better than green, but green is better than no color at all.

How Many Different Styles of Beer Are There?

Approximately 30 major brewing styles exist in the world. Many of these styles also have substyles (for example, bock beer has five derivations: Maibock, helles bock, weizenbock, eisbock, and doppelbock). All told, you'll find about 70 individual beer styles in the world. They all fall loosely into either the lager or ale category.

Chapter 19

Ten Favorite U.S. Brewpubs

As you can tell by the title, this chapter is not very objective. You must consider so many variables when compiling a "favorite" list of brewpubs that specific criteria become necessary. Here are some of the criteria that I used:

- ✔ **Beer:** The beer has to be good, above all else. The beer not only has to be drinkable but also has to be offered in a variety of styles. And the brewpub has to have a certain reverence or appreciation for beer beyond a secondary role as an accompaniment to the pub's food. Gotta have passion.

- ✔ **Food:** Although I'm not always able to enjoy a meal at each and every brewpub I visit, I make a point of perusing the food menu and taking mental notes on food presentation. Solid pub grub served in generous portions scores higher in my book than *haute cuisine* served in stingy morsels any day.

- ✔ **Ambience:** Though I don't mind if the brewery aromas aren't quite completely contained, I prefer a brewpub to reek of beer in the figurative sense. Brewery antiques and lithographs are more conducive to beer enjoyment than some outlandish conceptual motif.

- ✔ **History:** The brewpub must have an established track record for quality and consistency. So I avoid touting a Johnny-come-lately or the latest flash in the pan. Every brewpub on this list has been open for at least two years.

- ✔ **Region:** I tried to choose brewpub locations spread across the U.S. Very often, regionality plays an important role in each brewpub, especially in the beer. The fact that I am shining the spotlight around the country undoubtedly means that several brewpubs with great reputations in the same region as one that is mentioned must be passed over.

Ultimately, any list such as this one can't be completely objective and objectively complete. It is being provided solely as a starting point for those who have never experienced a brewpub and don't know what to expect (for more on that, see Chapter 5). If you need help finding more, try any one of the several excellent guides to brewpubs around the country, especially the one that *I* wrote: *Beer Across America.* Please.

Ten Top Spots

Here, then, are the brewpubs that stand out in my memory as highlights in my pub-jumping career (listed east to west).

Commonwealth Brewing Company: Boston, Massachusetts

It was a cold December night, and we had just witnessed the lighting of the city Christmas tree. We stopped in for a hearty meal and shared pint after pint of delicious ales — the darker they got, the better they got! Phone 617-523-8383.

Stoudt Brewery (Black Angus Restaurant): Adamstown, Pennsylvania

Just being here was a high point — I have great respect for industry leader Carol Stoudt and the beers she brews. Enjoying them all afternoon left me no less in awe. Phone 717-484-4386.

Great Lakes Brewing Company: Cleveland, Ohio

The GLBC had been on my "hit list" for a couple of years. When I finally visited, I was warmly received by Pat Conway and treated to some of the most outstanding beer I had ever tasted. I really hated to leave. This stop was one of the high points in my travels. Phone 216-771-4404.

Bluegrass Brewing Company: Louisville, Kentucky

The BBC was one of four brewpub visits I had to make that day. Too bad it wasn't my last. I would have loved to have stayed. Brewmaster David Pierce makes a beer to suit everyone's taste. Phone 502-899-7070.

Goose Island Brewing Company: Chicago, Illinois

Because "the Goose" is practically in my backyard, I've become spoiled. Any brewpub that produces 40 beer styles every year is likely to have that effect on someone. Goose Island is the standard by which I measure other brewpubs. Phone 312-915-0071.

Sherlock's Home: Minnetonka, Minnesota

Sherlock's is billed as "London without the airfare" for a good reason. Bill Burdick has recreated a thoroughly British pub inside and out, and a very classy one at that. His ales are worth their weight in pounds. Phone 612-931-0203.

Wynkoop Brewing Company: Denver, Colorado

As much as I was enjoying my sampler tray at the bar, I wouldn't have missed for the world the opportunity to join brewmaster Russell Schehrer (who recently passed away) in the cellar to sample some new beers fresh from the aging tanks. It doesn't get any better than that. (This brewpub is now the largest in the world, having sold over 5,000 barrels in 1995.) Phone 303-297-2700.

Rogue Brewery & Public Ale House: Ashland, Oregon

Boasting a panoramic view of the Rogue River, the Rogue Brewery has been called "America's most beautiful brewery site." Who am I to disagree? Rogue Ales are legends in the making. Phone 503-488-5061.

Mendocino Brewing Company: Hopland, California

Visiting Mendocino is like standing at ground zero; this brewpub was the very first in the modern craft brewing movement (and the building has even more history than the brewery). The beers of Mendocino are American classics. Phone 707-744-1361.

Trolleyman Pub (Redhook): Seattle, Washington

The Trolleyman is another touchstone in the U.S. beer renaissance: Ya sure, you betcha! The original brewery opened in 1982 in the historic Freemont Trolley Barn. It's now a draught-only facility — bottling is done in the new state-of-the-art brewery in Woodinville. Phone 206-548-8000.

Honorable Mentions

The following brewpub locations didn't quite fit all the preceding criteria but are well worth visiting for the beer alone, should you be in the area.

Boston Beer Works: Boston, Massachusetts

Across the street from Fenway Park, the Beer Works has established a reputation for quality and consistency, offering a long and tempting list of well-made brews. Can't beat fun near the old ballpark. Phone 617-536-2337.

Broad Ripple Brewpub: Indianapolis, Indiana

Transplanted Briton John Hill has introduced the Circle City to some of his tasty Yorkshire-influenced ales. Good traditional pub grub and beer. Phone 317-253-2739.

Appleton Brewing Company: Appleton, Wisconsin

Resurrecting the old Adler Brau name, Appleton Brewing honors its legacy with an incredible lineup of award-winning brews. A new bottling line allows for carry-out and mail order, too. Phone 414-731-3322.

St. Louis Brewery: St. Louis, Missouri

Formerly known as Schlafly's, the St. Louis Brewery gets consistent high praise for the beers produced there. Noted brewer and author Dave Miller had a hand in setting up the brewery and formulating the recipes. Phone 314-241-2337.

Oasis Brewery: Boulder, Colorado

A theme park for sedentary adults; check out a Tut Brown ale, a Scarab Red, or a Zoser Stout. Unique Egyptian decor and tasty beers are no mirage. Phone 303-449-0363.

Preston's Embudo Station Brewery: Embudo, New Mexico

Few brewpubs in the U.S. can match Preston's for location and scenic grandeur, situated as it is in a canyon by the Rio Grande, with ancient Native American burial grounds right behind. Though the brewery is the working definition of low-tech (it's one step above a homemade homebrew operation), the beers are eclectic in style and taste delicious. Phone 505-852-4707.

Bridgeport Brewing & Public House: Portland, Oregon

Bridgeport Brewing is a solid member of the old guard. The Public House offers an impressive list of brews from one of the industry's pioneers. Phone 503-241-7179.

Anderson Valley Brewery "The Buckhorn Saloon": Boonville, California

Though Boonville is on the road to nowhere, Ken Allen's oft-awarded beers are worth searching out. As they say in the local Boontling dialect: "Demand only the bahlest." Phone 707-895-2337.

Ones to Watch

The following locations have opened within the last two years and have been well received so far. Watching these pubs blossom should be fun.

Heartland Brewing Company: New York, New York

The Heartland, on Manhattan's Union Square, isn't just another upscale urban pretender. Brewmaster Jim Migliorini is serious about producing traditional beers, and he's succeeding. Phone 212-645-3400.

Park Slope Brewing Company: Brooklyn, New York

Opened in a space the size of a postage stamp, Park Slope is the little brewpub that could. Good food is bested only by great beer. Just opened a sister operation in nearby Brooklyn Heights (good luck parking) and soon will offer bottled beer, no less. Phone 718-788-1756.

Liberty Brewing Company: Akron, Ohio

Brewer Tim Rastetter earned his wings at the Great Lakes Brewing Company in Cleveland; now that he's in Akron, it's his turn to soar. Try a flight of Tim's award-winning brews. Phone 216-869-2337.

Blue Cat Brewpub: Rock Island, Illinois

Chemist Dan Cleaveland chucked it all to open his own brewpub. With his sister Martha running the operation, Dan concentrates on making some of the best beer in the region. In Rock Island, it's either drink Dan's beer or cruise on the riverboat casino (the Blue Cat is the odds-on favorite). Phone 309-788-8274.

Great Dane Brewing Company: Madison, Wisconsin

The Historic Fess Hotel is the perfect backdrop for Mad-town's first brewpub. Among a litter of beer styles, there are no dogs here! Phone 608-284-0000.

Tommyknockers Brewery & Pub: Idaho Springs, Colorado

Aggressive list of interesting beers from this upstart pub-brewery high in mountain country. Come for the beer; stay for the scenery. Phone 303-567-2688.

Rio Bravo Brewing Co.: Albuquerque, New Mexico

Rio Bravo offers a mix of traditional and contemporary in ambience and cuisine. Brewmaster Brad Kraus honed his skills elsewhere in the New Mexico scrub; now he's perfecting them in the big city. Phone 505-242-6800.

Part VII

Appendixes

The 5th Wave   By Rich Tennant

Let me just check this one more time. "Pour the water into a brewing vat and season with"... oh wait...it's "hops"-"...season with hops", not hogs.

In this part . . .

The rubber meets the road here, the cap comes off the bottle, the die is cast. . . .

In this part, you find the kind of information that leads directly to a purchase — a phone number or an address, including some e-mail and World Wide Web addresses. You might call this part the *action* "Part."

Need to pick a specific beer to drink? See Appendix A. Wonder what some beer style tastes like? See Appendix B. Want assistance on a beer question or problem? See Appendix C. Want to read or learn more? See Appendix D. Want to start homebrewing? See Appendix E. Want to know how strong your beer is? See Appendix F. Want to impress the folks at the local bar with your incredible grasp of beer history? See Appendix G.

Appendix A
Beer's Greatest Hits

● ●

*A*fter you've digested all the information in this book — heck, once you've glanced at it for a few minutes — you're going to want to start trying different beers. And one of the great delights of being a beer drinker today is that a tremendous choice of beers is available. But delightful though that may be, it's also a little daunting, so the following tables include some suggestions for you to try, by style. The last column in each of these tables lists (whenever possible) a European or Canadian brand name (an import in the U.S.) and/or a U.S. brand name (a U.S. domestic), with the country or state of origin.

The really driven among you may even want to photocopy these tables and work your way through them, one beer at a time. You will be the darling of the beer store if you do. Don't worry if you can't get the specific brand noted here — each one is just one of many suggestions that could have been made. These tables are just a start. But these beers can give you an idea of what each style should taste like, a sample with which you can compare all the others of that particular style.

Happy beer exploring!

Table A-1		Ales
Style	*Substyle*	*Brand Names*
Barleywine		Young's Old Nick (England); Sierra Nevada Bigfoot Barleywine (California)
Belgian Beer	Belgian ale	Chimay (Belgium); New Belgium Fat Tire (Colorado)
	Belgian strong ale	Duvel (Belgium); Celis Grand Cru (Texas)
	Faro	Lindeman's (Belgium)
	Flanders brown ale	Corsendonk (Belgium)
	Flanders red ale	Rodenbach (Belgium)

(continued)

Table A-1 *(continued)*

Style	Substyle	Brand Names
	Gueuze	Lindeman's Cuvée René (Belgium)
	Lambic (fruited)	Boon Kriek/Framboise (Belgium)
	Saison	DuPont (Belgium)
	Trappist dubbel	Affligem (Belgium)
	Trappist tripel	LaTrappe (Belgium); New Belgium Trippel (Colorado)
	Witbier	Hoegaarden (Belgium); Celis White (Texas)
Bitter	Ordinary bitter	Tetley's (England); Redhook Ballard Bitter (Washington)
	Special bitter	Fuller's London Pride (England); Hale's Special Bitter (Washington)
	Extra special bitter	Fuller's ESB (England); Oasis Capstone ESB (Colorado)
Brown Ale	English brown ale	Samuel Smith Nut Brown Ale (England); Lost Coast Downtown Brown (California)
	American brown ale	Brooklyn Brown Ale (New York)
Pale Ale	Classic pale ale	Bass (England); D.L. Geary's (Maine)
	American pale ale	Mendocino Red Tail Ale (California)
	India pale ale	Eldridge Pope Royal Oak (England); Grant's I.P.A. (Washington)
Porter		Samuel Smith Taddy Porter (England); Edmund Fitzgerald Porter (Ohio)
Stout	Dry (Irish style)	Guinness Extra Stout (Ireland); Rogue Shakespeare Stout (Oregon)
	Sweet (London style)	Mackeson XXX (England); New Haven Blackwell Stout (Connecticut)
	Oatmeal	McAuslan Oatmeal Stout (Canada); Oasis Zoser Oatmeal (Colorado)
	Russian Imperial	Samuel Smith's Imperial Stout (England); Grant's Imperial Stout (Washington)
	Foreign	Dragon Stout (Jamaica, England); Old Dominion Stout (Virginia)

Style	Substyle	Brand Names
Strong Ale	English old ale	Old Peculier (England); Hampshire Special Ale (Maine)
	Scotch ale	MacAndrew's Scotch Ale (Scotland); Samuel Adams Scotch Ale (Massachusetts)
Wheat Beer	Kristallclar	Schneider Weisse (Germany); Heartland Weiss (Illinois)
	Hefeweizen	Franziskaner (Germany); Tabernash (Colorado)
	Dunkelweizen	Hopf. Dunkel Weisse (Germany); Sprecher Dunkel Weizen (Wisconsin)
	Berliner Weisse	Berliner Kindl Weisse (Germany)
	American wheat	Mountain Wheat (Colorado)

Table A-2	Lagers	
Style	**Substyle**	**Brand Names**
American Lager	American pale lager	Leinenkugel's (Wisconsin)
	American dark lager	Frankenmuth Dark (Michigan)
Bock	Traditional bock	Spaten (Germany); Dock St. Bock (Pennsylvania)
	Doppelbock	Paulaner Salvator (Germany); Blue Ridge Subordinator Doppelbock (Maryland)
	Helles bock	Scheidmantel Silber (Germany); Sierra Nevada Pale Bock (California)
	Maibock	Ayinger Maibock (Germany); Stoudt's Honey Double Maibock (Pennsylvania)
	Weizenbock	Aventinus (Germany); Anderson Valley Whamber (California)
	Eisbock	E.K.U. Kulminator Urtyp Hell "28" (Germany)

(continued)

Table A-2 *(continued)*

Style	Substyle	Brand Names
German Pale Lager	Munchener Helles (pale Munich style)	Spaten (Germany); Capital Garten Brau Lager (Wisconsin)
	Dortmunder	D.A.B. (Germany); Berghoff (Illinois)
German Dark Lager	Munchener Dunkel (dark Munich style)	Altbayerisch Dunkles (Germany); Capital Garten Brau Dark (Wisconsin)
	Schwarzbier	Köstritzer (Germany); Sprecher Black Bavarian (Wisconsin)
Märzen/Oktoberfest		Paulaner Oktoberfest Märzen Amber (Germany); Capital Garten Brau Oktoberfest (Wisconsin)
Pilsner	Pilsner	Pilsner Urquell (Czechoslovakia); Hübsch Pilsner (California)
	German Pils	Bitburger Pils (Germany); Baderbrau Pilsner (Illinois)
Rauchbier		Aecht Schlenkerla (Germany)
Vienna Lager		Gösser (Austria)

Table A-3   Hybrids

Style	Brand Names
Altbier	Pinkus Alt (Germany); St. Stan's Alt (Calfornia)
Cream Ale	Liebotschaner Cream Ale (Pennsylvania)
Kölsch	Küppers Kölsch (Germany); Pyramid Kälsch (Washington)
Steam	Maisel's Dampfbier (Germany); Anchor Steam (California)

Table A-4	Specialties
Style	*Brand Names*
Fruit	Pyramid Apricot Ale (Washington)
Herb and Spice	Hoegaarden Wit (Belgium); Left Hand JuJu Ginger (Colorado)
Red Beer	McQueen's Nessie Red Ale (Austria); Boulevard Irish Ale (Missouri)
Smoked	Adelscott (France); Alaskan Smoked Porter (Alaska)
Wassail	Pete's Wicked Winter Brew (California)

Appendix B
Beer Style Chart

• •

*H*ere are the most popular and easily recognized beer styles in the world, with brief descriptions of their taste profiles. The styles are listed alphabetically, each with a style identifier: *A* is for ale, *L* for lager, *H* for hybrid (made with mixed fermentation methods), and *S* for specialty beers (ales and lagers to which special ingredients have been added).

These styles and descriptions are based on the American Homebrewers Association guidelines, modified to make them more accessible to the average reader. Beer styles are always subject to debate.

Style	Substyle	Type	Description
Altbier		H	Copper to dark brown, with noticeable maltiness and bitterness. Very little hop flavor or aroma. Traditionally fermented warm but aged at cold temperatures.
American pale lager	Diet/Light	L	Very pale, light-bodied beer with only a trace of malt flavor. No hop presence in taste or aroma.
	Standard	L	Very pale, light-bodied beer with mild malt flavor and a hint of hop aroma and flavor. Effervescent.
	Premium	L	Very pale to golden, with mild malt flavor and low to medium bitterness. Light-bodied with low hop flavor and aroma.
American dark lager		L	Deep copper to dark brown. Mild hop and malt flavors and aromas. Light- to medium-bodied.

(continued)

Style	Substyle	Type	Description
Barleywine		A	Ranges from copper to deep amber. Pungent nose; a cornucopia of fruit and malt aromas and hop bouquet. Copious amounts of hop bitterness are required to properly balance the bold malty character. The finish is long, complex, and warming in the throat.
Belgian beers	Belgian ale	A	Golden to deep amber, with subdued malt and hop character. Light- to medium-bodied, with some fruitiness and a bit of caramel or roasted malt flavor. Slightly acidic.
	Belgian strong ale	A	Pale to dark brown (darker Belgian strong ales may be colored with candy sugar). High maltiness is balanced by high hop bitterness. Fairly alcoholic beers (8% to 9% by volume).
	Faro	A	Lambic with rock sugar candy added for sweet and sour taste.
	Flanders brown ale	A	Deep copper to brown. Very fruity with no hop flavor or aroma; some vinegary sourness or spiciness is evident. Light- to medium-bodied.
	Flanders red ale	A	Pale red to ruby red. Definite vinegary aromas and sourness present, with no noticeable hop aroma or flavor. Light- to medium-bodied.
	Gueuze	A	Blend of young and old lambics; extremely sour.
	Lambic (fruited)	A	Cloudy or hazy. Intensely but cleanly sour, with no hop bitterness, flavor, or aroma whatsoever. Very fruity and effervescent. Kriek (cherry), framboise (raspberry), and pêche (peach) are most popular.

Style	Substyle	Type	Description
	Saison	A	Coppery-orange. Medium to high maltiness and fruitiness balanced by medium to high hop bitterness, along with some spice. Medium-bodied.
	Trappist dubbel	A	Dark amber to brown. Complex nose with sweet, malty, and nutty notes and a bit of fruitiness in the background. Medium- to full-bodied with mild bitterness.
	Trappist tripel	A	Pale gold, with a light malt and hop aroma. Banana flavors are noticeable, as is a sweet finish. Medium- to full-bodied with a fairly high alcohol content (8% to 9% by volume).
	Witbier	A	Hazy pale yellow. Mild sweet malt and spice character with low to medium hop bitterness. Light- to medium-bodied, with a dry finish.
Bitter	Extra special bitter (E.S.B.)	A	Gold to copper. Noticeable maltiness as well as hop flavor, aroma, and bitterness. Mild alcohol taste. Full-bodied, low carbonation.
	Ordinary bitter	A	Gold to copper. Mildest type of bitter, with low maltiness and medium bitterness. Light- to medium-bodied, low carbonation.
	Special bitter	A	Gold to copper. Stronger than *ordinary bitter* but milder than *E.S.B.,* with noticeable bitterness and moderate strength.
Bock	Traditional bock	L	Deep copper to dark brown. Malty sweetness dominates the palate, with some toasted chocolate malt character. Medium- to full-bodied.

(continued)

Style	Substyle	Type	Description
	Doppelbock	L	Amber to dark brown. Intense malty character in aroma and flavor, offset somewhat by a noticeable alcohol flavor. Very full-bodied.
	Eisbock	L	Deep copper to black. A stronger version of *doppelbock,* with rich and intense malt flavors and aromas balanced by high alcohol content and taste.
	Helles bock	L	Pale to amber. Malty sweetness in both flavor and aroma; low hop flavor and bitterness. Medium-bodied.
	Maibock	L	Pale to amber. Malty sweetness in taste and aroma balanced by medium bitterness and low to medium hop flavor. Medium-bodied.
	Weizenbock	A	Amber to dark brown. Banana and clove notes are apparent in this very malty beer, while hop flavor and aroma are absent. Dark versions have mild roasted and chocolate flavors and aromas. Medium- to full-bodied. Brewed with wheat malt.
Brown ale	American brown ale	A	Medium to dark brown. High hop bitterness, flavor, and aroma balanced by a chocolate-accented medium maltiness. Medium-bodied.
	English brown ale	A	Light amber to very dark brown. Low hop bitterness, flavor, and aroma don't overwhelm the mild malt character. Light-bodied with low alcohol.
California common (Steam)		H	Light amber to copper. Toasted or caramel-like maltiness, with medium to high hop bitterness and flavor and medium hop aroma. Medium-bodied.

Style	Substyle	Type	Description
Cream ale		H	Very pale. Faintly sweet malt character with low hop flavor and aroma. Highly carbonated and light-bodied.
Fruit		S	Generally light- to medium-bodied lagers or ales that have been given a fruity flavor by way of real fruit or fruit extract. Cherry, raspberry, and blueberry are the popular flavors.
German dark lager	Munchener Dunkel (dark Munich style)	L	Copper to dark brown. Nutty, roasty, chocolaty, and malty notes are evident in the taste and aroma. Low hop flavor and aroma with medium bitterness. Medium-bodied.
	Schwarzbier	L	Dark brown to black. Low malt sweetness and aroma. Low to medium hop bitterness may be accompanied by a low astringent bitterness from kilned malt. Medium-bodied.
German pale lager	Munchener Helles (pale Munich style)	L	Pale to golden. Medium malty sweetness with little bitterness and slight hop character. Medium-bodied.
	Dortmunder	L	Pale to golden. Medium malty sweetness balanced by medium bitterness and slight hop character. Some alcoholic warmth is evident. Medium-bodied.
Herb/spice		S	Colors and tastes can run the gamut. Anything from cinnamon to tarragon (or both) may be used; any beer style can be made with herbs or spices. Summer and winter seasonal brews are typical.
Kölsch		H	Pale, hazy gold. Wheat malt imparts a wheaty taste. The palate is clean, dry, sour, and winey, with medium bitterness. Light- to medium-bodied.

(continued)

Style	Substyle	Type	Description
Märzen/ Oktoberfest		L	Amber to coppery orange. Very malty, with a toasty taste and aroma, offset by low to medium bitterness. Medium-bodied.
Pale ale	Classic pale ale	A	Golden to deep amber. Low to medium maltiness is dominated by high hop bitterness, flavor, and aroma. Very fruity; medium-bodied.
	India pale ale (IPA)	A	Golden to deep amber. Medium maltiness with high hop bitterness. Hop flavor and aroma are medium to high. Alcoholic strength is evident in this medium-bodied beer.
	American pale ale	A	Pale to deep amber to copper. Low to medium maltiness with medium hop flavor and aroma. Fruity flavors, with a hint of caramel, are offset by high hop bitterness. Medium-bodied.
Pilsner	Bohemian Pilsner	L	Pale to golden. Low malt aroma and flavor, with some caramel notes. High hop bitterness; low to medium hop aroma and flavor. Light- to medium-bodied.
	German Pils	L	Pale to golden. Low malt aroma and flavor. High hop bitterness. Light- to medium-bodied; crisp.
Porter	Robust porter	A	Opaque black. Sharp, bitter black malt taste with a hint of burnt charcoal. Medium to high hop bitterness, medium- to full-bodied.
	Brown porter	A	Medium to dark brown. Low to medium malt sweetness with medium hop bitterness. Light- to medium-bodied.
Rauchbier		L	Dark amber to dark brown. Very smoky aroma and flavor, which can range in intensity from medium to high. This is smoked Oktoberfest beer.

Style	Substyle	Type	Description
Red beer		S	Not a style unto itself. Usually copper-amber with orange-red highlights. The dominant flavor is a toasty, nutty maltiness from the specialty malt that gives the beer its color. Some hop bitterness. Body and alcohol levels run the gamut from light and low to full and high.
Smoked		S	Any beer style can be given a smoky character. The flavor profile of the underlying beer should always be recognizable through the smoke. Porter, in particular, takes to smoke quite nicely.
Stout	Dry stout (Irish style)	A	Opaque black. Roasted barley character. Medium to high hop bitterness; a slight acidity or sourness is possible. Medium-bodied.
	Foreign style stout	A	Opaque black. Some fruity tastes, along with slight malty sweetness, are balanced by mild sourness or acidity. Medium- to full-bodied.
	Oatmeal stout	A	Not a style unto itself; any stout that's been brewed with oats in addition to the usual grains.
	Russian Imperial stout	A	Dark copper to very black. Very fruity and chewy due to a rich and complex maltiness. Hop bitterness, flavor, and aroma medium to high. Full-bodied with definite alcoholic strength.
	Sweet stout (London style)	A	Opaque black. Sweet maltiness and caramel flavors with a mild roasted barley character. Low hop influence. Medium- to full-bodied.

(continued)

Style	Substyle	Type	Description
Strong ales	English old ale	A	Light to deep amber. Very malty and fruity, with an equally assertive hop flavor and aroma. Alcoholic strength is very notice-able; medium- to full-bodied.
	Scotch ale	A	Deep copper to dark brown. Intense, almost overwhelming malt character is offset not by low hop flavor and aroma but rather by a clean, strong alcohol taste. Faintly smoky and full-bodied.
Vienna lager		L	Amber to coppery orange. Very malty, with a toasty taste and aroma, offset by low to medium bitterness. Medium-bodied.
Wassail		S	Traditional spiced ale brewed only during the Christmas season. Taste is predominately fruit and spice.
Wheat beer	American wheat beer	A	Golden to light amber. Malt and hop flavor and aroma are subdued; low to medium fruitiness. Light- to medium-bodied and effervescent.
	Berliner Weisse	A	Pale straw. Fruity aromas and flavors with an absence of hop flavor or bitterness. Palate is dominated by a sharp sourness and a dry finish. Light-bodied and very effervescent.
	Dunkelweizen	A	Deep copper to brown. Roasted malt and chocolate flavors evident, as well as banana and clove notes. Little hop flavor or aroma. Medium-bodied.

Style	Substyle	Type	Description
	Weizenbier	A	Pale to golden. Very fruity, with clove and banana aromas and flavors. Vanilla, nutmeg, smoke, and cinnamonlike notes may also be present. Low bitterness; mildly tart or sour. Light- to medium-bodied and very effervescent. Weizenbiers (wheat beers) are often interchangeably called weissbiers (white beers), depending on the whims of the brewer.
	Hefeweizen	A	An unfiltered *weizenbier.* Cloudy, with distinct yeast odors.
	Kristallklar	A	Literally means "crystal-clear." A filtered *weizenbier.*

Appendix C

Beer Associations, Clubs, Guilds, and Societies

● ●

*O*ne thing about us beer folks, we like to get together. Forming associations seems to come as naturally to beer people as forming a head does to good beer. Whether you wish to further the cause of collecting, drinking, or brewing (see Appendix E for homebrewers' groups), you can find like-minded beer enthusiasts to help you.

Consumer Groups

Beer consumers generally are a happy (and hoppy?) lot, and some of their groups do wonderful jobs of creating beer festivals and competitions or publishing beer-related information, all in the name of bringing good beer to more people. Sometimes various governments or market forces get beer enthusiasts frustrated. Maybe too many small breweries seem to be getting pushed out of distribution systems, or perhaps the bigger brewers (many of whom have bought up smaller breweries) may appear to be brewing only a few styles where previously many had been available. Or government regulations may inadvertently get out of whack and appear to be doing a disservice to the consumer — whatever the situation, consumer groups can seek to identify and solve the problem.

U.S. and Canada

Beer Drinkers of America: 915 L St., Ste. C-414, Sacramento, CA 95814; phone 800-441-BEER; publishes *Heads Up,* a politically driven newsletter

CAMRA Canada: 1440 Ocean View Rd., Victoria, British Columbia V8P 5K7, Canada; phone 604-595-7728

Chicago Beer Society: P.O. Box 1057, LaGrange Park, IL 60526; phone 847-692-BEER, Web site http://www.mcs.com/shamburg/cbs/cbshome.html

England

The Beer Lovers Club: 9 Windsor Rd., Finchley, London N3 3SN

CAMRA (The Campaign for Real Ale): 230 Hatfield Rd., St. Albans, Hertfordshire, AL1 4LW; phone (011-44) 01727 867201, fax (011-44) 01727 867670, e-mail camra@camra.org.uk, Web site http://www.camra.org.uk

Northern Europe

De Objectiv Bierprovers: Postbus 32, B-2600 Berchem 5, Belgium

PINT: Postbus 3757, NL-1001 AN, Amsterdam, The Netherlands; phone (011-33) 010 212262

Svenska Olframjandet: P.O. Box 16244, S-103 25, Stockholm, Sweden; phone (011-46) 08 669 36 30

Breweriana Collectors Clubs

If any beer enthusiasts are in need of company, it is breweriana collectors. They find one another at auctions and meet at other times to swap items and information. Some of the following groups publish terrific newsletters.

American Breweriana Association (ABA): P.O. Box 11157, Pueblo, CO 81001; phone 719-544-9267

Beer Can Collectors of America (BCCA): 747 Merus Ct., Fenton, MO 63026-2092; phone 314-343-6486

British Beermat Collectors Society: 30 Carters Orchard, Quedgely, Gloucester, Gloucs GL2 6WB, England

Just For Openers: 701 E. Audubon Lake Dr., Durham, NC 27713

Microbes: P.O. Box 826, South Windsor, CT 06074-0826; phone 860-644-9582

National Association for Breweriana Advertising (NABA): 2343 Met-to-Wee Ln., Wauwatosa, WI 53226; phone 414-257-0158

Stein Collectors International: 3530 Mimosa Ct., New Orleans, LA 70131-8305

U.S. Mail-Order Beer Clubs

This phenomenon seems almost strictly American, at least for now (Beer Around the World, in Luxembourg, is the only one outside the U.S. at press time). Keep in mind that some clubs require a two- or three-month minimum membership, and don't forget to ask about any premiums (books, videos, and so on) that you may get if you sign for a half-year or more. You usually get 8 to 12 bottles per month, and some of the clubs even publish their own newsletters or magazines, delivered along with the beer. Most feature U.S. brews, but some send international beers. And finally, receiving beer in the mail is restricted or illegal in certain states. Be sure to ask.

Ale in the Mail: Phone 800-573-6325

Beer Across America, Inc.: 55 Albrecht Dr., Lake Bluff, IL 60044; phone 800-854-BEER, Web site http://www.beeramerica.com

The Brew Tour: P.O. Box 471, Oregon City, OR 97045; phone 800-660-TOUR

Brewmasters International: Phone 800-571-7133

Great American Beer Club: 480 C Scotland Rd., Lakemoor, IL 60050; phone 800-879-2747

Hog's Head Beer Cellars: 620 S. Elm St. #112, Greensboro, NC 27406; phone 800-992-CLUB

MicroBrew Express: 2222 Calle del Luna, Ste. 4, Santa Clara, CA 95054; phone 800-962-3377, fax 408-748-9099

Worldwide Beer Club: Phone 888-2 BUY BEER

Professional Brewers Groups

If you want detailed information about beer or if, now that you have devoured every word of this book, you are determined to devote the rest of your waking hours to brewing or selling beer (and your sleeping hours to dreaming about it), then contact the following groups. Note that the Association of Brewers has several affiliates and divisions: the American Homebrewers Association, the Institute of Brewing Studies, Brewers Publications, and the Great American Beer Festival.

U.S.

American Society of Brewing Chemists: 3340 Pilot Knob Rd., St. Paul, MN 55121; phone 612-454-7250

Association of Brewers: P.O. Box 1679, Boulder, CO 80306-1679; phone 303-447-0816, Web site http://www.aob.org/aob

Brewers Association of America: P.O. Box 65908, Washington, DC 20035-5908; phone 202-467-6350

Institute for Brewing Studies: P.O. Box 1679, Boulder, CO 80306-1679; phone 303-447-0816, Web site http://www.aob.org/aob

Canada

Association des Brasseurs de Quèbec: 1981 av. McGill College, Montreal, Quebec H3A 2W9; phone 514-284-9199

Brewing and Malting: Barley Research, 206 167 Lombard Ave., Winnipeg, Manitoba R3B OT6

Saskatchewan Brewers Association: 380 Dewdrey Ave E, P.O. Box 3057, Regina, Saskatchewan S4P 3G7

England

The Brewers Guild: 8 Ely Pl., London EC1 N 6SD; phone (011-44) 171 405 4565

The Brewers Society: 42 Portman Square, London W1H 0BB; phone (011-44) 171 486 4831

France and Switzerland

Association des Brasseurs de France (ABF): 25 Blvd. Malesherbes, F-75008 Paris; phone (011-33) 01 42 66 29 27

Swiss Brewers Association: P.O. Box 6325, CH-8023, Zurich; phone (011-41) 01 221 2628

Japan

Brewer Association of Japan: 2-8-18 Kyobashi, Chuo-ku, Tokyo 104; phone (011-81) 03 3561 8386

Brewing Society of Japan: 6-30, Takinogawa 2-Chome, Kita-ku, Tokyo 114

Australia

The Institute of Brewing (chapter of the U.K.-based organization): P.O. Box 229, Brooklyn Park, South Australia 5032; phone (011-61) 08 356 0996

Lobbying Organizations

Some groups, such as the following two, devote themselves to promoting beer interests to various governments as well as the public.

The Beer Institute: 1225 Eye St. NW, Washington, DC 20005

Oregon Brewers Guild: 510 N.W. Third Ave., Portland, OR 97209; phone 503-295-1862, e-mail beer@teleport.com

Brewing Schools

If you want to learn brewing from professionals, here are a few leads.

American Brewers Guild: 1107 Kennedy Pl., Ste. 3, Davis, CA 95616; phone 800-636-1331 or 916-753-0497, e-mail abgbrew@mother.com, Web site http://www.mother.com/abg

Master Brewers Association of the Americas: 2421 N. Mayfair Rd., Milwaukee, WI 53226; phone 414-774-8558

United States Brewers Academy: Siebel Institute of Technology, 4055 W. Peterson Ave., Chicago, IL 60646; phone 312-463-3400

Institute of Brewing: 33 Clarges St., London, W1Y 8EE, England; phone (011-44) 171 499 8144

Technische Universitat Weihenstephan: Technische Universitat Munchen, Verwaltungsstelle, Weihenstephan, Freising 8050 Germany

Appendix D
Beer Media

●●●

*B*eer folks love to write, and you won't find any shortage of yeasty information in various forms of media. Following is a list of some sources that you may want to check out.

Homebrewing writers are the most prolific among beer writers, and they merit their own section: Appendix E. Homebrewing software is specifically covered in Chapter 12, although software relating to beer in general, which is covered in this appendix, often includes homebrewing subjects, too.

Beer Periodicals

You can read about beer on a regularly updated basis quite easily, either with the free papers that are often found at brewpubs *(brewspapers)* or with the purchase of some fairly glossy magazines, many of which are found on better newsstands around the country. The world of beer makes plenty of real news and, with all the various beer styles and beer's long history, certainly provides plenty of material for features. Besides, you need something to read when you're drinking alone.

U.S. brewspapers

Alephenalia Beer News: 140 Lakeside Ave., Ste. 300, Seattle, WA 98122. Colorful newsletter published by brewer and beer entrepreneur-importer Merchant Du Vin.

Ale Street News: P.O. Box 5339, Bergenfield, NJ 07621; e-mail alestreet@aol.com, Web site http://www.alestreetnews.com. Largest circulated brewspaper in the U.S. Bimonthly tabloid taps beer "hoppenings," primarily in the East. Excellent source of information and inspiration for special sales and promotion folks.

Barleycorn: P.O. Box 2328, Falls Church, VA 22042. Bimonthly tabloid covering beer and brewing in the mid-Atlantic states.

Beer & Tavern Chronicle: 244 Madison Ave., Ste. 164, New York, NY 10016. "America's First Monthly Beer Periodical" covers beer news for most of the Northeastern seaboard, with additional articles from afar.

Beer Travelers Newsletter: P.O. Box 187, Washington, IL 61571; e-mail `Beertrav@aol.com`, Web site `http://www.n-vision.com/beertravelers`. Regular reviews and listings of new and old brewpubs and festivals.

Celebrator Beer News: P.O. Box 375, Hayward, CA 94543; e-mail `tdalldorf@celebrator.com` or `CBeernews@aol.com`, Web site `http://celebrator.com/celebrator`. Celebrated tabloid brewspaper, published bimonthly. Covers West Coast beer scene.

Great Lakes Brewing News: 214 Muegel Rd., East Amherst, NY 14051. Brand-new brewspaper to cover the Great Lakes region. From the same people who do the *Southwest Brewing News*.

Midwest Beer Notes: 339 Sixth Ave., Clayton, WI 54004. Bimonthly brewspaper serving beer lovers throughout the Midwest. Good regional coverage of micros and beer festivals.

Rocky Mountain Beer Notes: 339 Sixth Ave., Clayton, WI 54004. For those in quest of a Rocky Mountain high. This bimonthly is published by the same people who produce *Midwest Beer Notes*.

Southern Draft Brew News: P.O. Box 180425, Casselberry, FL 32718-0425; Web site `http://realbeer.com/sodraft/`. Brewspaper covering the South and Southeast.

Southwest Brewing News: 11405 Evening Star Dr., Austin, TX 78739; e-mail `swbrewing@aol.com`. Bimonthly tabloid covers brewing industry and festivals in the South and Southwest.

Yankee Brew News: P.O. Box 520250, Winthrop, MA 02152-0005. "New England's Beeriodical since 1989." Bimonthly paper covering microbrewing in the Northeast.

U.S. national brewmags

All About Beer: Chatauqua, Inc., 1627 Marion Ave., Durham, NC 27705; phone 919-490-0589, e-mail `AllAbtBeer@aol.com`, Web site `http://www.allaboutbeer.com.aab`. America's foremost beer publication. Bimonthly, circulated magazine covers brewing industry at large, with special focus on microbreweries. Other features on beer festivals, liquor stores, pubs, and so on.

American Breweriana Journal: P.O. Box 11157, Pueblo, CO 81001. Bimonthly magazine of the American Breweriana Association. Focus is on brewery collectibles, but also includes good updated coverage of microbrewing industry.

BEER: the magazine: 1049 B St., Hayward, CA 94541; phone 800-646-2701 or 510-538-9500, e-mail `BeerMag@aol.com`. Slick, colorful, articulate bimonthly magazine, one of two produced by brewing personality Bill Owens (the other is the more professionally oriented *American Brewer*). Good coverage of entire industry.

Brew: All-American Publishing, 1120 Mulberry St., Des Moines, IA 50309; phone 515-243-4929, e-mail `brewmag@netins.net`, Web site `http://realbeer.com/brew/`. New bimonthly magazine blends U.S. travel with beer trekking, focusing on the latter.

Malt Advocate: 3416 Oak Hill Rd., Emmaus, PA 18049; phone 610-967-1083, e-mail `maltman999@aol.com`, Web site `http://maltadvocate.com/maltadvocate`. Up-and-coming magazine dedicated to the discerning consumption of beer and whiskey. Beer gets the lion's share of coverage.

Pint Post: 12345 Lake City Way NE, Ste. 159, Seattle, WA 98125. Quarterly publication of Microbrew Appreciation Society. Features micros of the Pacific Northwest.

Beer Books

Beer is an inspirational subject, and there seems to be no shortage of books on subjects ranging from discussions of its colorful history to discoveries of the best places to drink it. Here are some of the more interesting books on beer.

History and musings

The Ale Trail: Roger Protz.

The Secret Life of Beer: Alan Eames.

A Short, But Foamy, History of Beer: William Paul and Robert Haiber.

A Taste for Beer: Stephen Beaumont.

Guides to brewpubs, beer bars, and microbreweries

Beer Across America: A Regional Guide to Brewpubs and Microbreweries: Marty Nachel.

Beer Travelers Guide: Stan Hieronymus and Daria Labinsky.

Coop's Road Map Guides to Microbreweries and Brewpubs: Six regional versions. If you can't find these guides in your bookstore, contact Lone Mountain Designs, P.O. Box 153, Menlo Park, CA 94026.

Good Beer Guide: Edited by Jeff Evans. Annual. Indispensable for any trip to the U.K. CAMRA Books also publishes *The Good Beer Guide to Munich and Bavaria, The Good Beer Guide to Belgium and Holland,* and others on U.K. pub food and homebrewing.

On Tap Field Guide: Steve Johnson. Addresses and phone numbers of locations throughout the U.S.

On Tap **regional series of guidebooks:** Steve Johnson. Detailed coverage of specific areas.

Cooking and dining with beer

Great American Beer Cookbook: Candy Schermerhorn.

Great Cooking With Beer: Jack Erickson.

Jay Harlow's Beer Cuisine: Jay Harlow.

Reference and critical reviews

The Beer Directory: Heather Wood.

The Beer Enthusiasts Guide: Gregg Smith.

The Beer Log: James Robertson.

Encyclopedia of Beer: Christine Rhodes and Pamela Lappies.

Evaluating Beer: Compiled by Brewers Publications.

Michael Jackson's Beer Companion: Michael Jackson.

Simon & Schuster Pocket Guide to Beer: Michael Jackson.

Videos

Here's a short list of educational videos on beer and brewing; check your local homebrew shop or favorite homebrew catalog for these and other titles:

Beer and Ale: A Video Guide: Michael Sparks, with Michael Jackson. St. Clair Productions. $19.95 + $4.50 shipping and handling.

The Beer Hunter: (As seen on the Discovery Channel.) Michael Jackson. May be hard to find because the CD-ROM by the same title is now available (see "CD-ROM" in this appendix).

Here are a few entertaining videos that you should be able to rent at larger video stores:

Beer: Not an instructional video but a Hollywood movie. A send-up of the world of beer marketing and a wonderfully wicked satire on the industry at large.

Strange Brew: A Hollywood movie that has less to do with beer than *Beer,* but contains some hilarious references to fictitious Elsinore Brewery and its beer.

Take This Job and Shove It: Based on a true story of the sellout of a small-town brewery to a rich out-of-towner. Much of the movie was filmed in Dubuque, Iowa, and at the Dubuque Star Brewery, the actual brewery in question.

CD-ROM

***The Beer Hunter* (CD-ROM for Windows and the Macintosh):** Michael Jackson. The Discovery Channel Multimedia. $39.95

This virtual primer teaches veterans and neophytes alike how to taste and appreciate fine beers. Users can get information on homebrewing, peruse a video and photo gallery on the history of beer, or search for a particular beer by style, region, or country.

According to a media industry source, *The Beer Hunter* was the fastest-selling general-interest CD-ROM on the market as of December 1995.

The Internet and World Wide Web

The Internet is a sprawling network packed with information on a vast variety of topics. How useful you find the Internet in your search for beer information depends a great deal on how patient you are and how sophisticated your search is. I can't even begin to give you a primer on the Internet and the World Wide Web (one of the services on the Internet) in just an appendix. Whole books are devoted to the topic — check out the Internet section in your bookstore, and you'll be sure to find one that suits your needs. One such book is *The Internet For Windows For Dummies Starter Kit,* 2nd Edition, by Margaret Levine Young and John Levine (IDG Books Worldwide, Inc.), which shows you how to cruise the Internet and the Web and even includes the access software you need.

Appendix E lists sites that deal exclusively with homebrewing, but many of the following sites also cover that subject.

The rapidly expanding microbrewing industry appears to be going at warp speed where the Internet is concerned. More and more businesses are turning to the Net's far-reaching audiences to get the most bang for their advertising buck, and beer groups are easy to find (probably because beer nuts are naturally gregarious). Lists such as the ones in the following sections are going to grow exponentially over the coming months and years.

Commercial online services

The two largest commercial services in terms of participants, America Online and CompuServe, have their own beer forums. (For more information on these services, check out *America Online For Dummies,* 3rd Edition, by John Kaufeld, and *CompuServe For Dummies,* 3rd Edition, by Wallace Wang — both published by IDG Books Worldwide, Inc.) Other networks offer casually managed beer information.

> **America Online:** Food and Drink Network (keyword **FDN**), moderated by the Beverage Testing Institute (see Chapter 4). Includes folders for homebrewers and beer and brewery reviews as well as a section reserved for professional brewers.

> **CompuServe:** Very active beer and brewing forum (keyword **GO BEER**), with technical sections on beer styles, homebrew recipes, and more.

Usenet (beer newsgroups)

Newsgroups are where you can join conversations on select topics. You can read and post messages on an electronic "clipboard," or you can communicate with individuals via e-mail.

> `rec.food.drink.beer` is simply about consuming beer, with tips on storage, beer ranking and tasting notes, brewpub and beer bar recommendations, and lots more. In short, this newsgroup can be a tremendous resource for the beer nut.

> `alt.beer` is in a class all its own. Here, beer is a lifestyle, not a beverage. *Note:* Some postings in this newsgroup are not related to beer and may be of an obscene, prurient, or distasteful nature.

World Wide Web sites

Eric's Beer and Homebrewing Page, by Eric Wooten:
`http://pekkel.uthscsa.edu/beer.html` was one of the first beer Web sites ever, featuring beer reviews, brewpub listings for around the world, different homebrew labels, tasting notes, recipe exchanges, message boards, and an extensive and well-chosen set of links to a variety of credible and useful sources — publications, AOB, AHA, and so on. A great starting point for surfing the Net.

The Real Beer Page: `http://realbeer.com` is an essential stop for beer-nut Net surfers and also a home for many beer publications and breweries (see Figure D-1). Contains helpful and interesting resources ranging from games to shopping opportunities to travel ideas. Totally awesome, amazingly comprehensive assortment of links.

Virtual Library for Beer/Commercial Breweries:
`http://www.beerinfo.com/~jlock/wwwbeer.html` is a resource library that provides listings of and links to a ton of beer topics.

U.S. breweries online

I guess because they're so hip, brewers seem to have embraced the ultra-modern, high-tech online world with a vengeance (to trumpet their adherence to old-fashioned, traditional ways?). You can "virtually" visit many breweries. Here are a few:

Appleton Brewing Co., Appleton, Wis.: E-mail `adlerbrew@aol.com`

Arcadia Brewing Co., Kalamazoo, Mich.: E-mail `tsuprise@aol.com`, Web site `http://kalamazoo.inetmi.com/cities/kazoo/arcadia.html`

Bloomington Brewing Co., Bloomington, Ind.: E-mail `OneWorldEn@aol.com` or accessible through AOL's Food and Drink Network (see "Commercial online services")

Golden Prairie Brewing Co., Chicago, Ill.: Web site `http://www.mcs.com/~nr706/gp.html#story`

Grant's Yakima Brewing Co., Yakima, Wash.: Web site `http://www.Grants.com`

Hart Brewing Co., Kalama, Wash.: Web site `http://www.HartBrew.com`

Long Island Brewing Co., Jericho, N.Y.: E-mail `brewer@libc.com`, Web site `http://www.libc.com`

McAuslan Brewing Co., Montreal, Quebec: Web site `http://www.mcauslan.com`

Figure D-1:
The Real Beer Page is one of the best places to find information about beer on the World Wide Web. Easy and fun to use, it also has a great set of linked pages.

Nor'Wester Brewing Co., Seattle, Wash.: Web site
`http://www.norwester.com`

Portland Brewing Co., Portland, Oreg.: Web site
`http://realbeer.com/portland/`

Rock Bottom Brewpubs (Chicago, Ill.; Cleveland, Ohio; Denver, Colo.; Houston, Tex., Indianapolis, Ind.; Minneapolis, Minn.; Portland, Oreg.): Web site `http://realbeer.com/rockbottom/`

Rogue Ales, Newport, Oreg.: Web site `http://realbeer.com/rogue/`

Shipyard Brewing Co., Portland, Maine: Web site `http://realbeer.com/shipyard/`

SLO Brewing Co., San Luis Obispo, Calif.: E-mail `BrewHoffa@aol.com`

Spring Street Brewing Co., New York, N.Y.: E-mail `witbeer@interport.net`, Web site `http://www.interport.net/witbeer`

U.S. brewing and import businesses

Coopers Beers: E-mail `cooperbrew@aol.com`

Merchant Du Vin: E-mail `info—v-beer.com`

Paulaner-North America: E-mail `cincin@interserv.com`, Web site `http://www.paulaner:com/bier`

List of beer importers, wholesalers, distributors, and so on: Web site `http://www.classicbeer.com`

Clubs and organizations

Here's a list of clubs and organizations (for profit and not for profit) from which you can get information:

Association of Brewers (and Great American Beer Festival): Web site `http://www.aob.org/aob`

CAMRA (The *Cam*paign For *Real Ale*): E-mail `camra@camra.org.uk`, Web site `http://www.camra.org.uk`

Miscellaneous

Applied Brewing Technologies, Inc.(consultants): E-mail `ABTInc@aol.com`

Chicago B.O.P. (Brew On Premises): Web site `http://www.mes.com/chomsky/beer.html`

Appendix E
Homebrewing Information Sources

● ●

*I*f you're a homebrewer or you've decided to become one, you're probably eager for some reliable resources on the subject. Rest assured that plenty of resources are available to help you out. This appendix covers a number of those resources. Don't forget to check out Part IV, too, which is devoted to homebrewing, as well as the other beer magazines and books listed in Appendix D.

Homebrewing Magazines

Here are some homebrewing magazines that can provide you with helpful, up-to-date information:

American Brewer Magazine: 1049 B St., Hayward, CA 94541. First of two magazines produced by Bill Owens, created for the serious homebrewer and aspiring microbrewer.

Brewing Techniques: New Wine Press, P.O. Box 3222, Eugene, OR 97403. Focuses on homebrewing as well as microbrewing.

Brew Your Own: Niche Publications, 216 F St., Ste. 160, Davis, CA 95616; e-mail edit@byo.com, Web site http://realbeer.com/. Up-and-coming homebrewer magazine with a big-league editorial review board.

Zymurgy: American Homebrewers Association, P.O. Box 1679, Boulder, CO 80306-1679; phone 303-447-0816, Web site http://www.aob.org/aob. Journal of the American Homebrewers Association. Published quarterly, with a fifth "Special Issue" every year. Also covers national micro scene.

Homebrewing Books

Homebrewers of any level need a serious homebrewing bookshelf along with their carboys and hydrometers. Here are some of the best books available on the topic. They're loaded with technical detail, plenty of recipes, and sage advice.

The Brewer's Companion, Randy Mosher

Brewing Lager Beer, Gregory J. Noonan

Brewing the World's Great Beers, Dave Miller

Classic Beer Style Series, Brewers Publications, 1990 to present

If you're really into one particular style of beer, you may get a kick out of this series put out by the Association of Brewers. Current titles include *Bock* by Darryl Richman, *Belgian Ale* by Pierre Rajotte, *Continental Pilsner* by Dave Miller, *German Wheat Beer* by Eric Warner, *Lambic* by Jean-Xavier Guinard, *Pale Ale* by Terry Foster, *Porter* by Terry Foster, *Scotch Ale* by Gregory J. Noonan, *Stout* by Michael J. Lewis, and *Oktoberfest, Vienna, Märzen,* by George and Laurie Fix.

Dave Miller's Homebrewing Guide, Dave Miller

Designing Great Beers, Ray Daniels

Homebrew Favorites, Karl F. Lutzen and Mark Stevens

The Homebrewer's Companion, Charlie Papazian

Home Brewing Made Easy, Al Korzonas

Making Beer, William Mares

The New Complete Joy of Home Brewing, Charlie Papazian

Homebrew-Supply Mail-Order Catalogs

If you can't find a conveniently located homebrew-supply shop, you may want to try one of the more established mail-order catalogs listed here. Besides homebrewing ingredients and equipment, they sell a wide range of beer books and related media.

American Heritage Beer Co.: 6 Blackstone Valley Pl., Ste. 401, Lincoln, RI 02865-9933; phone 800-261-2739, fax 401-333-8845

Bacchus & Barleycorn, LTD: 6633 Nieman Rd., Shawnee, KS 66203; phone 913-962-2501

Brew & Grow: 2379 Bode Rd., Schaumburg, IL 60194; phone 847-885-8282

Great Fermentations of Marin: 87M Larkspur, San Rafael, CA 94901; phone 800-570-BEER

Liberty Malt Supply Co.: 1419 First Ave., Seattle, WA 98101; phone 800-990-6258 or 206-622-1880, fax 206-322-5185

William's Brewing: P.O. Box 2195-Y9, San Leandro, CA 94577; phone 800-759-6025

Homebrewing Electronic Media

Some companies, particularly those that sell homebrew equipment and supplies, offer how-to videotapes as part of a start-up kit package deal. The "Beer Machine" homebrewing kit and Beer Across America's Homebrewing Club come to mind.

Homebrewing software is covered in Chapter 12, but the best online stuff is listed here. You should also check out the general beer listings in Appendix D because so many of those sites also have information on homebrewing.

Homebrew newsgroups and Web sites

Homebrewing tips, recipes, ideas, and gossip abound on the Information Superhighway. First-timers and grizzled wort warriors alike can satisfy their thirst for knowledge (but not beer) at these newgroups and Web sites:

`rec.crafts.brewing` caters to the homebrewer of any level. Whether you want to increase hop growth by manipulating soil acidity or you're a novice brewing your first batch, you'll find an answer here.

`http://www.dna.lth.se/EHP/kurt/rcb.faq` recaps and answers the 26 most frequently asked questions from the `rec.crafts.brewing` newsgroup.

`http://www.primenet.com/~johnj/Howtobrew.html` is a great site for the beginning homebrewer. Contains glossaries, recipes, book and magazine recommendations, and links to relevant sources.

`http://alpha.rollanet.org/Library.html` (The Brewery) contains homebrew information, a substantial software library (particularly for Windows users), and links to other sites.

Homebrew clubs

Homebrewing is popular around the world. A list of registered homebrew clubs worldwide is available from the American Homebrewers Association (address is included under U.S. in the following lists). Here are the names and addresses of some clubs to get you started (don't you just love the names?):

Australia & New Zealand

Amateur Brewers of Victoria: 10 Aston Heath, Glen Waverly, VIC 3150

Auckland Guild of Winemakers: 426 Sandringham Rd., Auckland 3

Brisbane Amateur Beer Brewers: 20 Anna Marie St., Rochedale South, QLD 4123; phone 07223-8573

North Shore Fermenters Club: 13 Sundown Ave., Whangaparaoa, Auckland

Redwood Coast Brewers: 35 Chalmsford St., Tamworth, NSW 2340; phone 067-66-7852

Canada

The Brewnosers: 2325 Clifton, Halifax, NS B3K 4T9; phone 902-425-5218

Canadian Amateur Brewers Association: 146 First Ave., Toronto, ON M4M 1X1; phone 416-462-9981

Canadian Association for Better Ale and Lager (CABAL): P.O. Box 631, Toroto, ON M5C 2J8; phone 416-287-0195

Edmonton Homebrewers Guild: 10932 130th St., Edmonton, AB T5M 0Z3; phone 403-451-7633

Montreal Association of Serious Homebrewers (MASH): 1385 Garneau St., Bruno, PQ J3V 2V5; phone 514-441-9529

Royal Canadian Malted Patrol: 828 E. 17th Ave., North Vancouver, BC V7L 2X1; phone 604-987-8262

Thunder Bay Homebrewers Association: 160 Iris Crescent, Thunder Bay, ON P7A 8A1; phone 807-767-5077

Germany

German Homebrewers Association: c/o Dipl. Brm. Christian v. der Heide, Adlzreiterstr 27, Munchen D-80337

Japan

Far East Brewers: Nakagusuku son, Kita Hama, 381 Ban Chi, Okinawa

Japan Homebrewing Promotion Association: c/o Miyanaga-Biru 301, Motoakasaka 1-5-1 Minato-Ku, Tokyo

Sweden

Heimbrewed: Rådhusgatan 60, 83134 Östersund

Swedish Homebrewers Association: c/o Hakan Lundgren, Vallstanåsvägen 75, S-195, 70 Rosenberg; phone 046 8 590 35 727, e-mail lundgren@shbf.se

U.K.

CAMRA (The Campaign for Real Ale): 230 Hatfield Rd., St. Albans, Hertfordshire, AL1 4LW; phone 01727 867201, fax 01727 867670, e-mail camra@camra.org.uk

Craft Brewing Association: c/o James McCrorie, 82 Elmfield Rd., London SW17 8AN; phone 0181-675-0340

U.S.

American Homebrewers Association: P.O. Box 1679, 736 Pearl St., Boulder, CO 80306-1679; phone 303-447-0816, fax 303-447-2825, e-mail aha@aob.org

Beernutz: c/o Brew & Grow, 33523 W. 8 Mile #F5, Livonia, MI 48152; phone 313-442-7939

Bidal Society of Kenosha: 7625 Sheridan Rd., Kenosha, WI 53143; phone 414-654-2211

Bloatarian Brewing League: 7012 Mt. Vernon Ave., Cincinnati, OH 45227; phone 513-271-2672

Bluff City Brewers: 8927 Magnolia Leaf Cove, Cordova, TN 38018; phone 901-756-5298

Bock 'n' Ale-ians: 7404 Hummingbird Hill, San Antonio, TX 78255; phone 512-695-2547

BOSS (Brewers of South Suburbia): P.O. Box 461, Monee, IL 60449; phone 708-KEG-BEER

Boston Wort Processors: c/o John Dittman, P.O. Box 397198, Cambridge, MA 02139-7198; phone 617-547-5113 ext. 900, e-mail jason@world.std.com

Brew Free or Die: P.O. Box 1274, Merrimack, NH 03054-1274; phone 603-778-1231

Brewers United for Real Potables (BURP): 8912 Jandell Rd., Lorton, VA 22079; phone 703-339-8028

Capitol Beermakers Guild: 405 Fairview Dr., Charleston, WV 25302; phone 304-343-0350

Chicago Beer Society: P.O. Box 1057, LaGrange Park, IL 60526; phone 847-692-BEER, fax 847-699-7537, e-mail cbsbeer@aol.com (1996 Homebrew Club of the Year)

Covert Hops Society: c/o David Feldman, 5150 Vernon Springs Trail N, Atlanta, GA 30327; phone 404-377-3024

Crescent City Homebrewers: 2001 Neyrey Dr., Metairie, LA 70001; phone 504-831-2026

Dukes of Ale: 11524 Manitoba NE, Albuquerque, NM 87111; phone 505-294-0302

Great Northern Brewers: 3605 Arctic Blvd. #1204, Anchorage, AK 99503; phone 907-337-9360, e-mail docherty@arco.com

Green Mountain Mashers: 10 School St., Essex Junction, VT 05452; phone 802-879-6462

Hudson Valley Homebrewers: P.O. Box 285, Hyde Park, NY 12538

Impaling Alers: 7405 S. 212 #103, Kent, WA 98032; phone 206-872-6846

Kansas City Beer Meisters: 8206 Bell Rd., Lenexa, KS 66219-1631; phone 913-894-9131

The Keystone HOPS: Montgomery Farmers Market, Rte. 63, Montgomeryville, PA 18936; phone 215-614-HOPS

Madison Homebrewers & Tasters Guild: P.O. Box 1365, Madison, WI 53701-1365; phone 608-249-7126

Maine Ale & Lager Tasters (MALT): P.O. Box 464, Topsham, ME 04086-0464; phone 207-666-8888

Mid-Atlantic Sudsers and Hoppers (MASH): P.O. Box 105, Flagtown, NJ 08821; phone 908-359-3235

Oregon Brew Crew: 7260 S.W. 82nd, Portland, OR 97223; phone 503-293-6120

San Andreas Malts: P.O. Box 884661, San Francisco, CA 94188-4661; phone 415-885-1878, e-mail allison2@gene.com

Snowy Range Foamentors: 810 S. 23rd, Laramie, WY 82070; phone 307-742-0516

Society of Northeast Ohio Brewers (SNOBS): 515 High St., Wadsworth, OH 44281; phone 216-336-9262

Sonoma Beerocrats: 840 Piner Rd. #14, Santa Rosa, CA 95403; phone 707-544-2520

South Florida Homebrewers: 441 S. State Rd. 7, Margate, FL 33068-1934; phone 305-968-3709 or 305-968-3591

St. Louis Brews: 9 Adams Ln., Kirkwood, MO 63122; phone 314-822-8039

Sultans of Swig: 412 Lamarck Dr., Buffalo, NY 14225; phone 716-837-7658

Three Rivers Alliance of Serious Homebrewers (TRASH): 3327 Allendorf St., Pittsburgh, PA 15204; phone 412-331-5645

The Unfermentables: c/o Chris Galvin, Wine and Hop Shop, 705 E. 6th Ave., Denver, CO 80203; phonc 303-831-7229

Western Oregon Regional Tasters Society (WORTS): 2459 S.E. Tualatin Valley Hwy. #167, Hillsboro, OR 97123

Zion Zymurgists Hops (ZZ HOPS): 667 E. 1200 North, Bountiful, UT 84010; phone 801-298-4339

Homebrew clubs on the Web

Here are some clubs that have their own Web pages or sites.

American Homebrewers Association at

`http://www.aob.org/aob`

Barley Bandits at

`http://www.gordian.com/users/scott/brewstuff/bandits.html`

Boston Brew-ins at

`http://www.mit.edu:8001/people/cmqklein/brew-ins.html`

Boston Wort Processors at

`http://www.rsi.com/wort/`

The Brews Brothers at

`www.dfw.net/~arnie`

Chicago Beer Society at

`http://www.mcs.com/~shamburg/cbs/cbshome.html`

Fermental Order of Renaissance Draughtsmen at

`http://oeonline.com/~pbabcock/ford.html`

The Foam Rangers Homebrew Club at

`http://www.foamrangers.com`

Gulf Coast Brews Brothers at

`http://www.he.tdl.com/~murray/gcbb.html`

Hawaiian Homebrewers Association at

http://www.lava.net/~brew

HOPS at

http://www.netaxs.com/~ktoast/hops.html

Maltose Falcons Homebrewing Society at

http://www.silicon.net/~homebrew

Mystic Krewe of Brew at

http://www.neosoft.com/~dosequis/homepage.html

Palmetto State Brewers at

http://www.scsn.net/~psbrewer

Appendix F
Alcohol Content and Gravity of Various Beer Styles

● ●

*U*ntil quite recently, brewers in the U.S. have been prevented by law — despite their protests — from showing the alcohol content of their beer on labels, leaving consumers in the dark. But strength — as indicated by percentage of alcohol by volume, as well as the original gravity — is largely dictated by the recipe for each style of beer, so the figures can be made available to you even if they are not found on labels. The following tables show general parameters for both gravity and strength; keep in mind that these figures may vary from brewer to brewer even for the same style. Only some of the more common styles are listed.

While this information may not be essential, as you become more interested in beer, you'll find yourself needing more information, if not out of curiosity, then out of need for means of comparison and description. Many reviewers cite these figures, and some labels list the gravity, for example (sometimes it acts as a code, where "high gravity" translates as "strong"). So it helps to have these numbers.

Beer *gravity* is basically the density of the brew, as measured by a hydrometer. Specific gravity figures are based on ordinary water at 60 degrees F (15 degrees C), which has a specific gravity of 1.000.

The tables also indicate *degrees Plato* (the parenthetic number in the second column), which is another way of measuring gravity. The Balling scale on triple-scale hydrometers measures in degrees Plato. A homebrew with an original gravity of 1.048, for example, has a density of 12.5 degrees Plato. See Chapters 4 and 10 through 12 for more information on gravity.

Alcohol content is indicated both by volume and by weight (weight is the number in parentheses).

Source: *American Homebrewers Association 1996 Style Guidelines*

Ales

Table F-1 — American-Style Ale

Beer Style	Original Gravity (Degrees Plato)	Alcohol Content by Volume (Weight)
American pale ale	1.044–1.056 (11–14)	4.5–5.5 (3.5–4.2)
American amber ale	1.044–1.056 (11–14)	4.5–5.5 (3.5–4.2)
Barleywine	1.090–1.120 (22.5–29)	8.5–12 (6.7–9.6)

Table F-2 — Belgian and French Ale

Beer Style	Original Gravity (Degrees Plato)	Alcohol Content by Volume (Weight)
Flanders brown/red	1.044–1.056 (11–14.5)	4.8–5.2 (3.8–4.1)
Trappist dubbel	1.050–1.070 (12.5–17.5)	6–7.5 (4.7–5.9)
Trappist tripel	1.060–1.096 (16–24)	7–10 (5.5–7.9)
Belgian ale	1.044–1.054 (11–14)	4–6.2 (3.2–4.9)
Belgian strong ale	1.064–1.096 (16.5–24)	7–11 (5.5–8.6)
Witbier	1.044–1.050 (11–13)	4.8–5.2 (3.8–4.1)
Bière de Garde	1.060–1.080 (16–21)	4.5–8 (3.5–6.3)
Saison	1.044–1.080 (13–20)	4–7.5 (3.2–6)

Table F-3 — Belgian-Style Lambic

Beer Style	Original Gravity (Degrees Plato)	Alcohol Content by Volume (Weight)
Belgian gueuze	1.044–1.056 (11–14)	5–6 (4–5)
Belgian fruit lambic	1.040–1.072 (10–18.5)	5–7 (4–6)
Belgian faro	1.044–1.056 (10–14.5)	5–6 (4–5)

Table F-4 — Brown Ale

Beer Style	Original Gravity (Degrees Plato)	Alcohol Content by Volume (Weight)
Mild	1.030–1.038 (7.5–9.5)	3.2–4 (2.7–3.2)
English brown	1.040–1.050 (10–13)	4–5.5 (3.3–4.7)
American brown	1.040–1.055 (10–14)	4–5.9 (3.3–4.9)

Table F-5	English-Style Pale Ale	
Beer Style	*Original Gravity (Degrees Plato)*	*Alcohol Content by Volume (Weight)*
Classic English pale ale	1.044–1.056 (11–14)	4.5–5.5 (3.5–4.2)
India pale ale (IPA)	1.050–1.070 (12.5–17.5)	5–7.5 (4–6)

Table F-6	English Bitter	
Beer Style	*Original Gravity (Degrees Plato)*	*Alcohol Content by Volume (Weight)*
Ordinary bitter	1.033–1.038 (8–9.5)	3–3.7 (2.4–3)
Special bitter	1.038–1.045 (9.5–11)	4–4.8 (3.3–3.8)
Extra special bitter (ESB)	1.046–1.060 (11.5–15)	4.5–5.8 (3.8–4.6)

Table F-7	Scottish Ale	
Beer Style	*Original Gravity (Degrees Plato)*	*Alcohol Content by Volume (Weight)*
Scottish light ale	1.030–1.035 (7.5–9)	2.8–3.5 (2.2–2.8)
Scottish heavy ale	1.035–1.040 (9–10)	3.5–4 (2.8–3.2)
Scottish export	1.040–1.050 (10.5–13)	4–4.5 (3.2–3.6)

Table F-8	Porter	
Beer Style	*Original Gravity (Degrees Plato)*	*Alcohol Content by Volume (Weight)*
Brown porter	1.044–1.050 (11.5–13)	4–4.5 (3.2–3.6)
Robust porter	1.050–1.060 (13–15 .5)	4.8–5.8 (3.8–4.6)

Table F-9 English and Scottish Strong Ale (Old Ale and Scotch Ale)		
Beer Style	*Original Gravity (Degrees Plato)*	*Alcohol Content by Volume (Weight)*
Old ale	1.055–1.075 (14–19)	6–8 (4.8–6.4)
Scotch ale	1.072–1.085 (18–21.5)	6.2–8 (5.2–6.7)

Table F-10	Stout	
Beer Style	*Original Gravity (Degrees Plato)*	*Alcohol Content by Volume (Weight)*
Dry (Irish)	1.038–1.048 (9.5–12)	3.8–5 (3.2–4.2)
Foreign style	1.052–1.072 (13–18)	6–7.5 (4–8.6)
Sweet (London)	1.044–1.056 (11–14)	3–6 (2.5–5)
Russian Imperial	1.075–1.090 (19–22.5)	7–9 (5–5.7)
Oatmeal	1.052–1.072 (13–18)	6–7.5 (4–8.6)

Table F-11	German Wheat Beer Styles	
Beer Style	*Original Gravity (Degrees Plato)*	*Alcohol Content by Volume (Weight)*
Berliner Weisse	1.028–1.032 (7–8)	2.8–3.4 (2.2–2.7)
Weizen (incl. Hefeweizen)	1.046–1.056 (11.5–14)	4.9–5.5 (3.9–4.4)
Dunkelweizen	1.046–1.056 (11.5–14)	4.8–5.4 (3.8–4.3)
American wheat beer	1.030–1.050 (9.5–12.5)	3.5–4.5 (2.8–3.6)
Weizenbock	1.066–1.080 (16–20)	6.9–9.3 (5.5–7.5)

Lagers

Table F-12	Bock	
Beer Style	*Original Gravity (Degrees Plato)*	*Alcohol Content by Volume (Weight)*
Traditional bock	1.066–1.074 (17–19)	6–7.5 (5–6)
Helles bock/Maibock	1.066–1.068 (17–17.5)	6–7 (5–5.8)
Doppelbock	1.074–1.080 (18.5–20)	6.5–8 (5.2–6.2)
Eisbock	1.092–1.116 (23–29)	8.6–14.4 (6.8–11.3)
Weizenbock	1.066–1.080 (16–20)	6.9–9.3 (5.5–7.5)
Triple Bock	1.176–1.180 (43.5–44.0)	17–18 (13.6–14.4)

Table F-13	German Dark Lager	
Beer Style	**Original Gravity (Degrees Plato)**	**Alcohol Content by Volume (Weight)**
Munchener Dunkel	1.052–1.056 (13–14)	4.5–5 (3.8–4.2)
Schwarzbier	1.044–1.052 (11–13)	3.8–5 (3–3.9)

Table F-14	German Light Lager	
Beer Style	**Original Gravity (Degrees Plato)**	**Alcohol Content by Volume (Weight)**
Munchener Helles	1.044–1.050 (11–13)	4.5–5 (3.8–4.4)
Dortmunder	1.048–1.056 (12–14)	5–6 (4–4.8)

Table F-15	Classic Pilsner	
Beer Style	**Original Gravity (Degrees Plato)**	**Alcohol Content by Volume (Weight)**
Bohemian Pilsner	1.044–1.056 (11–14)	4–5 (3.6–4.2)
German Pilsner	1.044–1.050 (11–12.5)	4–5 (3.6–4.2)

Table F-16	American Lager	
Beer Style	**Original Gravity (Degrees Plato)**	**Alcohol Content by Volume (Weight)**
Light (diet) lager	1.024–1.040 (6–10)	3.5–4.4 (2.8–3.5)
Standard lager	1.040–1.046 (10–11.5)	3.8–4.5 (3.2–3.8)
Premium lager	1.046–1.050 (11.5–13)	4.3–5 (3.6–4)
Ice beer	1.046–1.050 (11.5–13)	4.5–5.8 (3.7–4.8)
Dry lager	1.040–1.050 (10–13)	4.3–5.5 (3.6–4.5)
Dark lager	1.040–1.050 (10–13)	4–5.5 (3.2–4.5)
Malt liquor	1.044–1.052 (11.5–13)	4.8–5.8 (3.8–4.8)

Table F-17	Vienna, Märzen/Oktoberfest	
Beer Style	**Original Gravity (Degrees Plato)**	**Alcohol Content by Volume (Weight)**
Vienna	1.048–1.056 (12–14)	4.8–5.4 (3.8–4.3)
Märzen/Oktoberfest	1.050–1.056 (13–14.5)	5.3–5.9 (4–4.7)
Rauchbier	1.048–1.052 (12–13)	4.3–4.8 (3.6–4)

Hybrids and Specialty Beers

Table F-18	Hybrids	
Beer Style	**Original Gravity (Degrees Plato)**	**Alcohol Content by Volume (Weight)**
Kölsch beer	1.042–1.046 (10.5–11.5)	4.4–5 (3.8–4.1)
Altbier	1.044–1.048 (11–12)	4.3–5 (3.6–4)
Cream ale	1.044–1.056 (11–14)	4.2–5.6 (3.4–4.5)
California common	1.040–1.055 (10–14)	3.6–5 (2.8–3.9)

Table F-19	Specialty Beers	
Beer Style	**Original Gravity (Degrees Plato)**	**Alcohol Content by Volume (Weight)**
Smoked beer	Refer to individual classic styles	
Fruit/vegetable beer	1.030–1.110 (7.5–27.5)	2.5–12 (2–9.5)
Herb/spice beer	1.030–1.110 (7.5–27.5)	2.5–12 (2–9.5)
Wassail	No standard	No standard

A Short History of Beer (For the True Beer Nut)

• •

*T*his little review of beer through the millennia is dedicated to all you beer nuts who never liked history in grammar school.

Beer history goes back beyond recorded history. Beer has been speculated to be the oldest alcoholic beverage known. It's been through many, many incarnations and has been both revered and reviled. (Fortunately, a beer renaissance is currently going on, meaning that now is one of the "revering" times.)

Some significant events throughout the course of history have been inspired by (or at least have involved) this magical, fabulous brew.

Beer = Civilization

According to Dr. Solomon Katz, a professor of anthropology at the University of Pennsylvania, the realization that grain could be used to make beer was what provided the motivation for the major transition from hunting and gathering to agriculture.

In becoming stationary, primitive people established communes. Eventually, commerce took place between these communes. The communes prospered and attracted more inhabitants to become towns, and the paths that linked these towns became roads, leading to more inhabitants.

Crude though it may have been, beer was an important source of nutrients in the diet of early hominids. This same grain that was used in the baking of bread was made more nutritious after having undergone the beermaking process, in which the starchy insides of the kernel were transformed into proteins and soluble sugars not otherwise available. Smart folks, those cavepeople!

Ancient races — Africans, Assyrians, Babylonians, Chinese, Egyptians, Hebrews, Incas, Saxons, Teutons, and various wandering tribes throughout Eurasia — all made a rough form of beer. Wherever cereal grains could be grown, beer could be made. In Africa, beer was made with millet and sorghum; in the Middle East, with wheat and barley; in Asia, with rice; and in the Americas, with corn.

From its discovery to the present, beer has been used in religious rituals, depicted on coins, and honored in epic sagas.

Ancient beer history

Here are some interesting tidbits:

- Babylonian clay tablets more than 6,000 years old depict the brewing of beer and give detailed recipes.

- A 3,000-year-old Egyptian clay tablet shows that beer was believed to have been invented by the gods. Beer gods and goddesses, deities of high rank and honor, received regular praise and offerings in ancient Babylon, Sumeria, and Mesopotamia. These spiritual beings wielded power and authority over the sun, the rain, and the soil — all things necessary to provide a bountiful harvest of grain.

- The world's oldest narrative tale, the 5,000-year-old Epic of Gilgamesh, tells us that "he drank seven goblets of beer and his spirit loosened. He became hilarious. His heart gladdened and his face shone." Those ancient Mesopotamians really knew how to party, man.

- Archaeological excavations at Ninevah (the ancient capital of Assyria, in modern-day Iraq) uncovered clay tablets that listed beer among the food items taken aboard the ark by Noah. (This begs the question: Did he bring *two* six-packs?)

- In Pharaoh's Egypt, beer was often used as a form of liquid currency. Tax debts were paid with jugs of beer; the king's laborers were paid with daily stipends of beer. According to an Egyptian saying in the time of the Pharaohs, "Happy is the man whose mouth is filled with beer."

- An Egyptian papyrus from the 3rd century BC describes the making of a strong beer called Zythum. It was flavored with juniper berries, ginger, cumin, saffron, and other herbs. Additionally, there were directions for making a stronger Dizythum, a palace variety called Carmi, and a mild family beer called Busa.

- Beer was believed to have medicinal properties. One Sumerian clay tablet contains a prescription that specifically calls for beer in the healing process, and in a medicinal text from 1600 BC, 100 of the 700 prescriptions contain beer. These medicinal applications run the gamut from a laxative to a cure for scorpion stings. Placing half an onion in beer froth was considered a remedy against death (but consuming the two together is tantamount to death).

- Venetian traveler Marco Polo wrote about Chinese beer, and an ancient Chinese manuscript states that beer, or Kiu, was known to the Chinese as early as the 2nd or 3rd century BC.

- So highly did early Europeans regard beer that Norse legends promised outstanding warriors the ultimate reward in the afterlife:

(continued)

(continued)

a brimming ale horn. The typical Norse ale horns bore "ale runes," inscriptions to ward against poisons. Norse ales were often served with garlic in them to ward off all evils (thus creating a new one, no?).

✔ Hops have been used in beermaking since the 8th century, in central Europe, replacing other flowers, leaves, berries, spices, and odd items used to bitter the beer. Hops were not widely accepted, though, until the 1500s.

In 15th-century England, ale brewers were just beginning to use hops in the beermaking process. Ale drinkers made a clear distinction between brewers who steadfastly refused to use hops and those who used them, and so fervently opposed to hop usage were many ale drinkers that in 1436, the king had to issue a writ to the sheriffs of London, ordering them to protect the brewers of "hopping beer" against acts of violence.

✔ With the rise of commerce and the growth of cities during the Middle Ages, brewing became more than a household activity. Municipal brewhouses were established, which eventually led to the formation of the brewing guilds. Commercial brewing on a significantly larger scale began around the 12th century in Germany. By the late 1300s, beer was well established as the national drink of England. Its refreshing qualities were enjoyed by both common folk and nobility.

✔ According to city records, commercial brewing in Plzen and Budweis dates back to the 1200s. By the 1500s, the Budweis brewery was supplying beer to the Royal Bohemian Court, thus giving foundation to its motto "Beer of Kings."

✔ In 1502, Christopher Columbus discovered something more important than America: Native American beer, made from corn and tree sap. He is said to have hoisted a few with the locals.

U.S. Beer History

When the U.S. celebrated its 50th birthday in July 1826, hundreds of breweries were in operation. By the turn of the century, over a thousand existed. By 1920, there were none producing beer — legally, that is. An industry that was over two centuries in the making was decimated in less than a decade and a half, thanks to the efforts of the prohibitionist Carry Nation and her like-minded friends in Washington.

Colonial times

The first beer brewed by American colonists was at Sir Walter Raleigh's Roanoke, Virginia, colony in 1587. The beer must not have been very good, though: Colonists continued to request shipments of beer from England.

The world's oldest beer recipe?

A 4,500-year-old tablet covered with hieroglyph-ics that was discovered recently in Egypt con-tains a beer recipe in the form of a love poem to the Sumerian beer goddess, Ninkasi. A few California brewers have attempted to brew from it, with some interpretation, but the word is that recipes and techniques have improved some-what since ancient times.

(Unfortunately, most of the ships' consignments of beer were drunk on the trans-Atlantic crossing by thirsty sailors.) And in 1609, colonists placed America's first "help wanted" ad in a London paper, asking for brewers to come to America.

Beer was far more healthful than the impure water sources available to Ameri-can colonists. Dr. Benjamin Rush, a noted physician and a signer of the Declara-tion of Independence, wrote, "Beer is a wholesome liquor compared with spirits. It abounds with nourishment. . . . While I wish to see a law imposing the heaviest taxes on whiskey distilleries, I should be glad to see breweries wholly exempt from taxation." (Amen!)

Breweries in the New World were among the first businesses established. American breweries preexisted American government; some of the breweries' staunchest supporters were also the leaders of the new nation.

In colonial America, the alehouse was second only to the church in importance. (As Martin Luther once said, "'Tis better to think of church in the alehouse than to think of the alehouse in church.") Aside from being where the brewer plied his trade, the tavern also served as the unofficial town hall and the social and political focal point of every town. It was here that the townsfolk gathered to deliberate and debate, to socialize and share news and information with the community. To the colonists, the alehouses were "cradles of liberty," while to the British, the alehouses were "hotbeds of sedition." As early as 1768, the Sons of Liberty were holding meetings at the Liberty Tree tavern in Providence; the Green Dragon Inn in Boston was called the headquarters for the revolution. George Washington made his headquarters at Fraunces Tavern in New York, where it still stands and serves beer, now in the heart of the financial district.

Most of the early breweries were small, house-based operations. Traditional ingredients, hard to come by in the New World, were often replaced with maize, molasses, bran, persimmons, potatoes, spruce twigs, birch bark, ginger, and allspice.

Beer as history maker

Rather than continue on to their destination in Virginia, the pilgrims on the Mayflower made their landing at Plymouth Rock for lack of beer. A December 19, 1620, entry in the diary of a Mayflower passenger tells the story: "We could not now take time for further search or consideration, our victuals being much spent, especially our beere."

The first real brewery in the New World was founded in New Amsterdam (New York) in 1633. Boston's first brewery debuted in 1637 and was a favorite among colonial leaders, who believed that beer was a moderate alternative to distilled spirits. The city of Philadelphia got its first brewery in 1685 (but made up for lost time, as Philadelphia has had more breweries in its history than any other U.S. city). This date is confirmed by an entry in the diary of William Penn, who was a brewer himself. Historians have studied Penn's ledgers and concluded that he ran malt and brew houses at his Pennsbury mansion in Pennsylvania's Bucks County.

Other early politicos liked to brew, too:

- George Washington had his own brewhouse on the grounds of Mount Vernon. His handwritten recipe for beer, dated 1757 in a diary he kept during his days as a Virginia colonel, is still preserved.

- Thomas Jefferson was another homebrewer, at Monticello. He collected all the books he could find on the subject and added them to his extensive library.

- Benjamin Franklin proposed the idea of a national brewery (talk about bloated government!).

- James Madison expressed hope that the brewing industry would "strike deep root in every state in the union."

Early colonists stayed true to the belief that beer was of great importance and an integral part of everyday life. This influence is witnessed in some of the colonial laws:

- Beer, beer bottles, brewers, and beer properties were exempt from taxation.

- Only voters and church members could brew and dispense beer.

- No tapping of beer was allowed during divine services.

- No person without skill and mastery of brewing was allowed to brew beer.

- Beer debts were excluded from court.

The introduction of lagers

Lager beer swept Europe like a plague, albeit a welcome one. This new style of beer was lighter in color and body than ale and thanks to the aging process, mellower. Eons of ale-drinking traditions gave way to the "new and improved" beer with the smooth, drinkable nature. Only the British Isles and Belgium resisted, and they continue to resist, with their loyalty to ale.

✓ Beer had to be served in standard half-pint, pint, and quart vessels.

✓ In 1789, the Massachusetts Legislature passed an act to encourage the manufacture of "strong beer, ale, and other malt liquors. . . . The wholesome qualities of malt liquors greatly recommend them to general use as an important means of preserving health of the citizens of the commonwealth."

✓ The price of beer was fixed to be "not more than one penny a quart at most" by the Massachusetts Bay Colony legislature in 1637.

As the U.S. became an instant magnet for people looking to start a new life, breweries opened as quickly as each ethnic enclave settled. Throughout the 1800s, most of the arrivals came from the "beer belt" countries of northern Europe (Ireland, Germany, Poland, Czechoslovakia, The Netherlands — the majority of brewers were of German origin), and with them came the knowledge of brewing and an appreciation for the craft.

In 1840, about 140 breweries were operating in the U.S., at least 1 in each of the 13 original colonies. Annual output totaled about 200,000 barrels. The American brewing industry boasted as many as 1,400 breweries by 1914 and employed more than 75,000 people.

The Volstead Act

The single most destructive force in U.S. brewing history was the Volstead Act — Prohibition — which completely shut down the industry for 13 long years (January 18, 1920, to December 5, 1933). Imagine having to endure the stock market crash of 1929 without a beer to cry in. No wonder they called it a depression!

Prohibition not only ruined a legitimate and successful American industry and put thousands of workers out on the street but gave rise to underworld figures who capitalized on the situation to brew and sell "bootleg" beer for millions of dollars in ill-gotten profits. In Chicago, over 700 deaths during Prohibition were attributed to mob-related "business."

Another side effect was American Prohibition's transformation of the Mexican siesta town of Tijuana into a beer boom town — a dubious distinction. More than 75 storefront bars operated on a main street only 600 feet in length.

Prohibition was the "great experiment" that went terribly wrong. According to government statistics, it cost the country more than $34.5 billion dollars in lost tax revenue and enforcement costs. And it didn't work.

Of the breweries that narrowly survived Prohibition to reopen in 1933, most got by on meager income from producing ice, soda pop, near-beer, and malt syrups (ostensibly used for baking but often used by clandestine homebrewers) or from brewing illegal beer for the thousands of speakeasies operated by the mob.

Post-Prohibition blues

When brewing beer again became legal, the laws governing its sale and distribution had changed drastically. Prior to Prohibition, the *tied house system,* under which a brewery also owned the local taverns and served its own brands exclusively, provided the larger breweries with an unfair advantage over the smaller ones. Lawmakers sought to break up the tied house system by instituting a *three-tier system,* in which the brewer, the distributor, and the retailer had to be independently owned; not even family members were allowed to own another tier in the system. This change was effective in opening up the market to small brewers but would later prove to be a major obstacle for the brewpub industry.

Of the 400 or so breweries that reopened following Prohibition, about half never regained the financial ground that had been lost; they eventually shuttered their doors. Even as new breweries continued to open, most found that the market had changed considerably. Several factors came into play: the introduction of the beer can, World War II, improved shipping methods, television, industry mergers and buyouts, and consumer preferences.

The can comes

The introduction of the beer can to the consumer market back in 1935 helped to change the way Americans drank their beer — or at least *where* they drank their beer. Previously, most of the beer consumed in the U.S. was drunk in draught form, usually at a neighborhood tavern or saloon or carried home in a bucket. It was always fresh. With the convenience of the beer can, Americans began to buy it in stores, and in bulk, and to drink it at home. Breweries that could not afford the expensive equipment necessary to can their beer lost a piece of the pie.

Kilroy wasn't here

World War II had a major impact on the brewing industry for a number of reasons. For starters, a huge chunk of the beer-drinking demographic was off to war. Replacing the young men down at the munitions plant were young women, many of whom didn't drink beer or only drank the lightest stuff available — which was just as well, as a general conservation effort was going on and brewing ingredients were in short supply. The men stationed at U.S. military bases were all drinking the only beer available down at the PX, one that was contract-brewed for the government. Ironically, while stateside military personnel were all forced to drink the "government-issue" beer, troops stationed in Europe brought home a taste for western European brews.

Gravy train

Immediately following the war, and for many years beyond, over-the-road and rail transportation systems were greatly improved. In addition to greater access and higher speeds, refrigerated trucks and rail cars were a boon to the industry. This meant that big breweries could ship their beer much farther, much faster, with limited adverse effect on the beer. The new interstate highway system introduced in the 1950s only made things better for the big guys.

Boob tube

Television, believed to be a vast wasteland when it was first introduced, is at least partly to blame for creating a wasteland in the American brewing industry. TV proved to be an invaluable medium for large, high-resource breweries looking to capture a greater share of the marketing pie. In raising advertising competition to a new level, TV helped to create the concept of "national brand" beers and galvanize the concept of beer product recognition and brand loyalty.

Lords of the ring (of foam)

Following the four-hit combination of beer cans, World War II, better shipping methods, and TV, all landed over a 20-year period, many welterweight breweries were either KO'd or were hanging on the ropes and given a standing 8-count. This is when the heavyweights took off the gloves for the finishing blow. Most of the remaining small breweries in the 1960s and 1970s were beaten to a pulp by the brewing titans and became pawns in a high-stake game of mergers and acquisitions. Brewing plants were shut down, and brand names and labels became movable property.

Ongoing U.S. breweries

Only a couple dozen regional breweries survived the beer wars of the 1970s and continue to operate. Among the survivors are

- ✔ August Schell and Cold Spring in Minnesota
- ✔ Genessee and F. X. Matt in New York State
- ✔ Hudepohl and Schoenling in Ohio (which merged in the late 1980s)
- ✔ Blitz-Weinhard in Oregon
- ✔ D. G. Yuengling, Jones, LaTrobe, Straub, and The Lion, Inc., in Pennsylvania
- ✔ Spoetzl in Texas
- ✔ Rainier in Washington
- ✔ Huber, Leinenkugel (bought by Miller in 1990), and Steven's Point in Wisconsin
- ✔ Dixie in New Orleans
- ✔ National in Baltimore

In addition, brewhouses in Dubuque, Iowa, and Evansville, Indiana, were founded over a century ago and are operating today, but they have undergone many ownership changes and much restructuring since Prohibition.

The majority of the rest of the beer, accounting for about 80 percent of all the beer produced in the U.S., is brewed by the four Goliaths in the industry:

- ✔ Anheuser-Busch (Budweiser, Bud Light, Michelob, Lowenbrau under license)
- ✔ Miller (Miller High Life, Lite Beer, Miller Genuine Draft)
- ✔ Coors (Coors Banquet Beer, Coors Light, Keystone)
- ✔ Stroh (Stroh's, Stroh's Light, Augsburger, Schlitz; G. Heileman and subsidiaries Old Style, Old Style Light, Mickey's Malt Liquor)

And about 2 percent of U.S. beer is craft brewed (see Chapters 1, 2, and 17).

Consumer preferences

Not long after the beer wars of the 1960s and 1970s, the U.S. was swept into a health and fitness craze. Beer never did rank high on any fitness buff's list of desired foods, so it had to gain acceptance or fall by the wayside. Along came light beer, perhaps the least beer-like product ever to be made at a brewery, in this author's opinion.

By around 1980, beer drinkers were left with a half-dozen major brewing companies and a handful of regionals producing millions of barrels of very light, very stable, very consistent beer. Interestingly, this style of beermaking has now become a double-edged sword for the industry. Despite megabrewed beer's popularity, beer drinkers began to complain that this level of lightness, stability, and consistency had turned much of the world's beer into a very dull and lifeless product. This pallid mediocrity in the beer marketplace eventually led to the demand for tastier beer and the U.S. beer renaissance.

Contemporary U.S. Beer Renaissance

Americans not only expect choices but demand them. In the world of cars, for example, many people began choosing Saabs, Volvos, and BMWs, even with their inflated sticker prices, over bland American-made cars, and this clamoring for better quality and selection was noticed by some American entrepreneurial spirits, who then created American-made cars that met the standards of cars made elsewhere. Demand for a well-made, interesting, classic product is high. Similar circumstances precipitated the birth of micro and craft breweries.

Consumer backlash against light beer, the dull product of the late 1970s and early 1980s, fueled the current U.S. beer renaissance (other factors also contributed, of course, especially the U.K. consumer movement for traditional ale — see the profile of CAMRA at the end of this appendix — and the trend toward gourmet food and coffee as well as increased interest in cooking).

Throughout the course of events in the U.S. brewing saga, the phenomenon of "mystique" beers — however few there were, coming from a small number of regional breweries — has held strong. Mystique beers are those with a limited distribution area and are often believed to be better than they really are by those who can't get them. Some beer lovers have gone as far as to bootleg these beers across state lines to share with family or friends (or to hoard for themselves). I remember how friends were willing to drive all the way out to Iowa to buy Coors or into Wisconsin's hinterlands to get their hands on some Point Beer (the gas to get there cost more than the beer).

The notion that these beers were somehow better than the products on the shelves of the local liquor store helped to pave the way for the great influx of imported beer. Foreign brewers anxious to cash in on America's beer-drinking habits managed to stoke the fires of consumer backlash in the late 1970s. The effects were almost immediate and eventually profound. Several high-profile brands, such as Heineken, Beck's, and Corona, experienced a meteoric rise in popularity that prompted a quick reaction by foreign brewers and importers everywhere. Soon, the market was flooded with foreign beer. The belief was that any beer in a green bottle with a foreign label on it would sell. Later on, clear bottles with silk-screened labels were all the rage.

At about the same time, many disillusioned beer lovers took to brewing their favorite beers right in their own kitchens. Brewing beer at home, though it became quasilegal in 1979, was still considered a clandestine hobby. In time, the craft grew, clubs and associations formed, information was shared, and homebrewing came out of the closet. So far out of the closet, in fact, that many novice brewers made the leap to professional brewing.

The people who made the leap from brewing in their homes to brewing professionally became the pioneers of the microbrewing industry. Like trails in the Old West, the road to small-brewing success was rough and rocky. Two major pitfalls stunted the early growth:

> ✔ **The three-tier system of distribution:** Laws dating back to the end of Prohibition stipulated that the brewer, the distributor, and the retailer had to be independently owned. Opening a small brewery or brewpub in most states guaranteed a fair amount of legal jousting.

> ✔ **The average beer drinker's lack of understanding and appreciation of craft brewing:** Without the consumer's elementary understanding of beer and its many examples of style, the small brewer could not profitably produce a wide range of flavorful lagers and ales.

Most of the earliest microbrewers hailed from the West Coast, already noted for its trend-setting ideas. Northern California, Oregon, and Washington — especially Portland and Seattle — have been on the cutting edge of this movement since its inception.

In 1977, the first of what would later come to be known as microbreweries opened in Sonoma, California. Though the New Albion brewing company managed to survive for only five years, it fired the first salvo in the war against mass-marketed beer. Following closely on New Albion's heels were the DeBakker Brewing Company (1979) in California and the Boulder Brewery (1980) in Colorado. Later in 1980, Cartwright Brewing opened in Oregon. In 1981, the Sierra Nevada Brewing Company in California began brewing high-quality ales and hasn't looked back since; along with Boulder (now called Rockies Brewing), it is the only one of these pioneering brewers still operating.

Soon thereafter, the idea caught on in the East and, finally, in the Midwest. With the notable exceptions of Florida and Texas, the southern states have been slow to jump on the beerwagon. In the beginning, for obvious reasons, the movement gravitated toward the larger cities, but now some microbrewers and pub brewers have found a home in rural America.

Today, many of the prohibitive distribution laws have been altered to allow for considerably easier startup. Where cash investment for such an undertaking was initially scarce, investors are now practically tripping over each other trying to throw money at small brewers in need of capital. Many microbrewers have even gone public, offering shares of stock in the company in exchange for investment money, and are doing very nicely, thank you.

Even the well-established brewing industries in western European countries have begun to sit up and take notice of the beer revolution taking place here in the U.S. The tail is wagging the dog, for sure, as the big commercial brewers are beginning to bring more flavorful beers to market, beer brewed with a nod to tradition.

Key players in the early days of the U.S. beer renaissance

With each year that went by, the U.S. beer renaissance picked up momentum and created small-town heroes in the craft-brewing industry. Here are some of the key players from early in the game (all of these breweries had opened by 1983):

✔ Jack McAuliffe, New Albion Brewing, California (extinct)

✔ Tom DeBakker, DeBakker Brewing, California (extinct)

✔ David Hummer and Randolph Ware, Boulder Brewery, Colorado (still operating as Rockies Brewing Co. — the oldest craft brewery in the U.S.)

✔ Charles Coury, Cartwright Brewing, Oregon (extinct)

✔ Ken Grossman and Paul Camusi, Sierra Nevada Brewing, California (still in operation)

✔ Charles and Diana Rixford, Thousand Oaks Brewing, California (extinct)

✔ Bill Newman, Newman's Brewing, New York (extinct)

✔ Michael Laybourn, Mendocino Brewing, California (still in operation)

✔ Bill Owens, Buffalo Bill's Brewpub, California (still in operation)

✔ Bert Grant, Yakima Brewing & Malting, Washington (still in operation)

✔ Paul Shipman, Redhook Brewing, Washington (still in operation, with ties to Anheuser-Busch)

✔ Mike Hale, Hale's Ales, Washington (still in operation)

Beer Seer (The Future of Suds)

The microbrewing industry is now into its second decade of existence and is alive and very well. The industry's popularity is such that the number of craft brewers in the U.S. has doubled every two years. In 1996, the U.S. boasts 900 small breweries, with new startups reported every week. While some self-styled prophets claim that the microbrewing revival is nothing more than a prolonged flash-in-the-pan, many industry experts are forecasting anywhere between 2,000 and 5,000 small breweries dotting the U.S. landscape by the turn of the century.

Even more impressive at this point in time is the ratio of openings to closings. For every six brewpubs that open, only one will not celebrate a second anniversary. That's a phenomenal success rate for new restaurants, and the ratio is only slightly less encouraging for packaging microbreweries (those without attached dining areas).

The line forms way to the right

As of January 1996, Bernd Helbig of Halle, Germany, was still looking for investors in his new company.

Helbig is marketing "Beer on a Stick," something like a beer Popsicle. If this venture is successful, he also has high hopes for beer pudding, beer jelly, and beer cream with pineapple.

Another indication of how popular and widespread this renaissance is are the ripple effects taking place:

- ✔ The American fat-cat brewers, who practically own the whole beer market, are showing real concern about losing mere single digits of market share to the microbrewers (of course, these mere single digits represent millions of dollars). So concerned are they that they're focusing a great deal of attention on producing beers that can compete with the craft brews, going so far as to create new divisions and buy small breweries.

- ✔ Contract brewing continues to fill in gaps on the map where no real hometown brewery exists. Contract beers are relatively quick and inexpensive to develop and market; expect to see many more in the future.

- ✔ Imported beers continue to stream into the U.S. marketplace, but they are no longer just Olde Foamy clones from distant shores. Though Heineken and Beck's still sell significant amounts of beer in the U.S., they pale in comparison to the hearty, sometimes exquisite (if not esoteric) beers now being imported from Belgium (such as Chimay), Germany (such as Ayinger), and the U.K. (Shepherd-Neame).

- ✔ Where American brewers have traditionally stood in awe of German brewing technology and expertise, the German brewing industry is now taking note of the revival taking place in the U.S.

- ✔ Though the Japanese may not aspire to become the craft-brewing zealots that the Americans have become, they have developed a keen interest in the beers produced in the U.S. and are willing to pay big yen for their pleasure (perhaps we can discuss the trade imbalance over a couple of brews?).

U.S. microbrewers may yet lead the world beer renaissance.

Elsewhere in the World

Beer is enjoying minirenaissances all over the world:

✔ The isolated island country of Iceland finally ditched an archaic law forbidding the open consumption of beer. Beer was viewed by the government as conducive to heavy drinking and alcoholism. Breweries have existed in Iceland, but they could brew only low-alcohol beer that was sold to tourists. Meanwhile, wine and spirits could be easily obtained and consumed anywhere in Iceland.

✔ Many second- and third-world countries continue to develop their brewing industries. As Asian countries continue to develop brisk trade with the West, there is every reason to expect them to acquire a thirst for good beer and to build state-of-the-art breweries as needed. Of course, the megabrewers are getting there first: Budweiser is now being brewed in Wuhan, China. China is also one of the big beneficiaries of the decline of large American breweries. A handful of these old behemoth brewhouses have been dismantled and rebuilt in the People's Republic — China is now a world second in beer production!

✔ The outlook for northern Africa and the Middle East is not so rosy. Islamic law prohibits alcohol consumption. One oasis is the new $1.2 million brewery opened in Taybeh, in the Israeli-occupied West Bank. Palestinian entrepreneur Nadim Khoury studied microbrewing in the U.S. and ran a liquor store in Boston before returning to his homeland in 1994. Taybeh Beer is scheduled to be marketed in Golden, Amber, and Wheat versions.

Landmark dates in the history of beer

Here are some dates and figures to throw around with your beer pals:

✔ **1118:** The first known record of a brewery, in Bohemia, is made.

✔ **1351:** Eingeck beer is introduced to the cities of the Hanseatic League.

✔ **Fourteenth or 15th century:** The Weihenstephan brewery is founded.

✔ **1516:** Duke Wilhelm IV writes the German Purity Law, the Reinheitsgebot.

✔ **1589:** The Hofbraühaus is commissioned in Munich, Germany.

✔ **1759:** The Guinness Brewing Company begins brewing in Dublin, Ireland.

✔ **Circa 1777:** The Bass Ale triangle becomes the first international trademark.

✔ **1829:** The D. G. Yuengling Brewery is founded in Pottsville, Pennsylvania (making it the oldest American brewery still in operation today).

✔ **1842:** The Urquell brewery in Plzen introduces its famed Pilsner to the world.

(continued)

(continued)

✔ **1850:** The Bernhard Stroh brewery opens in Detroit, Michigan. By **1852,** Anheuser-Busch, brewer of Budweiser, has begun its operations in St. Louis and later makes an arrangement with the Budweis brewery in Czechoslovakia.

✔ **1872:** Jacob Schueler and Adolph Coors form the Golden Brewing Company in Colorado, later to be renamed the Adolph Coors Brewing Co. Two years later, Joseph Schlitz begins brewing in Milwaukee.

✔ **1888:** Milwaukee's Plank Road Brewery is renamed the Frederick Miller Brewing Co. The following year, the Best Brewing Company in Milwaukee is renamed the Pabst Brewing Co.

✔ **1892:** The Pabst Brewing Company becomes the first brewery to produce more than a million barrels in one year. Miller becomes the second to reach the million-barrel mark in **1900,** and Anheuser-Busch reaches that plateau in **1901.**

✔ **1939:** Anheuser-Busch goes on to become the first brewer to produce two million barrels in one year. In **1942,** Schlitz and Pabst both reach the two-million barrel mark, only to watch Anheuser-Busch sell three million barrels of beer the same year. A-B is now the world's largest brewer, producing about 80 million barrels per year.

✔ **1966:** Pieter Celis revives the witbier style at the De Kluis Brewery in Hoegarrgen, Belgium.

A Toast to Important Folks in the History of Beer

For better or for worse, the following brewers, scientists, inventors, writers, and historically significant others have influenced the brewing business, particularly in the U.S.:

Duke Wilhelm IV was the protectorate of Bavaria in 1516, the year he penned the famous Reinheitsgebot, or German Purity Law. This law not only is believed to be the world's first ever consumer-protection law but has managed to hold sway over the vaunted German brewing industry for almost 500 years. Though the Duke wrote the Reinheitsgebot for several reasons (including producing revenue for Bavaria's war-depleted bank account), it is best remembered for defining the concept of "pure" beer.

Though the European Economic Community recently declared the Reinheitsgebot an unfair trade barrier, German brewers continue to abide by the purity law voluntarily. Swiss, Norwegian, and American microbrewers have been inspired by the Reinheitsgebot enough to brew beer according to the original decree.

Dutch naturalist **Anton van Leeuwenhoek** invented the microscope in the early 1700s, opening the door to bacteriology and leading to **Louis Pasteur's** idea of boiling liquids to kill off bacteria (pasteurization). Van Leeuwenhoek's invention would again prove useful when brewing scientists endeavored to isolate individual yeast strains, the foundation of modern brewing by recipe, especially lagers.

Pasteur, the man for whom pasteurization is named, was a great French scientist, well known for his pioneering work that made milk safer to drink. What most people don't know is that Pasteur's research was actually done on behalf of the brewing industry and was only later applied to the dairy industry.

Pasteur was the first to establish the scientific role of yeast in the fermentation process. He learned that by killing off the yeast and other bacteria with a rapid heating process, the bacteria and other microorganisms would be killed and the beer would not go bad so quickly. His work also laid the foundation for the isolation of yeast strains for lager beers.

In 1895, British brewing scientist Walter Sykes wrote, "More to him [Pasteur] than to any other man living or dead do we owe much of our present knowledge of that difficult, maybe even mysterious process carried on by the agency of living organisms *viz.* fermentation."

The 1800s witnessed an industrial revolution. This boom in industry brought about many technological advancements that helped to improve the business of brewing beer. Though mechanization played a vital role, the invention of compressed-gas refrigeration in the 1850s was a quantum leap for brewing. Where aging beer used to be stored in caves or kept cool with ice cut from frozen lakes and rivers, the lagering process could now be completed within the brewery and without seasonal interruptions.

A little after the discovery of artificial refrigeration, a few of Europe's finest brewers were working together to produce a new strain of yeast capable of fermentation in low temperatures. **Anton Dreher** of Austria, **Gabriel Sedlmayr** of Germany, and **Emil Hansen** of Denmark shared in this success. Sedlmayr and Dreher have been credited for their joint research that isolated *saccaromyces uvarum,* or bottom-fermenting lager yeast strain, and Hansen is credited with isolating the first single-cell yeast culture.

Sedlmayr came from a family that served as brewers for the Bavarian royal court. He excelled in the brewing field and was instrumental in creating the great Spaten beers of Munich in the mid–19th century. He was recognized as one of the first professional brewing chemists, bringing science to bear on the technique of the brewhouse.

Dreher, a Viennese brewer, met Sedlmayr when studying brewing techniques in Munich.

Hansen made the single most important discovery of the Carlsberg Brewery Laboratories in Copenhagen, Denmark. Hansen isolated the first single-cell yeast culture. Once the trick of isolating individual yeast species was known, the process of elimination allowed brewers to choose only those strains that made good beer. Success came in 1883, an accomplishment that ensured brand consistency by eliminating bad yeast strains.

In Vienna in 1873, Professor **Carl von Linde** presented the International Brewing Congress with an important paper on artificial refrigeration. On the Congress's executive committee were none other than Gabriel Sedlmayr, Anton Dreher, and Louis Pasteur.

The invention of a compressed-gas refrigeration system held huge implications for the brewing industry and provided much reason for the gentlemen on the executive committee to be excited. The invention was a serendipitous event, complementing and advancing the recent achievements made in the field of lager yeast culturing.

Today, the impact of von Linde's invention goes far beyond the brewing industry, but breweries were among the first businesses to put it to good use. Artificial refrigeration meant that lager beer could be brewed throughout the year rather than only during the cooler months, and beer could be easily transported for long distances without suffering from the effects of heat.

Jean De Clerck was not only Belgium's foremost brewing scientist but one of the greatest ever, anywhere. He was a professor at the Université Catholique de Louvain School of Brewing and a consultant to the brewing industry. His legacy to the industry was his highly regarded work *A Textbook of Brewing,* which was first printed in French in 1948 and reprinted in English in 1958. This two-volume set of books is the most detailed and comprehensive work on modern brewing, covering everything from production and brewery setup to analyses and quality control. To give you an idea of how influential this work was, the famous Siebel Institute of Brewing Studies in Chicago continues to use De Clerck's book as a classroom text for aspiring young brewers nearly 50 years after it was written.

So respected was De Clerck in his native Belgium that when he died, he was buried at the abbey of Scourmont in Chimay, brewer of Chimay Trappist ales.

Al Capone was unquestionably America's most notorious felon. His criminal exploits were simultaneously cheered and feared, depending on your perspective. Despite his deadly tactics and ruthless demeanor, Capone and his underworld associates should be properly credited with promoting and sustaining the American brewing industry during the 13 years that the federal government declared the practice of brewing illegal.

Were it not for the likes of **Carry Nation**, Capone might have been just another penny-ante thug. An impassioned prohibitionist, the ax-wielding Nation wreaked havoc on the saloons of Kansas, and her Women's Christian Temperance Union found friends in high places. U.S. legislator **Andrew Volstead** introduced the bill (the Volstead Act) that was to become the basis for the 18th amendment to the Constitution, which made alcoholic beverages illegal.

Fritz Maytag is one of the few people in the brewing industry with widespread name recognition, but ironically, the Maytag empire was built with washing machines, not brew kettles. It was the family fortune that allowed Fritz Maytag to rescue a floundering California brewery from financial ruin and turn it into a legendary American brewing success story.

In 1965, the Anchor Brewing Company of San Francisco was on the brink of collapse. Maytag bought it, reintroduced traditional recipes, and revitalized it into America's first craft brewery since before Prohibition. With an untarnished reputation as a producer of high-quality ales, Anchor Brewing serves as an inspiration for the American craft brewing movement. Anchor's flagship brand, Anchor Steam, is considered one of the few American indigenous beer styles.

In addition to running a successful brewery, Maytag sits on the board of directors for the Brewers Association of America as well as for the United States Brewers Association.

In 1971, four serious individuals were genuinely concerned about losing non-pasteurized, cask-conditioned Real Ale in England. **Michael Hardman, Bill Mellor, Graham Lees**, **Jim Makin,** and their supporters brought attention to their cause by staging protest marches and mock funerals at every closing of a cask-conditioned ale brewery. The increased public awareness resulted in one of the world's largest and most effective consumer organizations, which became known as **CAMRA** (Campaign for Real Ale) in 1973 (see Appendix C).

Current CAMRA membership is close to 50,000 beer lovers, divided among 150 chapters throughout Great Britain (Canadian, U.S., and Dutch counterpart organizations also exist). CAMRA sponsors one large national beer tasting every year and many smaller regional beer tastings in the U.K. throughout the year and publishes excellent guides to pubs serving traditional cask-conditioned ale in the U.K. and beer guides to other European countries (see Appendix D).

CAMRA has been the inspiration for many homebrewers and microbrewers in the U.S. and around the world and has been properly credited with planting the seeds of the U.S. beer renaissance.

The **Michael Jackson** — the world's foremost authority on beer and brewing, not the singer-dancer — began his writing career as a reporter for local newspapers in his native England. Concerned about the lack of attention and respect (not to mention print) given to beer and whiskey, Jackson began writing some of the first books on these subjects back in the mid-1970s. These works are still in print and continue to be the definitive works in this field. In search of beer knowledge, Jackson has also visited more breweries in more countries than anyone else alive and has even been instrumental in helping brewers rediscover old and forgotten beer styles.

In addition to his books, Jackson has done a six-part series on beer for the Discovery Channel *(The Beer Hunter)* as well as an interactive CD-ROM version of the same information. Jackson continues to tour and lecture extensively, having hosted beer fetes in places as unlikely as Cornell University and the Smithsonian Institute.

In 1978, **Charlie Papazian** founded the American Homebrewers Association in Boulder, Colorado. His mission was to promote public awareness and appreciation of the quality and variety of beer. Papazian began teaching homebrewing courses at the Boulder Free School in the early 1980s, spawning a great deal of local interest in homebrewing. As the craft of homebrewing grew, more and more people became interested in the revival of old beer styles — a cornerstone of the microbrewing industry. Many American microbrewers started out as homebrewers and are quick to acknowledge Papazian's inspiration and contribution.

Meanwhile, the AHA spawned several outgrowths, including the Institute for Brewing Studies, the Great American Beer Festival, and Brewers Publications (including *Zymurgy* and *The New Brewer* magazines), all under the aegis of the Association of Brewers, of which Papazian is still president.

Papazian, in addition to selling close to a million copies of his homebrewing manuals, continues to write for various beer and brewing magazines. He remains an active member of the American Society of Brewing Chemists and is an allied member of the Master Brewers Association of the Americas.

People of beer history, we beer nuts salute you!

Index

IDG BOOKS WORLDWIDE REGISTRATION CARD

RETURN THIS REGISTRATION CARD FOR FREE CATALOG

Title of this book: **Beer For Dummies™**

My overall rating of this book: ❑ Very good [1] ❑ Good [2] ❑ Satisfactory [3] ❑ Fair [4] ❑ Poor [5]

How I first heard about this book:

❑ Found in bookstore; name: [6]

❑ Advertisement: [8]

❑ Word of mouth; heard about book from friend, co-worker, etc.: [10]

❑ Book review: [7]

❑ Catalog: [9]

❑ Other: [11]

What I liked most about this book:

What I would change, add, delete, etc., in future editions of this book:

Other comments:

Number of computer books I purchase in a year: ❑ 1 [12] ❑ 2-5 [13] ❑ 6-10 [14] ❑ More than 10 [15]

I would characterize my computer skills as: ❑ Beginner [16] ❑ Intermediate [17] ❑ Advanced [18] ❑ Professional [19]

I use ❑ DOS [20] ❑ Windows [21] ❑ OS/2 [22] ❑ Unix [23] ❑ Macintosh [24] ❑ Other: [25]_____
(please specify)

I would be interested in new books on the following subjects:
(please check all that apply, and use the spaces provided to identify specific software)

❑ Word processing: [26]

❑ Data bases: [28]

❑ File Utilities: [30]

❑ Networking: [32]

❑ Other: [34]

❑ Spreadsheets: [27]

❑ Desktop publishing: [29]

❑ Money management: [31]

❑ Programming languages: [33]

I use a PC at (please check all that apply): ❑ home [35] ❑ work [36] ❑ school [37] ❑ other: [38] _____

The disks I prefer to use are ❑ 5.25 [39] ❑ 3.5 [40] ❑ other: [41]_____

I have a CD ROM: ❑ yes [42] ❑ no [43]

I plan to buy or upgrade computer hardware this year: ❑ yes [44] ❑ no [45]

I plan to buy or upgrade computer software this year: ❑ yes [46] ❑ no [47]

Name: _____ Business title: [48] _____ Type of Business: [49] _____

Address (❑ home [50] ❑ work [51] /Company name: _____)

Street/Suite# _____

City [52]/State [53]/Zipcode [54]: _____ Country [55] _____

❑ **I liked this book!** You may quote me by name in future
IDG Books Worldwide promotional materials.

My daytime phone number is _____

IDG BOOKS
THE WORLD OF
COMPUTER
KNOWLEDGE

❏ **YES!**

Please keep me informed about IDG's World of Computer Knowledge.
Send me the latest IDG Books catalog.